BETJEMAN

A.N. Wilson was born in 1950 and educated at Rugby and New College, Oxford. A Fellow of the Royal Society of Literature, he holds a prominent position in the world of literature and journalism. He is a celebrated biographer and novelist, winning prizes for much of his work. He lives in North London.

'Beautiful, inspiring and brilliantly perceptive . . . The masterpiece that A.N. Wilson was born to write'
Country Life

'Terrific . . . [Wilson's] book zeroes in on Betjeman's struggles with his faith, which he places dead centre of the life and work, and on his family difficulties, and does so with extraordinary imaginative sympathy . . . Essential'
Spectator

'A bold and lively survey'
Roger Lewis, 'Books of the Year', *Daily Express*

'A.N. Wilson, as one would expect from such a talented novelist, is brilliant at evoking even the marginal characters in the story'
Francis King, *Literary Review*

'Wilson provides a new sense of the fine detail of the depression and guilt by which his subject was permanently beset . . .
Absorbing'
The Times

'A sharp-edged triumph . . . This, it is safe to say, should be the final biography'
Times Literary Supplement

BETJEMAN

by

A.N. WILSON

'Poetry is the only possible way of saying anything
that is worth saying at all.'

ARTHUR MACHEN, *The Secret Glory*

arrow books

Published by Arrow Books in 2007

10 9 8 7 6 5 4 3 2 1

Grateful acknowledgment is made for permission to reproduce lines from the following:
Collected Poems, *Best Loved Poems* and *Summoned by Bells* by John Betjeman © The Estate of
John Betjeman 1955, 1958, 1960, 1962, 1964, 1968, 1970, 1979, 1981, 1982, 2001.
Reproduced by permission of John Murray (Publishers), a division of Hodder Headline

'Seventeenth Century Lyric', 'The Garden City', 'St Aloysius Church, Oxford', the
Shell Guides and other writings by John Betjeman are reproduced by kind permission
of the John Betjeman Estate

John Betjeman, Letters: Volume One: 1926 to 1951 and *Letters: Volume Two 1951–1984*
(ed.) Candida Lycett Green reproduced by kind permission of Methuen

The Letters of Evelyn Waugh edited by Mark Amory, by permission of Weidenfeld &
Nicolson, an imprint of the Orion Publishing Group

Memories by Maurice Bowra, by permission of Weidenfeld & Nicolson,
an imprint of the Orion Publishing Group

'Meditations in Time of Civil War', *The Poems* by W.B. Yeats, Macmillan,
by permission of A.P. Watt on behalf of Michael B. Yeats

The Secret Glory (Copyright © Arthur Machen) by permission of A.M. Heath & Co Ltd

'This Be the Verse', *Collected Poems*, by Philip Larkin, by permission of Faber & Faber Ltd

Lines for Christmas Sing-Song by W.H. Auden from an unpublished and undated letter to
John Betjeman, British Library (shelfmark: Add. MS 71646 f14), used by permission of
Curtis Brown, Ltd. All rights reserved. These lines have been published in a slightly
different form in *The Completed Works of W.H. Auden Plays and Other Dramatic Writings
1928–1938* by W.H. Auden and Christopher Isherwood, Princeton University Press, 1988

First published in 2006 in the United Kingdom by Hutchinson

Arrow Books
The Random House Group Limited
20 Vauxhall Bridge Road, London SW1V 2SA

www.rbooks.co.uk

Addresses for companies within The Random House Group Limited can be found at:
www.randomhouse.co.uk/offices.htm
The Random House Group Limited Reg. No. 954009

A CIP catalogue record for this book is available from the British Library

ISBN 9780099498377

Designed by Peter Ward
Printed in the UK by CPI Bookmarque, Croydon, CR0 4TD

To Paul and Candida
Bright as the morning sea those early days!

Contents

I

BEGINNINGS

The fashionable King's Road, Chelsea, on a Sunday morning in the 1980s was quiet. The shoppers who had milled about in their thousands during Saturday afternoon had returned to different parts of town, and the revellers of the previous evening, in clubs and restaurants and bars, were sleeping off their excesses. Dog-walkers or churchgoers were about. Such as these might have seen, as a regular occurrence on Sunday mornings, a large black car pull up in Radnor Walk, a small street off King's Road. Out of it would step a small woman in her early fifties, with auburn, almost bronzed hair in the perm-helmet fashion which had become obsolete twenty years before. She would ring a door-bell. From a tiny artisan's terraced cottage, built to house the workers at the Chelsea Pottery in the nineteenth century but now, in the late twentieth, occupied by the rich, there emerged a six-foot tall, aristocratic lady with a girlish face and springy, greying, short-cropped hair, struggling to help a stout, elderly man who by now needed the assistance of a wheelchair to make even rudimentary street walks. After getting him out of the front door and into the wheelchair, the three of them would process out of Radnor Walk, and down the King's Road, where only a few hours before, clubbers and young people out for a good time had staggered towards their mini-cabs. In one of his best poems, the man in the wheelchair had imagined a bleary-eyed nightclub proprietress coming into the club the next day and seeing the brimming ashtrays and unwashed glasses. 'But I'm dying now and done for', she exclaims. 'What on earth was all the fun for?'

All three in the little procession had in their different ways enjoyed life, though with the limitations of their office or class in society. The man in the wheelchair, who had recently wowed television audiences by complaining that he had not had enough sex in his life, was the Poet Laureate. His tall, willowy minder, lover and friend was Elizabeth Cavendish, sister of the Duke of Devonshire, a magistrate, and someone who had become his life-companion. The third party, known to the man in the wheelchair as 'Little Friend', was the Queen of England's sister, Princess Margaret. Before the onset of Parkinson's disease, the man in the wheelchair, with his tall companion, Lady Elizabeth Cavendish, and her 'Little Friend', had attended another church, the Grosvenor Chapel in Mayfair, but for the time being, Holy Trinity, Sloane Street, a church which could be reached on foot from Radnor Walk, was their destination.

Ever since a Chelsea boyhood, the man in the wheelchair, the Poet Laureate, had been aware of this church, designed by J. D. Sedding and built in 1888–90. Its Arts and Crafts architecture had fascinated and delighted him. Before his thirtieth birthday he had written a poem about it, and some time before his seventieth birthday he had found himself, together with, to use his own phrase, 'that excellent artist Gavin Stamp', campaigning for the salvation of this church from demolition. It was one of the hundreds of beautiful buildings which, during that vandalistic period of English history, the poet had campaigned to save. Now in the premature old age which Parkinson's disease had inflicted upon him, he seized eagerly upon this place both as a church which was within reach of his home, and as somewhere which adhered to the Book of Common Prayer – another bit of the past which the British seemed intent upon throwing heedlessly away.

John Betjeman, the man in the wheelchair, being pushed along by his lover, Lady Elizabeth Cavendish and her friend Princess Margaret (Cavendish was her lady-in-waiting), is the subject of the book which follows.

Although the medical diagnosis of his condition was that he had been suffering since he was sixty-five from Parkinson's disease, anyone seeing his face in the latter days could feel that more than simple disease had battered it. Because of his frequent television appearances in the previous thirty years, it had become one of the best-known faces in England – round, chubby, wistful, often lit up by a completely enchanting laugh, revealing appalling teeth. But the large eyes, as well as being humorous, were also full of fear. He was a depressive, who all his life had lived on cycles of mood swings from elation, when he loved clowning and showing off, to deep melancholy and self-doubt. Like many melancholics, he was of a very religious temperament. The churchgoing was no mere outward form; it was his bedrock and strength. But churchgoing did not prevent appalling consciousness of his own inadequacies, a morbid near-revelling in sin, and a deep, almost total doubt.

'I hang on to faith by my eyelids, a lot of the time I think it is all rot.'

The morbid guilt was deeply increased by the fact that this national icon, and pillar of the Church, was living apart from his wife, and by the fact that he was effectually estranged from his elder child, Paul. Both things preyed on his mind, and at times endangered sanity itself, driving out all capacity for happiness.

Such was the wish of the nation to make him an entirely jolly figure – the tiresome cliché 'the nation's teddy bear' was even applied to him – that no one really wanted to dwell on his private life. The public at large preferred the public image. In August 1974, the *Daily Express* had published an insinuating article alongside a photograph of Betjeman and the house in Radnor Walk – 'Old friend Lady Elizabeth comforts Betjeman'. On television, his wife Penelope gave an interview in which she spoke very firmly as if they were still married – which, canonically and legally, they were. Both of them believed they were, and he loved his wife to the end.

'The great thing about John', Lady Betjeman told the television audiences in her surprisingly cockney, albeit 'upper-class cockney', tones, 'is that he gets over rows very quickly, and my technique has usually been to pay no attention to him when he gets in a passion and that annoys him all the more. So on the whole it's probably better if I do have a bit of a row. I think we have less rows than we used to when we married.'

She neglected to mention that one possible reason for this was that they no longer lived together.

'I did not like all the probing and prying in the *Express*', Betjeman wrote to her. 'I felt very sorry for you, what business is it of theirs, fuck them.'

As long ago as 1964, John Osborne, then perhaps the most celebrated playwright in England, had written a play which everyone in the know recognised to be about Betjeman. 'I have always been afraid of being found out', says the hero of *Inadmissible Evidence* Bill Maitland, who is a married man with two children, two women (the mistress called Liz) and a furious obsession with the architectural wreckage of England.

When Betjeman said that he was afraid of being found out, he was not, of course, simply referring to his 'private life', which was an open secret among all his friends and a wider public. (Maurice Bowra, his old mentor from Oxford days, upon hearing that Betjeman's son Paul had become a Mormon, crisply commented, 'Excellent thing, excellent thing, Paul a Mormon, a Mormon. It combines the religious fervour of the mother and the polygamous tendencies of the father.')

What troubled Betjeman, surely, when he spoke of himself as a fraud, an *arriviste*, a poseur, was the sense that he might have thrown away his life in wasted time. Was he a 'proper' poet, or merely a rhymester? Intellectually snobbish critics dismissed him as little better than a joke, and he always believed them. For all his professed devotion to women, and his love poems to huge strapping athletic girls, and his perpetual talk of sex, was he particularly interested in it? And if he was, had he ever entirely shaken off the homosexuality of his youth? He once threatened a younger journalist friend with legal action if he went into print with the suggestion.

The public create favourites, especially television favourites, in the image they themselves require. There is a good example of this in the diaries of an Anglican priest, Victor Stock, who describes a very celebrated radio-speaker, Rabbi Lionel Blue, coming to speak at his church of St Mary Le Bow. The rabbi spoke to an audience of about 350 people, very movingly and frankly, about his sexual orientation. 'I'm an ungay gay.'

Stock overheard two old ladies speaking to one another afterwards.

"'He's a lovely man, isn't he?"

"I like him so much, don't you?"

"Yes, I like him, too."

"Mind you, I didn't like that what they said about him."

"No, I didn't like what they said about him either."

"You know what I mean?"

"Yes, they said he was one of those. Horrible wasn't it?"

"Nasty."

Well, "they" hadn't said anything. Lionel had said it himself. But his fans couldn't bear it and turned what they had heard into something they wanted to remember was said *about* him, not said *by* him.'

Psychopaths actually murder their favourite stars and celebrities, either because in private life the reality does not match their image, or simply to hug them to themselves. The cult of personality is such, however, that even devoted and healthy-minded fans place a tremendous burden on the object of their adulation. Betjeman in his wheelchair was punch drunk, not just from Parkinson's but from Publicity. What had begun as a habit of perpetual clowning, had attracted such a wide audience that he could barely cope with it. He was both addicted to it, right up to the end, not minding the humiliation of coming on television as an old dodderer in the wheelchair, but equally, hating it all, and especially hating the mountains of letters which arrived every morning.

The sheer weight of a nation's desire to make him into their 'teddy bear' screened from that nation what much of his work quite openly revealed. 'Angry Old Man' would be just as accurate a description. 'Unmitigated England' is viewed in much of his later writing with unmitigated hatred. The man who had written verses which called for the bombing of Slough just before the Second World War always *had* hated, as well as loved, England.

This isn't to deny his warmth, his humour, his infectious laughter. But lovers of the teddy bear evidently do not notice the fury of so much of the poetry. 'The women who walk down Oxford Street / Have bird-like faces and brick-like feet.' This one, 'Civilised Women', makes Kingsley Amis look pale. In 'Shattered Image', there is not only the most mordant sense of tragedy that a man has had his life, his career and his future ruined by his affair with an under-age boy; there is also a real hatred of the society which condemns him. Betjeman's hatred of the society which sent Oscar Wilde to prison was lifelong. The wreckers of England in Betjeman's vision are not just spiv developers who drive the firm's Cortina. They are landowners, and greedy farmers.

> God save me from the Porkers
> The pathos of their lives,
> The strange example that they set
> To new-rich farmers' wives.

No 'Green' protester of the present day, against factory farms or Genetically Modified Crops, could be angrier than the Betjeman who wrote 'Harvest Hymn'. 'We spray the fields and scatter / The poison on the ground.' His vision of life is as bleak as Larkin's. The tragic pair of English pensioners in the Costa Blanca have no future, no money, no hope –

> Our savings gone, we climb the stony path
> Back to the house with scorpions in the bath.

His life as a famous man on the lecture circuit is pure hell:

When I saw the grapefruit drying, cherry in each centre lying.

As for the three havens of his declining years – Chelsea, where he was cared for by his beloved Elizabeth, Cornwall, his childhood refuge, where he was to die peacefully, and the Church – each is seen with a vision jaded by disgust and disease.

Between the dog-mess heaps I pick my way
To watch the dying embers of the day
Glow over Chelsea . . .

Whereas, far away in the West in the 'Delectable Duchy' of Cornwall, 'a smell of deep fry haunts the shore', and Jan Trebetjeman, as he called himself sometimes, looks forward to the whole place being engulfed by the Atlantic, with only a few rocks, 'a second Scilly', jutting out of the angry sea. As for the consolations of Faith –

'I am the Resurrection and the Life':
Strong, deep and painful, doubt inserts the knife.

Yet while some of the sillier Betjeman fans wanted to overlook this dark side to his poetry, it is in part the darkness and the complication, both in his character and in his writings, which created the charm. When he died, there was a palpable sense of national loss in England, comparable to what happens when a member of the royal family or a very deeply loved screen-star meets death. A journalist called John Ezard noted in his home pub of Brentwood, Essex, that he had interrupted a conversation about the Cup Final with the question, 'Does everyone know John Betjeman is dead?' Everybody in that bar spoke about him, and although most referred to his television appearances 'a surprising number' knew him from his written poems. Comparisons with Byron are sometimes made, but the truth is that there has *never* been another English poet quoted by people in pubs. This, quite as much as the packed congregation at Westminster Abbey for his memorial service, with the Prince of Wales reading the lesson, was a mark of what an extraordinary figure Betjeman had become in the public consciousness. Elizabeth Cavendish likens his impact on a wider public to that of Diana, Princess of Wales. Tens of thousands of men and women and children felt they knew him, simply from seeing him on television. Those who met either figure, even for a few minutes, remembered it all their lives. Both Betjeman and Diana possessed a healing presence and were assiduous hospital visitors. His lifelong friend (briefly his fiancée) Billa Harrod wrote to him in the sadness of his sick, depressed last days, from her village in Norfolk, after a visit to see him in Chelsea.

> You've always had guilt, which is I suppose a sort of fear; you *shouldn't* have it now; you really are the tops – much more than you can know; you only know the official rather public, Londony side; but I know how you are regarded all over England by quite simple people who may, but not necessarily, have seen you on telly – but they've *heard* of you (not always even *heard* of you) and somehow your very extraordinary personality has come across and is now part of folk-lore. I really mean this, and it is no longer, 'Oh Mr Betjeman, you would love it, it is so *hideous*' – it is a sort of understanding and a deep affection that you have inspired. You may think this is all BALLS but it *ain't* . . . You have done more good to make people understand the English landscape, the architecture (including, but not exclusively, the formerly despised Victorian) the language, and the atmosphere than those others [she has just listed some of her cleverest or most famous friends] put together . . . So you of all people, should not have guilt or fear. If that is what is stopping you walking, I think you could get up and run.

'If Billa were here now', he remarked to a visitor to Radnor Walk at about this date, 'I'd like her to take me upstairs and give me a jolly good *talking-to*.' Perhaps this bracing letter is too kind for the sort of thrill he had in mind, but it is surely true. And it is to explain its truth, and expand upon it, that this book has been written.

⌘ ⌘ ⌘

When he was an old man, of seventy-two, John Betjeman wrote to his wife Penelope, 'I have just re-read Goldsmith's *Deserted Village* which influenced me more than any other English poem. Ernie [Betjemann, that is, the poet's father] used to read it to me almost daily when I was six or seven. I still think that it is one of the best English poems . . .' These words from the Poet Laureate in 1978 would have surprised many who saw him, rather crudely, as a throwback not to the eighteenth, but to the late nineteenth century. By then, he was seen as the defender of Victorian architecture and the lover of Victorian hymns, the celebrant of the suburban 'Nobodies', joked about in Victorian and Edwardian editions of *Punch*.

He had also projected himself, in his hugely popular verse autobiography, *Summoned by Bells*, as a man completely at odds with his father Ernest Betjemann (who hated being called Ernie), the third-generation manufacturer, in Islington, North London, of inlaid boxes, dressing-tables, onyx ashtrays, condiment-sets and, by the time of Betjeman's own birth, cocktail cabinets. The theme of the autobiography, indeed, was how he resisted his father's moral blackmail to take over the family business, and struck out on his own to become a poet. He was destined to be the most popular poet in England since the death of Tennyson. This very popularity, and the fact that it was enhanced by his genius as a television broadcaster, has led to some confusion about the nature of Betjeman's life and work. Some of his friends, and many of the literary establishment, took his self-depreciation and jokiness at face value and made the mistake (as in very different ways people mistook Byron) of not seeing that it was possible to be funny about serious matters. Many missed the point of his allusions in *Summoned by Bells* to T.S. Eliot, who, by a

bizarre chance, taught Betjeman at Highgate Junior School in 1916.
They fail to see the nature of Betjeman's jokey, but ironical,
relationship with modernism, both in literature and in architecture.
When he started to write his serious poetry, some time in his
twenties, he did not try to imitate the modernist masters. Instead,
he drew on the weakness of his own schoolboy attempts at poetry.
'The lines of verse / Came out like parodies of A & M.' That is, of
Hymns Ancient and Modern, a Victorian compilation of hymns widely
used in the Church of England in the lifetime of Betjeman and his
parents.

When we assess the life of a popular writer, we are doing rather
more than telling the story of their days from birth to death. We are
also describing someone who made a profound appeal to their own
contemporaries, and therefore we are seeing something about their
generation. Byron's subversive narrative poems were popular
because they were so well made, so funny, so euphonious, and so
raunchy, of course. They also, surely, owed their popularity to the
fact that their author had set himself up as the opponent of all that
the Tories and the British Government of his day had set out to do
in fighting the war against Napoleon and supporting the continuation
of the aristocratic hierarchies in Britain. In a later generation,
Victorians swarmed to buy Tennyson's *In Memoriam* partly, again,
because of its beauty and music, but partly because it voiced their
inmost fears that the new scientific learning might in fact be spelling
the end of Christianity.

Betjeman's vast popularity as a poet – over two and a half
million copies of his *Collected Poems* have sold – is not entirely to be
attributed to his skill as a television broadcaster. Nor can it be
explained by the fact that the British public shared his enthusiasms.
They might have thought they did, when he appeared on television
saying how much he liked seaside piers, or music-hall songs, but
many of his loves and obsessions – for the poetry of T.E. Brown,
for the arcane rituals of High Anglicanism, for Greek Revival

architecture or for the novels of Arthur Machen — were hardly calculated to appeal to the masses.

Nevertheless, he touched a chord which went very deep. No other poet, still less Poet Laureate, has spoken as he did. The reason for his popularity, in spite of the eccentricities of his tastes and the perhaps cultivated eccentricity of his mannerisms, is that at some visceral level he spoke for England. He did so more than any politician of his time, and more than any of the religious leaders either. And the confession to his wife, that he and his father were addicted to *The Deserted Village* by Oliver Goldsmith, is perhaps a useful starting-point for telling the story of his life, and for celebrating it.

Goldsmith's poem about the wrecking of rural Ireland (first published in 1770) is very far from being a gentle piece of 'pastoral'. It is an angry poem, and at the deepest level it is a highly political one. If all you see when you read Betjeman is a few brick suburban churches, and some strapping young girls in tennis-skirts, you have similarly missed the point that his whole work, as a poet and as a broadcaster, was a protest movement against the very phenomena which Goldsmith had been attacking. Goldsmith came in at the beginning. Betjeman came at very nearly the end, to cast his deep-seeing, large, laughing but also scathing eyes upon

> Dear old, bloody old England
> Of telegraph poles and tin,
> Seemingly so indifferent
> And with so little soul to win.

Betjeman, in his celebrations and elegies for a lost England, is both quintessentially English and completely an outsider, at one with the various classes to which he pretends, or aspires, to belong, such as the Pooters of North London, or the aristocracy, and not belonging to any of them; obsessed by celebrity but hiding behind masks; utterly self-confident in his own abilities while presenting himself as full of fear and doubt, and yet, too, full of fear and doubt;

a lover and a hater of what he depicted. Critics of Jane Austen's novels, both at the time and since, have tried to extract from her work a political attitude or lack of it from her failure to address the most glaring political event of her time – the war with Napoleon. Betjeman's attitudes to the political struggles of the twentieth century, to the two great world wars, to the class system, were so out of kilter with the stereotypical responses of his contemporaries that we can be forgiven for not seeing that he had any attitude at all. He responded to life instinctually, which is why, when his poems hit a bull's-eye they hit so very hard, staying in the mind, and making us laugh, but also disturbing us. They are about death, and failure, and disappointment, and greed. They see an old order, of 'men who never cheated, never doubted', passing away, and a new one of bombers in a pointless war, of spivs and speculators after it, coming to finish off what the greedy landlords had begun in Goldsmith's land 'where wealth accumulates and men decay'.

In the Preface to one of Betjeman's favourite novels, the work he says changed his life, Arthur Machen observes:

> In every age, there are people great and small for whom the times are out of joint, for whom everything is, somehow, wrong and askew. Consider Hamlet; an amiable and an intelligent man. But what a mess he made of it! Fortunately, my hero – or idiot, which you will – was not called upon to intermediate with affairs of state and so only brought himself to grief.

The Secret Glory, Arthur Machen's story, provided Betjeman with one of his earliest role-models, a man outside the general run, a man who in many ways found England with its boarding schools and class system and irreligion, hateful. In spite of, or perhaps because of, this perspective Betjeman, more than any of his contemporaries, grew up to be a writer who spoke for England.

The Betjemans were cabinet-makers who emigrated from Holland to the East End of London in the eighteenth century. The poet's great-grandfather, George Betjeman, founded the family firm which produced writing desks, dressing cases and cabinets in Aldersgate. His son, John Betjeman, invented the Tantalus, an elegant decanter-carrier with a lockable cage-like carrier, which enabled middle-class households to prevent their servants from taking nips out of the sherry or the port.

It was this John Betjeman who added an extra 'n' to the name. By now, with a more-than-half German queen on the throne of England, married to a German prince, there was what poet John called 'the craze for all things German'. Hence – *Betjemann*. To the actor James Fox, in an interview in the *Radio Times* in 1976, the poet said, 'I've never talked about these things before.' This is a typical Betjemanism, drawing both interviewer and reader into the sense that they alone are his confidants. In fact, the spelling of the name Betjemann had been described in *Summoned by Bells* in 1960.

> I was always rather ashamed of it all, you see, having a name with two 'n's which was carefully dropped by my mother during the 1914 war because I was thought to be German. I have a terrible guilt about not having any right to be in this country. My father insisted on keeping the two 'n's. It's been an awful nuisance. Now I'm rather pleased when I see it with two.

In the days of his fame, Betjeman's surname became synonymous with many people's idea of England itself, but there always remained the paradox that it was foreign. There were those who shared Malcolm Muggeridge's suspicion that Betjeman was really Jewish in origin, though there is no evidence for this. The fact the suspicion was voiced, however, points up the quizzical nature of our subject, the strange outsider-insider business of living in England.

Part of this is class. Edwardian England, into which Betjeman was born, was probably more class-bound than at any period in its history before or since. The social shibboleths and hierarchies were expressed in ways which were recognised as comic even at the time, but which nonetheless were not to be disregarded. 'Before the First World War, we never met any middle-class people, except for writers like Hilaire Belloc', Lady Diana Cooper used to say. Belloc himself, in his comical verses, spoke of the 'ancient social curse' becoming 'hoarier and hoarier, And it stinks a trifle worse *Than in* The days of Queen Victoria'.

Belloc himself, a Member of Parliament, the descendant of Dissenting intellectuals such as Joseph Priestley, was very much in the upper echelons of the middle class. Betjeman, with the family 'works' in the Pentonville Road, Islington, was much lower down the hierarchy. In *Summoned by Bells*, he recalled adolescent rows with his father, in which Ernie Betjemann accused him of being

> 'A rotten, low, deceitful little snob.
> Yes, I'm in trade, and proud of it I am!'

When, in his early twenties, Betjeman had launched himself upon the world, he made no attempts to hide from his aristocratic or high-bohemian friends that he came from a family in trade. Indeed, he played it up, made a joke of it. One of the themes running through all his poetry, and to which his English readers readily responded, was his awareness of the class system, both as a comic phenomenon, and as an observation of the way things were.

One of Betjeman's closest upper-class friends and most devoted admirers, Diana Mitford, got to know him when she was about twenty. She was so bewitched by his distinctiveness that she wanted to know what his family could possibly have been like. Among her wedding presents when she married Bryan Guinness was an onyx cigarette-box, made by Betjemann & Sons. With a screwdriver, she removed one of its hinges and went along with it to 36 Pentonville Road, asking if it was possible to have it repaired. The clerk to whom she spoke said he would fetch 'Mr Ernest'. A foreigner meeting Ernest Betjemann would probably have heard nothing in his speech patterns to suggest that he was 'below' a member of the upper-class.

Ernie Betjemann   *Bess Betjemann*

Penelope Betjeman who herself spoke a sort of cockney said that Ernie had a cockney accent. Diana Mitford said it was not especially marked. But to an upper-class girl, his courteous manners were those of a 'shop man'. She slunk away, feeling ashamed of herself for having spied on 'Betj''s family with unworthy motives, and she never told him of her visit to Pentonville Road.

The tragi-comedy of the English class system, in which everyone was trying to 'better' themselves, is that parents gave their children upbringings and education which were calculated to make them ashamed of their origins; or, if that is too strong a word, calculated to make them at home anywhere but home. Dickens is the greatest chronicler of this phenomenon, so familiar to English readers: 'It is a most miserable thing to feel ashamed of home.'

Betjeman's father Ernie Betjemann was a cabinet-maker. Mabel 'Bess' Dawson, his wife, was a Highbury girl. Highbury was a district of North London too far out to be fashionable. Her father was an artificial flower-maker. (Like Marie Lloyd's, though perhaps in a bigger way than her Dad.)

They were Church of England. The church in which they were married, St Saviour's, Aberdeen Park, is the subject of one of Betjeman's finest poems, as polychromatic as the brickwork itself in this Victorian (William White, 1856–7) Anglo-Catholic shrine. In two pages – just 36 lines – a good demonstration of Arthur Machen's doctrine that 'poetry is the only possible way of saying anything that is worth saying at all' – Betjeman evoked the vanished world of Edwardian tradesfolk, their prosperity in 'solid Italianate houses for the solid commercial mind'. Into this prosaic world of broughams crunching on gravel, and gardens bright with geraniums, a little-known Victorian architect and his clerical patron the Rev. R.W. Morrice created an interior successfully designed to shock the solid commercial mind into a vision of the supernatural:

> Wonder beyond Time's wonders, that Bread so white and small
>   Veiled in golden curtains, too mighty for men to see,
> Is the Power which sends the shadows up this polychrome wall,
>   Is God who created the present, the chain-smoking millions and me;
> Beyond the throb of the engines is the throbbing heart of all –
>   Christ, at this Highbury altar, I offer myself to Thee.

Ernie and Bess were far from being paupers, but their prosperity does not appear to have been as great as that of the grandparents. Their only son John Betjeman, the subject of this book, was born in a mansion flat at 52 Parliament Hill Mansions, on the borders of Gospel Oak and Highgate. This area of London forms the backcloth to much of Betjeman's best work. Connected by railways, underground and overground, by tram-rails and by road transport, one bricky area gives way to the next, each retaining some of the qualities of the small village it once was, and each demonstrating by its different level of size and grandeur the varying degrees of prosperity.

South of the River Thames, even before the bombs and the developers engulfed so much of it, the old London of Dickens and Charles Lamb had been covered with new building. The chokingly overcrowded 'Great Wen' which had given abruptly and refreshingly into meadows and woodland was now sprawled over for ever, with old Croydon and Deptford lost beneath identical stockbuilt streets. In the north, however, the extraordinary phenomenon of Hampstead Heath, acres of hilly woodland, retained, and retains, its life. When they moved house from 52 Parliament Hill Mansions, it was to one of the steepest streets in London, West Hill, which borders the section of the heath where supposedly parliaments met in the Middle Ages, Parliament Hill Fields. In Kentish Town, until the 1970s,

John Betjemann

there existed, abutting terraced houses, tenements, trafficky streets and railways, a copse of trees and a field looking much as it must have done when this part of London was still rural, as painted by Constable. The North London Railway, Tottenham Branch, had acquired the land in the nineteenth century, but in the end only used part of it for engine sheds. So it was that an area of pasture, covered in wood violets, survived in a crowded area of North London until the late twentieth century. Betjeman's London was a rural London under threat. His later pattern of life, dividing time between living in country villages and in London, was not really a break with childhood. This part of London quickens that sense, so acute in Betjeman the poet and Betjeman the conservationist, both of how close we all are to the pre-industrial, unwrecked England of Constable and

Keats, and how easily, by a piece of careless planning and ugly building, that England can be lost, destroyed for ever.

'Parliament Hill Fields', a poem in which he remembered childhood rides by tram through North London, is one of the best topographical evocations in the language, ending as it does with

> my childish wave of pity, seeing children carrying down
> Sheaves of drooping dandelions to the courts of Kentish Town.

To a member of the Camden History Society in 1971, Betjeman gave a detailed commentary on the poem:

The tram was a number 7 and it was brown when it was LCC . . . Hampstead Heath then had buttercups and dandelions and daisies in the grass at the Parliament Hill Fields end. Daniels was a kind of Selfridges and it was on the corner of Prince of Wales Road, or very near that corner. There was a cinema higher up on the same side and there I saw my first film, very early animated pictures; it was called the 'Electric Palace' . . . The Bon Marché was an old fashioned draper's shop . . . Opposite Kentish Town station was a Penny Bazaar and next to that was Zwanziger which always smelt of baking bread. Then there was an antique dealer and a picture framer and a public house . . . Then there was some late Georgian brick houses with steps up to their front doors, then the always-locked parish church of Kentish Town (that was the one I referred to in the poem. It was rebuilt in Norman style in 1843 by J.H. Hakewill and seems to have no dedication). It was very low. Then there was Maple's warehouse, always rather grim, then some squalid shops and a grocer's shop called Wailes which was very old-fashioned. Then came Highgate Road station with a smell of steam and very rare trains which ran, I think, to Southend from a terminus at Gospel Oak. Then there were some rather grander shops with a definite feeling of suburbia . . . I remember thinking how beautiful the new bits of Metroland Villas were in the newly built Glenhurst Avenue and my father telling me

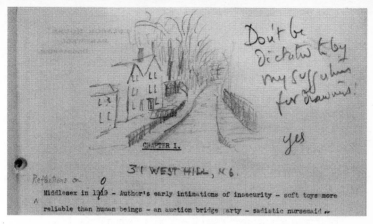

Typescript and sketch – Summoned by Bells

they were awful. Then there was the red brick gloom of Lissenden
Gardens and Parliament Hill Mansions . . .

This letter tells us so much of Betjeman. One can be fairly sure
that he did not look anything up in a book in order to write it. His
childhood world was totally vivid to him aged sixty-five. Vivid as
a topographical entity – the names of the shops, the architecture
old and new. We note, too, his father's 'good taste' in hating the
new mansion blocks, and Betjeman's perverse desire to like some
architecture which a sober judgement considered awful. And we
note too the fact that he must have often tried the door of the parish
church in order to know that it was 'always-locked'.

Behind 3 1 West Hill stretched miles of thick woodland, rolling
hills. On the other side of the road, beyond a well-planned neo-Tudor
housing development called Holly Lodge, is the rambling Highgate
Cemetery where so many great figures from the nineteenth century –
Christina Rossetti, George Eliot and Karl Marx among them – lie
buried. Betjeman himself, and his mother, were destined to be
buried far away in the west. But it was in this London necropolis that
Ernie would one day lie.

Betjeman's sketches for chapter headings
in Summoned by Bells

CORNWALL
– AND THE DRAGON

From quite early manhood, Betjeman gave lantern lectures, which were previews, really, of his later much more famous, televised, self. The slides would take the audience through the range of his enthusiasms for architecture and for places. The first of them would be a picture of a young man and a woman lolling in a punt, and across the screen, in gothic lettering, would be the single word PEACE.

This yearning for PEACE was fundamental to him as a child. A poem he wrote when he was aged nine, and dated 23 August 1915, is entitled PEACE.

> I [*sic*] was a quiret [*sic*] eve when I went out
> No people to see not a call nor a shout
> I thought of the places I had not seen
> As I sat upon the village green
> I sat & listend [*sic*] to the church bell chime
> And thought in my head this comferting [*sic*] line
>   O God be with me
>   Yet wretched I maybe [*sic*]
> And I sat by the village stocks
> And saw the waves dash over the rocks
> And the sunset made a blood red sky
> And I looked at the clowds [*sic*] that were up on high.

It is an instantly recognisable Betjeman poem. It has church bells. It has the sense of his own wretchedness in the presence of God. It has the mildly kinky need to be punished, in this case in village stocks. No doubt one of the reasons for being in the stocks was so that they could rhyme with rocks. The waves crashing on the rocks of the coast of North Cornwall were part of the inner music of Betjeman all his life.

In a mature poem, 'Harrow-on-the-Hill', he is in an electric train going through Wembley on the outer reaches of North London, and glimpsing the lights go on after tea in Harrow-on-the-Hill. Only, in the slightly dream-like state induced by the gathering dark, and the movement of the train, the urban sprawl has turned into Cornish sea and Atlantic rollers

> As they gather up for plunging
> >   Into caves.

It is one of the most successful of Betjeman's poems:

> There's a storm cloud to the westward over Kenton,
> >   There's a line of harbour lights at Perivale,
> Is it rounding rough Pentire in a flood of sunset fire
> >   The little fleet of trawlers under sail?
> >   Can these boats be only roof tops
> >   As they stream along the skyline
> >   In a race for port and Padstow
> >   With the gale?

If North London provided the background for Betjeman's birth and early experiences of fear and loss, there was always this other place, from the very beginning – Cornwall which, in his daughter's words, was 'the healer of all wounds'.

When his mother died, and Betjeman found himself in the unusual position, in 1951, of having a little money, he considered buying a house. 'I do want to buy a house in Trebetherick', he told a friend. 'Nowhere else. Not even Rock or Polzeath.' These are all small villages, within a few miles of one another on the North Cornish coast.

Bess and Ernie Betjemann had been going down to Trebetherick since before their son was born. South Cornwall is sub-tropical. Palm trees grow in its villa'd gardens and on the esplanade at Penzance. Its sea is good sailing sea, and in such ports as St Mawes and Falmouth, holiday-makers have sailed their dinghies alongside fishing boats for generations.

North Cornwall and its savage coast is completely different. The sea off these dramatic high cliffs is not man's friend. At the dividing line between Cornwall and Devon, some twenty-five miles from the Betjemanns' favourite haunt, Parson Hawker of Morwenstowe, a good minor poet, devoted much of his parish ministry in Victorian times to the burial of wrecked sailors. The living pursued by the fishermen of North Cornwall is, to this day, perilous. One of John Betjeman's most eloquent poems is the prose-description of the deserted fishing village of Port Quin.

> Here at the end of the last century, all the men of the village were
> drowned in the fishing boat owned by the village. So it is now a
> street of ruined cottages. Weeds choke the stream, fennel, valerian
> and mallow sprout among the ruined cottage walls and an occasional
> caravan pollutes a weedy garden. From the inland end of the street
> may be seen, like a village church tower, the Regency Gothick folly on
> Doyden Point. Down on the deserted quay the saltings and pilchard
> stores are empty and the few remaining old cottages are preserved by
> the National Trust. High hills enclose the sea which seems to be
> licking its chops and thirsting for more lives, so that one turns inland
> up the mild valley to the shrine of St Endelienta.

Trebetherick is in a more sheltered stretch of the coast, a few miles westward, just over the Camel estuary and over the water from Padstow. It nestles on a road which slopes steeply down to one of the most spectacular stretches of golden sand – Daymer Bay, which ends with the little headland of Pentire which he saw in his sunset-vision in the Harrow-on-the-Hill poem just quoted. At the top of Daymer Bay, above the dunes, is a golf course, also celebrated in his verse ('Lark song and sea sounds in the air / And splendour, splendour everywhere'). And in the middle of the golf course is a churchyard. The wobbly old spire of St Enodoc's Church was all that showed of this medieval granite fane in the eighteenth century. It had been completely buried in the drifting light sand. In order to collect his stipend, the parson had to read the service in St Enodoc's once a year. They used to dig a hole in the sand and lower him in through the roof. In 1863 the church was excavated, and, inevitably, restored. The golf course followed a few decades later.

At first, when the Betjemanns came to Trebetherick, the other holiday-makers, Harley Street doctors, Indian civil servants and head-masters (a little later in its history it was known as 'Beaks' Bay'), might have shown their awareness that the Londoners were 'in trade'. Little by little, as business prospered, Ernie bought more and more land in the village and along the coast, while continuing to stay in the Haven Guest House, or rented a house called, aptly, 'Linkside'.

One of Betjeman's childhood playmates remembered how Ernie stipulated that all the houses built on his land should be white. The Arts and Crafts architect C.F.A. Voysey built the finest house in Trebetherick. When in the 1920s Ernie Betjemann decided to build himself a holiday retreat, he commissioned his golfing friend Robert Atkinson, architect of the first Odeon cinemas, to design 'Undertown', itself a magnificent piece of Arts and Crafts, with its swooping roof and overhanging eaves, its mullioned windows and its whitewashed granite.

'The cosy fuschia-ed and tamarisk-ed [*sic*] gardens of Trebetherick with their sunken slate terraces set out for tea in the shade of macro-carpas' remained for Betjeman the landscape of his inner peace, his paradise. It was not a paradise lost; as a natural melancholic he was too canny to take risks by throwing away things which made him happy. Trebetherick was his secret 'other place', his soul-refreshment. It was the holiday place of his parents, even when they were quarrelling with one another and when he, as an adolescent, was finding them exasperating. It was the place where he took his own children on holiday, and to which he returned whenever he could in adult life; it was where he died, in 1984, and in St Enodoc's churchyard he lies buried.

Cornwall appealed to the mystic in Betjeman,

> And all the time the waves, the waves, the waves
> Chase, intersect and flatten on the sand
> As they have done for centuries, as they will
> For centuries to come, when not a soul
> Is left to picnic on the blazing rocks,
> When England is not England, when mankind
> Has blown himself to pieces. Still the sea,
> Consolingly disastrous, will return
> While the strange starfish, hugely magnified,
> Waits in the jewelled basin of a pool.

He continued, throughout life, to see the seashore with the amazed eye of the child. Cornwall was also a place where he had jolly friends. Among the first friends they made, at the Haven Guest House, were the Larkworthies. Joan, a year older than John Betjeman, remembered Bess, bustling into the guest house, followed by her four-year-old son who 'used to walk exactly like her, rather fast . . . I can see him now – coming in in a white suit, little anxious face, big eyes.'

Joan was one of the first female playmates who fell for his charm. He enjoyed emphasising, what was a genuine and ineradicable part of his nature, his timorousness. She remembered his being dragooned into a cricket match with the other children, and walking on the pitch 'in a very stiff painful way'. When she asked him if anything was the matter, the reply was, 'I'm covered in newspapers. I am afraid of being hurt.' He had completely padded himself, round arms and legs, with newspapers, giving himself the appearance of the Michelin man.

In London, cooped up in his private dream-world at 31 West Hill, the rough and tumble of other children could appear threatening. He had the statutory crush on a neighbour's little daughter, Peggy Purey-Cust – an admiral's daughter who lived at the considerably grander Number 82, West Hill. He was also bullied by two of the boys who attended the same kindergarten, Byron House. To his horror, when he moved on to Highgate Junior School, he found that the pair, Jack Shakespeare and Willie Buchanan, had arrived before him. He was a pupil there from September 1915 to March 1917. In *Summoned by Bells* he remembered them

> now red-capped and jacketed like me:
> 'Betjeman's a German – spy –
> Shoot him down and let him die:
> Betjeman's a German spy,
> A German spy, a German spy.'

Britain, which had been so fervently pro-German in the last years of Queen Victoria's reign, developed an insane anti-Hun mania from almost the moment war broke out in 1914. Much-loved German bakers' shops were torched. It became unpatriotic to like Beethoven. Little children, still taught German as a matter of course in many schools, seized the opportunity to torment their German teachers. The language itself was a joke, an excuse to find 'rude words' which might be permissibly yelled at the teacher ('Zucker *damn it*'). In such an atmosphere, it was bad luck to be called Betjeman, and to have the timorous clowning, cowering nature which appealed to the protective instincts in females and the bully in males.

Ernie Betjemann could not fail to have found it disturbing that his son was mocked because of his name, lured by Shakespeare and Buchanan to Swain's Lane, at the bottom of West Hill, where they ripped off his shorts and threw him in a holly bush.

I learned a lot from that tough London boys' school. I learned how to get round people, how to lie, how to show off just enough to attract attention but not so much as to attract unwelcome attention, how to bribe bullies with sweets (four ounces a penny in those days) – and I learned my first lessons in mistrusting my fellow beings.

The affectation of disliking England's greatest poet which he retained to the end of his days – 'I couldn't see why Shakespeare was admired' – makes more sense when one remembers Jack Shakespeare's taunts.

His flowering poetic taste was in the direction of narrative verse, such as might be found in 'Reciters' – volumes of verse designed, in schoolrooms or parlours, to be recited – 'Casabianca', 'The Wreck of the Hesperus', 'Soldier's Dream'. These, and the rhythms and cadences of the hymnal, were to be the formal inspiration of Betjeman the poet. And once again he is remarkable for the extent to which he did not need to move on, once he had discovered a formula to suit him. He tells us: 'I knew as soon as I could read and write / That I must be a poet'.

By the time Betjeman was a boy, English poetry, like the British Empire, had reached a division of the ways. It was not a division which was apparent for everyone. Versifiers like Masefield, who was destined to become Poet Laureate, could continue writing their anthology pieces. But in even the best of the so-called Georgian poets (named after George V) there was a feeling of the machine running down. It is a mistake to think of Betjeman writing in their wake or following in their footsteps, though he makes occasional echoes of the best of them – Housman, for example. In rather a similar way, it would be a mistake to try to find inspiration for Blake's poetry in the literary traditions of his contemporaries. Blake's *Songs of Innocence and Experience* grew out of ballad sheets, and the hymns of Nonconformist chapels. Betjeman's poetry grew out of music-hall songs, hymns and the Reciter. Meanwhile, waiting in the wings, to outshadow the etiolated offerings of the 'Georgians', was a poet of an altogether different order, an American called Thomas

Stearns Eliot. It is one of the most extraordinary coincidences in literary history that Eliot at this time was a master at Highgate Junior School. The child Betjeman had his verses bound up into a book, and presented them to 'The American master, Mr Eliot' . . . 'At the time / A boy called Jelly said, "He thinks they're bad".' In later life, Eliot apparently kept his counsel about his assessment of Betjeman's poetry. As a publisher, however, at Faber & Gwyer, later Faber & Faber, in 1936, he tried to publish Betjeman as a poet – before he was taken up by the firm which published most of his work, John Murray. Faber did, however, publish, for a while, another of Betjeman's great achievements, the *Shell Guides*. Different as the two men were in temperament, they met at a number of important levels. Both laughed at many of the same things. Both loved the English music hall – see Eliot's classic appreciation of Marie Lloyd. Both loved 'old London', the City, City churches, gentlemen's clubs. When Eliot taught Betjeman, he was still a young man, spiritually homesick and adrift, and locked into a disastrously unhappy marriage. He was to find his Rock in just such Anglican shrines as delighted Betjeman –

> where the walls
> Of Magnus Martyr hold
> Inexplicable splendour of Ionian white and gold.

On a level of faith, and loyalty to their church, the two men found a profound bond.

༖ ༖ ༖

If in London the young Betjeman nurtured the introspection of the only child, in Cornwall, with more congenial companions, he could develop that other, very usual quality in onlies, compulsive sociability.

It was in sociable Trebetherick that a solution was found to Betjeman's education, an escape route not only from the bullies of Highgate Junior, but also from the awkwardness of class. One of the ideas of Victorian boarding schools was to cement the class system. But those who attended them, all treated alike, all fed and clothed in the same austere manner, had mysteriously managed, whether or not their fathers were gentlemen, to make themselves a cut above.

Ernie and Bess Betjeman befriended A.E. 'Hum' Lynam and his wife May who had a house at Trebetherick called Cliff Bank. Hum's brother Charles Cotterill – 'Skipper' – Lynam was the headmaster of a school for dons' sons and daughters in North Oxford, called the Dragon. Skipper's children, Joc and Audrey, became Betjeman's friends at Trebetherick and remained his friends for life, as did the rest of the Trebetherick 'gang' – Joan and Roland Oakley, Vasey, Ralph and Alastair Adams, John and Biddy Walsham, the Larkworthies already mentioned (Joan and Tom), Phoebe and Alan Stokes . . . The difficulty of making a coherent chronicle of a gregarious man is comparable to trying to catch his attention at a crowded party, where everyone clusters around. It is important to remember the two sides, always – the need for solitude, and the fact that he wanted, so much of the time, to be in a crowd.

What are now called preparatory schools – preparing children for public school – were more often in those days called private schools. In most such places, the boys would still be dressed in stiff Eton collars, and varieties of Victorian school uniform: miniature bowler hats or top hats; blazers or tail coats. The Dragon was different from this. It was a disciplined, organised school, but written into its organisation was a studied bohemianism. The children wore 'sensible' clothes – corduroy shorts, aertex shirts. The lives of the pupils, in which cleverness was expected of them, but not too much care was given to outward appearances, matched the lives of their parents, mostly dons who lived with their wives in the rented, lumpy neo-Gothic redbrick villas of the surrounding North Oxford roads.

This too, like North London, and North Cornwall, became part of the Betjeman inner landscape and recurs frequently in his verse.

The portly figure of the don's wife, dying in 1940 at an Oxford bus stop, breathes her last within yards of the Dragon School –

> This dress has grown such a heavier load
> Since Jack was only a Junior Proctor,
> And rents were lower in Rawlinson Road.

In a May-Day Song, to be sung to the tune of 'Annie Laurie', the blossom is out in Belbroughton Road, the gardens are bright with prunus and forsythia

> And a constant sound of flushing runneth from windows where
> The toothbrush too is airing in this new North Oxford air
> From Summerfields to Lynam's, the thirsty tarmac dries,
> And a Cherwell mist dissolveth on elm-discovering skies.

The Cherwell is the river running past the playing fields at the edge of the Dragon. Summer Fields is another small private school, a little further north. It chiefly sends boys (such as the Prime Minister Harold Macmillan) to Eton. At the beginning of the war, its school magazine noted, 'Wavell mi has done well in North Africa'. Lynam's was another name for the Dragon School.

When Betjeman first went to the school, in May 1917, Skipper Lynam was still the headmaster, and he remembered 'the dramatic moment at a prize-giving when Skipper threw off his gown and Hum assumed it . . .'

> Hum was like a father to me. One always knew one could go to
> him if up the spout, although one never did. There was the feeling
> that he was there as a protection against injustice. He taught me how
> to speak in public and how to recite, 'Hands behind your back. Eyes
> on the clock. Stand at the front of the stage. Now speak up.' Hum's

preoccupation with religion and the school services, I realise now, greatly affected me. Here was this great, but never remote and always kind man, interested in religion. There must be something in it. Preoccupation with it since, for which I am especially grateful, must be due to Hum and always, of course, one was part of his family in holidays in Cornwall, Joc and Audrey, the Adams family and the Walshams, all of whom were at school.

To this extent, being at the Dragon was an extension of the Cornish experience. Betjeman was happy at the Dragon, in spite of the fact that, like all such establishments until the 1970s, it practised corporal punishment. *Summoned by Bells* recalls one of the masters, Gerard Haynes ('From his lower lip / Invariably hung a cigarette'), thwacking Betjeman with a slipper for talking after lights out in the dormitory.

> 'I liked the way you took that beating, John.
> Reckon yourself henceforth a gentleman.'

He was not reckoned a gentleman by all his friends and coevals.

Hugh Gaitskell, a future leader of the Labour Party, got on well with Betjeman, but his parents warned him against the friendship. Betjeman was said to have relations who lived in Polstead Road (the road where Lawrence of Arabia spent his childhood), too far north, too recently built, too far from the centre of Oxford to be quite the thing. When young Hugh Gaitskell still failed to pick up the hint, and met Betjeman during the holidays in London, his parents had to spell it out. They did not like him mixing with a child whose *father was in trade*.

Another friend, destined to become a Roman Catholic priest, was Ronald Hughes Wright with whom he enjoyed exploring the churches in the town. This incipient fascination with architecture was nurtured by Mr Haynes, who took favoured boys for jaunts on his motor-bike in search of Early English Gothic architecture.

At the Dragon, Betjeman enjoyed acting – his first appearance on the boards was as Ruth in the *Pirates of Penzance* – 'a pleasing buxom wench' said the school magazine – and, in spite of his distaste for Shakespeare, he was also successful in *Henry V*, as Charles VI of France and the Earl of Cambridge. 'The cleverest actor of all was John Betjemann', said the *Oxford Times*, 'he played the mad old king of France in such a way that, instead of being completely minor it became one of the most impressive parts in the whole play.'

Offstage, too, he was a noted eccentric.

'Betjeman first achieved notice when his father sent him an unusually sophisticated stationary steam engine which inspired me', remembered a contemporary, Per Mallalieu – like Gaitskell another future Labour politician – 'to some pyrotechnic mis-spellings.

> "Betgiman's engin was going tonight", I wrote to my mother, "and it has a lovely pump that pumps in water whill the thing is going". The "engin" drove a variety of tools including a miniature circular saw on which H. K. Hardy tried to cut his finger nails, spending a week in bandages after . . .'

Betjeman too got himself in bandages. He had been intoning some chant to himself in one of the classrooms and marking the beat by pulling and releasing the rope which opened and shut a glass skylight. They spent about a week in the school Sick Room picking bits of glass out of his head. 'This was a serious matter for the rest of us because no one was allowed to play with his "engin" until he returned, which, eventually, he did, looking like a Sikh.' 'Thereafter', Mallalieu added, 'Wright and Betjeman specialised in eccentricity.'

Laughter redeems boarding-school life, and for some reason the jokes are funnier when the children are between seven and thirteen than later on. At the Dragon, Betjeman was in his element. He had developed his incipient love of buildings. He had fallen, especially, in love with Oxford, and begun to see it through the eyes of an old illustrated book, purchased at the long-vanished shop of

Chaundy's, and illustrated with Victorian watercolours of wisteria-draped colleges, where gowned Doctors of Divinity entered the ancient porch of a college. 'All that was crumbling picturesque and quaint / Informed my taste.' He had also developed his histrionic gifts. The Betjeman phenomenon was beginning to be formed.

⚜ ⚜ ⚜

When he came home for the holidays, he found that his parents had left 31 West Hill, and abandoned North London in favour of Chelsea. The new house, 53 Church Street, was 'poky, dark and cramped' but fashionable. Bess now had friends 'whose friends had friends who knew Augustus John'. The advantage of the house, as far as Betjeman was concerned, was its proximity to his friend Ronald Wright, so he could continue trawling round churches and second-hand bookstalls even in the holidays. Though Bess groaned as 'more books' were carried into the tiny house, Ernest Betjeman encouraged his son. 'If you must buy books, then buy the best.' He inscribed George Goodwin's *The Churches of London* with the words, 'To my dear boy in the hope that his appreciation of all that is beautiful will never fade'. The hope was fulfilled.

One of the most successful passages in *Summoned by Bells* is the conclusion to chapter VI, when he describes seeking out City churches, following the sound of a single bell, tinkling down those still unbombed intersecting lanes of the City until he found 'St Botolph this, St Mary that', and heard the words of Evensong from the Book of Common Prayer read out as they had been for three hundred years.

> Thus were my London Sundays incomplete
> If unaccompanied by Evening Prayer.

Ronnie Wright and he were to go different ways. As early as twelve years old, Wright became a Roman Catholic. This was never to be

From Betjeman's sketchbooks:
St James's church, Holloway

Betjeman's way. The great city churches of Wren, with their gilded
Commandment Boards and sword-rests; the varied styles, from
medieval to Victorian neo-Norman of the Oxford churches, the
sand-lashed mysteries of Cornish shrines, all held something for

him, which could not, quite, be found anywhere else. At the same time, he felt it to be largely a longing for the past, certainly not a conscious search for God. But the longing continued until it grew into the search, even during the next phase of life, his inevitably miserable adolescence.

THE SECRET GLORY

'When I announce that I was at Harrow I always add "in all but fact", as I like the turn of phrase,' he told a friend in grown-up life. He loved the songs of Harrow School such as 'Five Hundred Faces and All So Strange' or 'Forty Years On'. He believed that Harrovians wrote the best prose, giving as proof the names of Winston Churchill, Wyndham Ketton-Cremer and Sir Bernard Docker. Surprisingly, given the splashy colours of Churchill's Macaulayesque rhetoric, Betjeman spoke of 'cool Harrovian prose'. 'I like things that are overshadowed – like Harrow', he once said in a speech.

But, in fact, Betjeman was not sent to the Alma Mater of Sir Winston Churchill, Lord Byron and the seventh Earl of Shaftesbury. He never attended that school which, from the train in the gloaming, resembled a rocky Cornish island, that outpost in North London of the Elizabethan age, which received its charter in 1572, but which had links with a much older foundation, that Harrow which, next to Eton, ranks as a school for the upper classes. He went instead to Marlborough College, an architecturally undistinguished boarding school in Wiltshire, founded by a Rugby master in 1843, in the first instance for the sons of the clergy. Betjeman arrived slightly older than the usual thirteen – just after his fourteenth birthday in September 1920.

Had he gone to Harrow, he would almost certainly have been bullied for snobbish reasons, as Anthony Trollope was in the previous century. Public schools were, and for all we know still are, brutal institutions. At the top, rather like an eighteenth-century

Deist's conception of the Almighty, was the headmaster, who preached sermons in the school chapel – the one good building at Marlborough, by G.F. Bodley; who probably taught classics to the sixth form but had very little to do with the actual running of his kingdom. The school was/is divided into houses of fifty or so boys. Housemasters profoundly resented any attempt by the headmaster to interfere in their fiefdoms. In Betjeman's day, a housemaster at Marlborough received the boarding fees directly from the parents and was expected, upon his retirement, to make a handsome profit. It paid the housemaster to be parsimonious. Food and bedding for the boys would therefore be on the verge of inadequate. The hunger, cold and discomfort suffered by the pupils was deemed to be good for the character, as was the frequent use of corporal punishment and bullying as a means of subduing independent spirits. In the house, while teachers could, and sometimes did, beat the boys, the overall running of the place was left in the hands of the older boys, who were allowed to beat younger boys with canes, to make them work as minor servants ('fags'), cleaning shoes, making toast, running errands. Moreover, these adolescent gauleiters could, and usually did, rule not merely by formal discipline but by terror and bullying.

Anyone who has been educated in such an institution will recognise the atmosphere of the Marlborough chapter in *Summoned by Bells* – 'Doom! Shivering doom' . . . 'The dread of beatings, dread of being late! / And greatest dread of all, the dread of games'.

Betjeman's adolescence was as stormy as most. At home, his parents were more than ever quarrelsome with one another, and with him. There were slammed doors and 'black waves of hate'. Ernest Betjeman, who had been the friend of his only son, was now perceived as a monster. The habits of bad temper which the two parents and their boy permitted themselves no doubt sharpened, in John Betjeman's mind, a sense of his father's imperfections. To the Dragon boy, Ernest had been the charming patron, who read aloud from Oliver Goldsmith and persuaded his son to buy old books and write poetry. He was the weekend painter who enjoyed the landscape of rural Hertfordshire and the Cornish coastline. Now, as knowing adolescence advanced in John, Ernie was seen as a tyrant, forcing him to shoot with his Hertfordshire friends and to play golf in Cornwall when he would prefer to be looking at old churches. The hatred between the two male Betjemans was perhaps quickened by the pathos of Bess, with her toothache and her psychosomatic illnesses. Was the adolescent Betjeman becoming aware that all was not well in his parents' marriage? When did he begin to discover, as he certainly knew in his undergraduate days, that Ernest had a mistress, possibly several?

Whatever the reasons for the estrangement between father and son it was a powerful ingredient in Betjeman's make-up. Perhaps it was genetically programmed that the younger should fight the elder. Betjeman himself did not learn from his experiences of psychological warfare with his father in teenaged years to be sensitive to his own son during adolescence. He was programmed to copy the same pattern of turning into a tyrant with his own son, at about the period of life, early teens, that he himself had come to hate Ernie.

Marlborough, with its hearty, gamesy ethos, appeared to be at war with everything the budding aesthete stood for. Moreover, it was relentlessly male in atmosphere, and Betjeman, in spite of enjoying and even loving the company of his own sex, was at his happiest in the company of females. The awful discomfort of a boys' boarding house derives not only from the rows of lavatories without cubicle-doors; not just from the icy dormitories, and the smell of sweaty clothes and boots; nor even from the total failure in any inch of such institutions to consider the look of the place. It was also, in those days, the complete absence of the tenderness which could be found in the company of girls.

Here were no Joan Larkworthies, still less Peggy Purey-Custs.

Gauche Marlburian

Some of his contemporaries were boys destined for very great distinction in their fields. Louis MacNeice, a little older than Betjeman, grew to be a very different sort of poet. Anthony Blunt, art historian, keeper of the Queen's Pictures and Soviet agent, was another contemporary, as was Frederick Copleston, later a Jesuit priest whose many-volumed *History of Philosophy* is unsurpassed.

ıs such as Marlborough like to advertise such famous
ıs typical products of the system. In fact, however, poets, and
ıs and aesthetes and philosophers, emerge in spite of, rather
than as a consequence of the public-school system. The only achieve-
ment of the men listed above which could certainly be
credited to Marlborough is Blunt's ability for so long to fool, and
undermine, the system as a communist agent. Resourceful children
learn deceit as the first lesson in such places, as a way of surviving.
They also learn, which must have quickened Betjeman's awareness
that his father had 'shop man's' manners, the deadly and indelible
lessons of snobbery.

Betjeman triumphantly survived it, using tricks he had already
mastered at Highgate Junior, evasiveness, buffoonery and charm. He
was also helped by his temperament, since, as well as being timor-
ous, he had a tremendous capacity to derive enjoyment from life.
There is a great deal of laughter in these schools, as he remembered
when thinking of the deaf invigilator in the Memorial Reading Room
at Marlborough –

> 'Do you tickle your arse with a feather, Mr Purdick?'
> 'What?'
> 'Particularly nasty weather, Mr Purdick.'

Although the bullying and the discomfort were memories, Betjeman
also developed a deep love of Marlborough, and its surrounding
country, as a place. The art master, Christopher Hughes, was a friend
for life, teaching him, as 'Tortoise' Haynes had done at the Dragon,
to take an interest in his surroundings, and to capture them in line
and wash. When he had children of his own, Betjeman taught them
to sketch, and 'as Hughes had taught him, how to effect a cloudy sky
by blotting the still wet blue wash with a rolled-up handkerchief '.

Marlborough and all such schools were specifically designed to
instil conformity.

Everybody thought that he had absolutely fallen into line; that he was absorbing the *ethos* of the place in the most admirable fashion, subduing his own individuality, his opinions, his habits, to the general tone of the community around him – putting off, as it were, the profane dust of his own spirit and putting on the mental frock of the brotherhood. This of course is one of the aims – rather *the* great aim – of the system . . .

'There is no system known to human wit that approaches in thoroughness and minuteness the supervision under which every single boy is kept all through his life at an English Public School.'

These words come from *The Secret Glory* by Arthur Machen, the book which was lent to Betjeman by a clergyman, met while cycling round to look at Cornish churches. The priest, the Reverend Wilfrid Johnson, was a tall, bearded figure, rector of St Ervan from 1915 to 1955.

The village upon which Betjeman had alighted was a long ride from Trebetherick. Dr Pevsner, his mind not attuned to the glories Betjeman was to discover there, found the village 'a picture of squalor and neglect'. The austere church, however, was a place where something rather more engaged was taking place than had been reflected in Betjeman's aimless pursuits of Evensong in almost empty City fanes, or among the comforting school hymns of Bodley's chapel at Marlborough. As Ambrose Meyrick, hero of *The Secret Glory*, discovers, Christianity 'was not a moral code, with some sort of metaphorical Heaven held out as a reward for its due observance, but a great mystical adventure into the unknown sanctity'.

The book contrasts the world of 'reasonable' Anglicanism and public school morality on the one hand, and the spiritual power-house which is hidden, but contained, in the old Celtic Church. Among the Welsh hills, the Holy Grail itself is hidden.

Boswell quotes Johnson as saying, 'When at Oxford I took up Law's *Serious Call to a Holy Life*, expecting to find it a dull book (as such books generally are), and perhaps to laugh at it. But I found Law quite an overmatch for me: and this was the first occasion of my thinking in earnest of religion, after I became capable of rational inquiry.' 'From this time forward', adds Boswell, 'religion was the predominant object of his thoughts; though, with the just sentiments of a conscientious Christian, he lamented that his practice of his duties fell far short of what it ought to be.'

Arthur Machen's *The Secret Glory* occupies a comparable place in the inner history of John Betjeman. It is in some ways a badly written and bizarre book, lurching from one melodrama to the next. The hero, as well as glimpsing the Holy Grail, elopes from the public school with a parlourmaid and ends up being crucified by the Kurds. But the overwhelming things about it which spoke to the schoolboy Betjeman were its dismissal of public-school and middle-stump Church of England conformity, and its embrace of Mystery as the fundamental reality of life, the Mystery of all Mysteries being the Blessed Sacrament of the Eucharist.

When we read *The Secret Glory*, we find Betjemanic echoes all the way through. The appalling sarcasm of Mr Horbury, upbraiding Meyrick for his interest in Gothic architecture against the finer points of Greek grammar, seems exactly like the hated A.R. Gidney, who taught Greek to the Lower Sixth at Marlborough.

> Still droned the voice of Mr Gidney on:
> That 'ὅτι'? Can we take its meaning here
> Wholly as interrogative?

There is the vision of Welsh loveliness, in which love of God and love of a woman are blended –

> I saw golden Myfanwy, as she bathed in the brook Tarogi . . .
> I gazed into her blue eyes as it were into twin heavens.
> All the parts of her body were adornments and miracles.
> O gift of the everlasting!
> O wonderful and hidden mystery!

This moment in Machen finds its echo in many of Betjeman's poems, including the late one ('Lenten Thoughts of a High Anglican') where he glimpses in the Mistress 'A hint of the Unknown God': but most obviously in the fantasy poems he wrote about an actual Myfanwy, Myfanwy Evans. The vision of loveliness on a bicycle becomes blended with the experience of Eucharistic worship –

> Tubular bells of tall St Barnabas,
>   Single clatter above St Paul,
> Chasuble, acolyte, incense-offering,
>   Spectacled faces held in thrall.
> There in the nimbus and Comper tracery
>   Gold Myfanwy blesses us all.

More than any specific echoes and influences, however, we find in *The Secret Glory* one of the most distinctive features of Betjeman's whole attitude to life, namely that life is funny; but that humour itself derives from a fundamentally religious viewpoint. 'No real mirth is possible without the apprehension of the mysteries as its antecedent.'

Although published in 1922, Machen's book gives off, like the almost stupefying reek of incense-smoke, the scent of three decades earlier, the atmosphere of the 1890s.

As far as the history of English literature was concerned, it was the decade of turning point. In their different ways, two of the three giants on the poetic scene when Betjeman was growing up – Ezra Pound and W.B. Yeats – both looked back to the 1890s as the time when everything changed. Modernism found its roots in the symbolist poets of the 1890s. Neither was to make any appeal to Betjeman: the symbolism which attracted the other giant, the early T.S. Eliot, or the full-scale modernism of Pound and Eliot's later manner.

> The age demanded an image
> Of its accelerated grimace,
> Something for the modern stage,
> Not, at any rate, an Attic grace.

As Pound and Yeats both acknowledged – Pound in his tribute to the Nineties in the Hugh Selwyn Mauberley poems, and Yeats in his autobiographies – it was in the personalities and lives of the Nineties poets, as much as in what they wrote that the novelty and shocking-ness of the Decadence was heralded forth.

Almost the central event in this mythology was the arrest, trial and imprisonment of Oscar Wilde. It was an event which had shaken England. Obviously, the sexual nature of Wilde's offences was what made them so excitingly shocking to those newspaper-readers who had previously flocked in such hordes to laugh at his comedies in the theatre. His trials, during which his witty exchanges with prosecuting lawyers had blurred the distinction between his dramas and his life, now made the bourgeoisie uneasy, as they laughed about young men having secret lives, concealed from Lady Bracknell or Canon Chasuble, as they invented friends called Bunbury and made rather improbable declarations of love to sexless young women, as the Ideal Husband turned out to be one who 'is as domestic as if he was a bachelor'.

The subversive nature of homosexuality was one of the things which made it frightening, its apparent capacity to undermine the solid fabric of family life and morals. Wilde's trial for offences under section eleven of the Criminal Law Amendment Act 1885 revealed, not that he was guilty of buggery – hitherto the chief, if not in effect the only, charge which could be brought against homosexuals – but that he had made various challenges to 'decency' in the presence of a strange galaxy of rent-boys and other juvenile hangers-on. The cause of his downfall, however, had been his romantic obsession with Lord Alfred Douglas, third son of the eighth Marquess of

Queensberry, and whom Wilde had met in 1891. Wilde was a married man of thirty-seven. Douglas, an undergraduate at Magdalen College, Oxford, was just short of his twenty-first birthday. It was when Douglas's father, the Scarlet Marquess, became obsessed by the relationship, and left a card at Wilde's club to 'Oscar Wilde, posing as a somdomite [*sic*]' that Wilde sued Queensberry for libel. Queensberry was acquitted, and the witnesses whom he had accumulated (and in some cases bribed) to provide evidence in his defence, also provided enough evidence to send Wilde to prison for two years' penal servitude.

Betjeman was imaginatively caught up in this story. When he was a schoolboy at Marlborough, his burgeoning emotional life took a homosexual direction. *Summoned by Bells* speaks of

> First tremulous desires in Autumn stillness –
>   Grey eyes, lips laughing at another's joke,
> A nose, a cowlick – a delightful illness
>   That put me off my food and off my stroke.
> Here, 'twixt the church tower and the chapel spire
> Rang sad and deep the bells of my desire.

That is the published version. In the original typescript, preserved in the British Library, Betjeman had written

> Electric currents racing through my frame –
> Was this the love that dare not speak its name?

The phrase, which had entered the language as a synonym for homosexuality, comes from the poem 'Two Loves', of 1896. Its author was Alfred Douglas.

Betjeman discovered Douglas's poems at Marlborough and began the affectation, which he carried into grown-up life, of considering Douglas a better sonneteer than Shakespeare. 'When I was at Marlborough, I discovered that Oscar Wilde was someone one ought not to mention; so naturally he had a great attraction for me

In Brighton: Bosie,
Nancy Mitford, JB

. . . Then I discovered that Lord Alfred Douglas was actually still alive.' The schoolboy wrote to the poet, then in his early fifties, and a correspondence ensued. It began when Douglas was living in Belgium with his mother to escape imprisonment for criminal libel. (He had accused Winston Churchill, when First Lord of the Admiralty during the First World War, of publishing a false report of the Battle of Jutland in order to satisfy the Jews.)

The correspondence continued into the holidays, and the letters, arriving at Trebetherick, must have been read by Bess Betjemann. One day after lunch, his mother and Nancy Wright, sister of his friend Ronnie Wright, left the room, and Ernest Betjemann, by now very deaf and getting on badly with his son, took him for a walk up a lane. He accused him of having a correspondence with Lord Alfred Douglas. The adolescent Betjeman admitted it. His father then asked him if he knew what Douglas was, going on to explain that he was a bugger. Although young Betjeman had heard the word he did not know its precise anatomical meaning. After the graphic description given by Ernest, his son 'felt absolutely sick and shattered'.

Ernest Betjemann confiscated the correspondence and locked Bosie's letters in a safe. After Ernest died, Betjeman gave them to a biographer of Lord Alfred. 'They weren't very interesting.'

The letters themselves might not have been interesting, but

the pen friendship, which turned into an actual friendship, was reveal-
ing, and typical of Betjeman. He delighted in collecting out-of-the-way
friends and making a cult of them – developing what he called 'manias'
for them. He was also a very loyal friend, and did not drop them
simply because someone disapproved. In fact, disapproval by prigs was
something which actively encouraged him to keep such friendships in
good repair – witness, after the Second World War, his continued
friendship with the 'disgraced' fascists Oswald and Diana Mosley.

Bosie was the perfect friend in all these respects for the school-
boy Betjeman. There was another thing, however, to be noted about
the relationship. It might be thought that when a fifty-something
poet, whose name was notorious for homosexuality (although Bosie
was a married man), starts a correspondence with a schoolboy, that
the man would be the more powerful or authoritative in the
relationship. What struck Bosie, however, about Betjeman from the
first was the surprisingly authoritative strength behind the larky,
whimsical mask. Also, behind a mask of vagueness was a sharp and
well-stocked mind. Bosie was the first to notice how *learned*
Betjeman was. In 1939, when Betjeman and Bosie were still friends,
Lord Alfred gave a flavour of their relationship to his perhaps
surprising friend Marie Stopes. 'He signs his name "Moth" because
that is the name I bestowed on him when he was a boy at
Marlborough, after Armado's page in Love's Labour's Lost . . . a
"well-educated infant". I called him that because even in those days
he was omniscient.'

And naturally it was his friendship with Bosie, and his lifelong
preoccupation with the tragedy of Wilde, which inspired one of
Betjeman's finest poems of his early maturity, published in 1937
– 'The Arrest of Oscar Wilde at the Cadogan Hotel'. Its nine
quatrains give a stronger sense of Wilde than many of the weighty
biographies.

Betjeman pasted into his copy of W. B. Yeats's *Oxford Book of Modern
Verse* one of Bosie's typically vitriolic telegrams, sent to the editor –

W.B.Yeats, Abbey Theatre, Dublin.Your omission of my name from
the absurdly named *Oxford Book of Modern Verse* is typical of the attitude
of the minor poet to the major one. Had Thomas Moore been editing
such a book he would have omitted Keats and Shelley. Incidentally
why drag in Oxford? Why not Shoneen Irish? Alfred Douglas

Presumably, too, it was the friendship with Alfred Douglas which
directed Betjeman, after school, to his choice of Oxford College –
Magdalen – that beautiful combination of medieval and eighteenth-
century buildings where first Wilde and then Bosie had studied. With
its large chapel, its surpliced choir singing daily renditions of the
Prayer Book Matins and Evensong, its deer park and its meadow,
where Addison in the eighteenth century had walked among the
purple fritillaries, it was surely the ideal setting in which a young
poet could spread his wings. Perhaps, like the Victorian novelist
Charles Reade, author of *The Cloister and the Hearth*, Betjeman was
destined to become a 'lay fellow' of this ancient foundation? Destiny,
or what Betjeman sometimes called The Management, had crueller
plans.

4

OXFORD

When John Ruskin went up to Oxford as a gentleman-commoner in 1837, he went as the son of a tradesman; but the money made by his father as a sherry-merchant purchased him the status of 'Gentleman-commoner', a rank normally occupied by sons of noblemen. (Being noble entitled the young men to wear golden tassels on their caps – the 'tufts' which snobs hunted when they were known as 'tuft hunters'.) No one in Ruskin's family, however, supposed that he would follow his father into trade. His life as an aesthete and a connoisseur had been assured since boyhood.

With the growth of public-school education, more and more members of the commercial classes aspired to the university education, which since the eighteenth century had tended to be the preserve of the professional and upper classes. The First World War, with its cataclysmic culling of young men, increased the proportion of middle-class boys who would leave boarding school and go on to university.

G. Betjemann & Sons was a firm which had been founded in the 1820s, and from generation to generation, during the reign of Queen Victoria, father had handed over to son. John Betjeman's decision not to take over the business from Ernest was seen by himself as an intensely personal crisis; but it was one which was replicated in middle-class families all over Britain. Trade brought them money. They used the money to 'better' themselves, by which they meant, send their sons to the actual schools (Eton, Harrow, etc.) or imitations of them (Marlborough, Lancing) which were designed to train not tradesmen but soldiers and professionals, not manufacturers but bishops and judges. There is no wonder, particularly after the trauma of the First World War, that Betjeman's generation felt a heady sense of liberation, but also a feeling of disorientation from their roots. Oxford confirmed a process which had begun when he first went to the Dragon School.

Moreover, Oxford itself, in its recovery from the devastation of the First World War, passed, in the early 1920s, through something like an extended festival or *mardi gras*. The generation following the Great War, those who came up and took their degrees immediately after the Armistice, included many who had been in the armed services. Figures such as C.S. Lewis, wounded at Arras in 1917, or Maurice Bowra, who had taken part in heavy fighting in the region of Villers Bretonneux, provided the backbone of the rising generation of dons. These men, who had endured experiences so terrible that often they could not talk about them, were different in kind from the ones who came after. The next intake, in which hearties threw aesthetes into ponds, and such figures as Harold Acton and Brian Howard posed and minced, signalled the coming of a new age. It was silliness with a purpose. Betjeman and the friends he was to make for life arrived immediately after these.

⤬ ⤬ ⤬

'My diary', Betjeman wrote desperately to a friend with whom he had been staying in April 1940, '(a red Oxford University one) I lost it and it has made me very sad and helpless.' Just as he liked to use stamps from the Isle of Man, a place he had only visited a few times, so he always, to the end of his life, carried an Oxford University pocket diary, a perpetual badge of exile from the university which he attended only for a few short years, and which he left without taking a degree. Samuel Johnson who likewise left Oxford without taking a degree, in poverty, and with little hope of promotion or preferment, retained an exaggerated devotion to his old university.

For all Betjeman's passionate interest in literature, Oxford taught him little, if anything, any more than it had taught Samuel Johnson, who arrived having a far wider knowledge of Latin literature than the dons, or any more than it taught the poet Shelley whom it expelled. In his jokey, mythologised version of events in *Summoned by Bells*, he makes

Magdalen undergraduate

it seem as if he was so frivolous, so devoted to parties and smart friends, that his own expulsion without a degree was almost inevitable. But in the decade or so after it happened, staying awake at night and thinking about it with uncontrollable rage, this was not how it seemed. Looking back aged thirty-three, he could see that he had been

> a very usual type of undergraduate, caught up with the latest fashions in 'art', pretentious and superficial. But all that, I have since discovered is quite right in this type . . . [he means the aesthetic temperament] . . . Indeed it should be encouraged, for it argues an awareness of what is going on and an incipient sensibility which can easily be crushed or misdirected for ever by an antipathetic tutor.

Betjeman was unlucky enough, when he came up to Magdalen College in the Michaelmas Term of 1925, to find that he had as his tutor C.S. Lewis, a figure who was as antipathetic as it was possible to be.

Oxford was the place where Betjeman met those who were to be his friends for the rest of his life. To that extent, it was a place

Osbert Lancaster

of incalculable importance to him. Without Oxford, he might never have met Maurice Bowra, 'Colonel' Kolkhorst, Father Frederic Hood, Osbert Lancaster, Kenneth Clark, Bryan Guinness, A.L. Rowse, W.H. Auden, Alan Pryce-Jones, Tom Driberg, John Sparrow, Henry Yorke, Billy Clonmore, Robert Byron, Frank Pakenham, Graham and Joan Eyres-Monsell, Lionel Perry, John Dugdale, Edward James, Randolph Churchill, and *their* friends, families, girlfriends, sisters who constituted his enormous 'circle' for the rest of his life. Almost instantaneously this compulsively sociable and gregarious young man entered into a social circle which saw the point of him, rejoiced in his humour and encouraged all that was best and worst in his character.

While most of these figures saw out their full three, or in the case of classicists four, years at Oxford, Betjeman did not. His friend and undergraduate contemporary Osbert Lancaster, who was at Lincoln College, spent most of his time, when not going to parties, studying drawing at the Ruskin School or acting in the OUDS (Oxford University Dramatic Society). He ended his time there having read as little as possible 'of the insufferable Beowulf or Sir Gawain and the Green Knight' with 'an honest Fourth'. Anthony Powell, another contemporary, at Balliol College, managed a third. Betjeman was not allowed to try.

He obviously was not good at passing exams. In those days, aspirant students had to pass an elementary test in Latin and

Mathematics called Responsions. It is inconceivable that, having been at the Dragon School and Marlborough, Betjeman did not have reasonable proficiency in both subjects, yet when he tried Responsions in the spring of 1925, he failed it not once, but twice. Fortunately, the President of Magdalen, Sir Herbert Warren, obviously liked the sound of Betjeman. Ernest suggested to his son that he send the President a sonnet for which he had won a prize at school. He received the reply:

> Dear Mr Betjemann,
> I am glad to have your poem. I am much interested in it. I shouldn't have called it a 'typical' Prize Poem at all and I have written one and read a great many in my time. I think the Marlborough authorities must have been open-minded and discerning to give it the prize.

In other letters, Warren urged Betjeman to read Matthew Arnold. ('It might be suitable to read "Tristan & Iseult" at Trebetherick.')

Warren was a legendarily snobbish man, who had been proud when the Prince of Wales came to the college as a commoner. At Christ Church, the Emperor of Japan had entered his son. When, however, the Crown Prince had, on some application form, been asked to name his father, he had written the word GOD, a blasphemy which the Dean of Christ Church, also dean of the cathedral, felt was inadmissible in so stoutly churchy an institution. When the Japanese Crown Prince applied rather to Magdalen he was welcomed by Sir Herbert, with the assurance that Magdalen was used to undergraduates of the most distinguished descent.

Nevertheless, Warren was not so snobbish as to turn down the son in Betjemann & Sons, manufacturers of luxury goods in Pentonville Road. He must have seen Betjeman's qualities in an interview and in the poems he sent in. Why, it might be asked, was the President of the College conducting so much of the admissions business himself in the case of the English Literature students? Because, until that summer, they did not have an English Literature tutor, and had only elected C.S. Lewis to the Fellowship a few months before Betjeman's eventual arrival.

Lewis might not come across as a man who was uncertain of himself, but as a fledgling university teacher, he was. He had seen himself getting a Fellowship in philosophy, and making a name as a poet. His first effort by way of verse was a long parricidal fantasy entitled *Dymer* at which he had been working since the end of the war. He had a relationship with his own father which made Betjeman's with Ernest appear harmonious by comparison. Since the end of the war, Lewis had been secretly living with a married woman, the mother of a comrade killed in action. Nowadays, when a completely different ethos prevails, it is hard to imagine that a man's whole career could founder because of such private matters. (The poet William Empson was asked to leave his Fellowship at Magdalene, Cambridge when a contraceptive was found in a drawer of his bedroom by a servant; Empson's name was expunged from the college lists, so deep was the disgrace considered.)

The Lewis, therefore, whom Betjeman met was an edgy twenty-seven-year-old with many personal problems. He was always awkward with poets, envious of them, and unable to see their merits because he so much wanted to be a poet himself. He disliked Betjeman's school contemporary Louis MacNeice. He made philistine jeers at T.S. Eliot. He once had a fight in a pub with Roy Campbell – admittedly on a non-literary question. He was also at this date a militant atheist, anti-religious as perhaps only those born in Northern Ireland can be.

Lewis took an instant dislike to Betjeman. The fledgling aesthete from Marlborough was equally horrified by Lewis, who had a barking voice, with just a trace of Ulster in it, and who organised 'Beer and Beowulf' evenings for his pupils to help them master sound change and other intricacies of Anglo-Saxon philology.

> Thus Æ to E they soon were fetchin'
> Cf, such forms as ÞÆC and ÞECCEAN,

Lewis boomed. (His nickname was 'Heavy' Lewis.) Soon his cantan-
kerous diary was making such entries as

> Betjeman appeared in a pair of eccentric bedroom slippers and said he
> hoped I didn't mind them as he had a blister. He seemed so pleased
> with himself that I couldn't help saying that I should mind them very
> much myself but that I had no objection to *his* wearing them – a view
> which I believed surprised him.

It would not be fair to say that Lewis had no humour. Once a term he
forced his pupils to 'the English binge'. Excuses were not accepted.
'Nothing above the belly or below the knee tonight!' he would call
out, as the drink flowed, and they were all obliged to indulge in what
he called bawdry. But humour of a more delicate kind often passed
Lewis by. On one occasion when, for the third week running,
Betjeman had failed to produce an essay, he was astounded when his
pupil threw himself down on the hearth-rug of Lewis's 'arid room'
in the New Buildings.

'What is the matter, Betjeman,' growled Lewis.

'I'm hopeless. I've failed to produce an essay yet again. I shall be
a failure. I shall have to take Holy Orders. But, you see, I am in such
an agony of doubt, I can't decide!'

'What can't you decide, Betjeman?'

'I can't decide whether to be a High Church clergyman with a
short lacy surplice or a very Low Church clergyman with long grey
moustaches.'

Like many of Betjeman's jokes, it was almost true. In the inter-
vals of getting to know almost everyone in Oxford, attending all the
parties, and wowing people with his charm and eccentricity,
Betjeman was sampling the church life of the place. He made a
particular cult of a Low Church, long since demolished, called Holy
Trinity, Gas Street. It was not a fervent or an evangelical church; it
was old-fashioned Low, with the Lord's Supper, on the rare occasions
when it took place, being celebrated, as the 1662 Prayer Book

demands, at the north end of the Holy Table. The incumbent of this church was called Arber. Betjeman, to the end of his days, liked to call Low Church clergy 'Father' and High Church clergy 'Rev.' or 'Revd', deliberately incorrectly omitting their initials or first name. So the High Church Frederic Hood would be Rev. Hood, and this was Father Arber. One of Betjeman's High Church friends stole a little notice from the Kardomah café and placed it on the altar at Holy Trinity, Gas Street. It read 'No service at this table'. This joke was not in Betjeman's style. His jokes about religion always held back just this side of mockery. He genuinely revered Father Arber – who became one of those many figures whom he discovered, invented, cultivated, of whom others either could not see the point, or had not hitherto seen the point until Betjeman invented it.

At the other end of the ecclestiastical spectrum from Holy Trinity, Gas Street, was Pusey House in St Giles's. When the venerable figure of Dr Pusey died, his High Church disciples believed, with the great Victorian churchman himself, that Christianity was about to be snuffed out in Oxford. The college chapels, they believed, would soon be emptied. Anglican worship would no longer be obligatory for undergraduates. Darwinism and cynicism would sweep away seven hundred years of Christianity from Oxford and its shrines. They therefore established a religious institution in St Giles's, the broad street going northwards out of Oxford which gives the place the air of a Cotswold market town. The architect of the chapel was Temple Moore, a figure whose work meant so much to Betjeman from this date onwards. When Betjeman was an undergraduate, Moore's somewhat austere Gothic chapel – a monastic chapel from Moore's native Yorkshire – had not yet been refurbished by another favourite architect of Betjeman's, Ninian Comper. (A glorious gilded baldachino, hung with fabric of 'Comper pink', came in 1937.) As well as the chapel, at Pusey House there was kept Dr Pusey's considerable theological library, to which a modern theological library had been added. There was a principal and a small community of priests known

as librarians. The Principal was
an ancient Victorian bigot,
always known as The Darwell,
the Reverend Dr Darwell Stone,
a bearded figure who resembled
Melchisedek, according to a
contemporary. He was unworld-
ly to a degree, enjoying contro-
versies about such esoteric
questions as the Reservation of
the Sacrament, but not much
understanding the world. (He
once said the greatest day of
his life was when he was asked
to contribute an article to *The
Smart Set* – though no one could
tell whether he had accepted the

Father Freddy Hood

invitation.) Once, when a breezy undergraduate told the Darwell that
he had been to see the Dolly Sisters during the vacation, he received
the reply, 'That is a religious order of which I have not heard.'

It was the younger priest-librarians at Pusey House who made an
impression upon Betjeman, especially Frederic Hood (Freddy) who
conducted a service of 'Devotions' to the Blessed Sacrament every
Saturday evening to prepare the congregation for the awesome
moment next morning when they would receive Holy Communion.
Many who laughed, or smiled, at the sight of Freddy sitting at the
harmonium singing 'Sweet Sah – crament Divine' with his strange
lisp on the letter 'r' would stay to pray among the incense-smoke.
The place made a huge impression upon Betjeman, as he recorded
in his autobiography. It was to Freddy Hood that he made his first
confession, a practice he continued until the end of his life.

Betjeman's religious life, however, went on against a background
of riotous sociability. And, unquestionably, Betjeman, in common

with all those lucky enough to know Maurice Bowra, learned more at his parties than he learned at lectures or tutorials. Isaiah Berlin, in his tribute at Bowra's memorial service in 1971, said,

> Those who knew him solely through his published works can have no inkling of his genius. As a talker he could be incomparable. His wit was verbal and cumulative: the words came in short, sharp bursts of precisely aimed, concentrated fire, as image, pun, metaphor, parody, seemed spontaneously to generate one another in a succession of marvellously imaginative patterns, sometimes rising to high, wildly comical fantasy. His unique accent, idiom, voice, the structure of his sentences, became a magnetic model which affected the style of speech, writing, and perhaps feeling, of many who came under its spell. It had a marked effect on some among the best-known Oxford-bred writers of our time.

Berlin was probably here thinking of Cyril Connolly, Evelyn Waugh, Peter Quennell, Robert Byron, Anthony Powell, Henry Green, to name only a few of the writers who first gathered at Bowra's feet as undergraduates.

'But', Berlin continued,

> his influence went deeper than this. He dared to say things which others thought or felt but which they were prevented from uttering by rules or convention or personal inhibitions. Maurice Bowra broke through some of these social and psychological barriers, and the young men who gathered round him in the twenties and thirties, stimulated by his unrestrained talk, let themselves go in their turn. Bowra was a major liberating force.

A young don, who had been through the war, Bowra was teaching classics at Wadham College when Betjeman came up. He was a clever man, even a learned one, who was prodigiously well read in a wide variety of languages. He was noticeably small. ('Arise Sir Maurice', the wags imagined the Queen saying, when he was knighted, to receive the curt, barked retort, 'I have arisen, Your Majesty.') Anthony Powell brilliantly captured his appearance – 'this lack of stature emphasised by a massive head and tiny feet, Bowra – especially in later life – looked a little like those toys which cannot be pushed over because heavily weighted at the base, or perhaps Humpty Dumpty whose autocratic diction and quick-fire interrogations were also paralleled'. Born in China, he had mastered Russian as a boy when crossing the great Russian land mass by train. He read Pushkin and Lermontov in the original. He knew all the great German, French, Italian and Spanish poets. He was a serious intellectual who despised bluffing or pseudery and who spent every morning at his desk. His parties, riotously enjoyable as they were, with all the malice and jokes for which he was famous ('Don't tell me – let me guess', he said to the porter when he saw the college flag at half mast) were interspersed with readings from favourite poets, especially Yeats for whom he had a passion.

Through Lionel Perry, his best friend at Magdalen, Betjeman met a schoolfriend of Perry's, John Dugdale. Both young men belonged to the smart set, accustomed to dining at the George restaurant in Broad Street, and known as the Georgeoisie. Dugdale's parents lived at the extraordinary Sezincote, built by a nabob during the Regency, a sort of Brighton Pavilion set down in the Gloucestershire countryside. Designed by Samuel Pepys Cockerell for his 'nabob' brother Sir Charles in the very early years of the nine-teenth century, the house is an amazing Moghul extravaganza, onion-domed, fretted, carved. 'Indian without and coolest Greek within', Betjeman described it. John Dugdale's father, Colonel Dugdale, was a farmer; the mother, Ethel, was an ardent socialist, and here Betjeman renewed his old friendship with Hugh Gaitskell, and came across 'Major' Attlee, the future Labour Prime Minister. This was Betjeman's first taste of country-house life, and he loved it. There is no mystery about why this generation of middle-class boys found country house life so exciting. Boys of Betjeman's class (unless they happened to be geniuses such as Turner, kept at Petworth House) simply were not asked to such houses before the twentieth century. Who could not be excited by houses of such architectural splendour as Sezincote, with its large rooms, and the opportunities which parties in such a house can provide, of hugely enhancing and expanding one's social circle? No wonder they were so-called 'snobs'. The Dugdales also provided Betjeman with an example of something of which he had no first-hand experience in his own tiny family, a harmonious marriage, and a happy family atmosphere. Sezincote, he tells us, became a second home.

As his memoirs show, Bowra was happy to be asked to the country houses and London dinner tables of such luminaries as Sibyl, Lady Colefax, or Lady Ottoline Morrell. In Bowra's company, Betjeman's keen social ambitions became a possibility. He shared none of Darwell Stone's hesitancy about wishing to get into *The Smart Set*. Anthony Powell, pondering in old age the success, or otherwise, of his middle-class friend's social climbing, picked out Betjeman as 'in a sense the most socially successful, particularly because at the same time avoiding almost all opprobrium for being snobbish, anyway to the extent of cases such as Waugh, Beaton, and other fellow-climbers'.

In the summer of 1926, Pierce Synnott, one of Bowra's favourites, asked Betjeman and Bowra to stay at Furness, Naas, County Kildare. Bowra was in love with Synnott, but the only occasion he had manifested physical affection, putting an arm around Synnott's shoulder, he was told firmly, 'Take it away.' Synnott's father had died in 1920, and he had inherited Furness, a fine old house of 1740, with delicate plasterwork ceilings, a park or demesne as they are called in Ireland, complete with ice house and hermitage. The New Buildings, that is, the crumbling eighteenth-century buildings at Magdalen, with their view over the deer park always reminded Elizabeth Bowen of Irish country houses. Having sampled such architectural beauty at Oxford, Betjeman was now seeing the Irish country house for himself, with all its beauty, all its tragedy. At this date, 1926, the Irish Civil War was just over. Many of the great houses owned by Anglo-Irish gentry had been torched, and landowners threatened with death. Nevill Coghill, an aesthete don at Oxford, came from the Protestant enclave of West Cork. During the Troubles, he was taken by the IRA to a tree on his estates, blindfolded, and told to prepare for death. Being a 'High Church nancy' – to use the contemporary jargon – he made the sign of the cross. The men rushed forward, removed the bandage from his eyes and apologised. 'Sure, Mr Nevill, and we never knew you were a Catholic.'

Synnott introduced Betjeman to the world celebrated by Yeats in his poetry, the 'rich man's flowering lawns', threatened with destruction not merely by the Troubles, but by the march of the Modern.

> What if the glory of escutcheoned doors,
> And buildings that a haughtier age designed,
> The pacing to and fro on polished floors
> Amid great chambers and long galleries, lined
> With famous portraits of our ancestors;
> What if those things the greatest of mankind
> Consider most to magnify, or to bless,
> But take our greatness with our bitterness?

Some of Betjeman's greatest friends came from the Anglo-Irish gentry or aristocracy, or from the Scottish, like Patrick Balfour, later third Baron Kinross. There was Billy Clonmore: 'Cracky Clonmore. He was about the least known peer there was.' There was Basil Dufferin and Ava, whom Betjeman called Little Bloody. In grown-up life, some time in his fifties, Betjeman met Lady Caroline Blackwood, 'Little Bloody's' daughter. He 'was so moved by her resemblance to Ava, and so attracted to her, that he decided he could never meet her again'. We learn this from the diaries of Betjeman's friend James Lees-Milne, who adds, then he told me that he was more in love with Ava than with any human being he had ever met in the world. His Oxford career was ruined by this unrequited love for 'Little Bloody'. He loved his gutter-snipe good looks, his big, brown, sensual eyes, sensual lips, dirtiness generally. Never received so much as a touch of a hand on the shoulder. He then said that in after-life no loves ever reached the heights of schoolboy loves.

Three things need to be considered as a footnote to this diary entry of 21 July 1980. One is that Lees-Milne is not a completely reliable source. Second, Betjeman, as we shall see in the course of this book, was a sympathetic conversationalist. If someone told him they loved redheads, he would turn out to have exactly the same taste. Sado-masochism? Likewise. In the company of his many gay friends, he liked to play up the homosexual side of his nature, but there is no evidence of his ever having had a full-blown love affair with someone of his own sex though there might have been school-boy or undergraduate fumblings. Third, and most importantly, if we take this confession as roughly speaking true, it tells us much about what Betjeman thought of 'love'. Nearly all his best love poetry is addressed, not to his wife or his long-term mistress, but to figures who were almost or actual strangers. The crush, the love from afar, were what inspired his muse.

The experience of being painfully and unrequitedly in love throughout university years, or indeed throughout one's twenties, must be very usual. In loving Little Bloody, Betjeman was undoubt-edly loving a person of huge charm and fascination, but also he was loving the whole world of the Anglo-Irish gentry and aristocracy. 'The Anglo-Irish are the greatest race of Western civilization', he wrote in 1938 to Elizabeth Bowen, herself an ornament of that race. He meant it. Among his other friends made at Oxford there was Bryan Guinness, later Lord Moyne, and Frank Pakenham, later seventh Earl of Longford. Of course, the grandeur of the ancestry, displayed in portraits lining long galleries and old libraries, was exciting to a middle-class boy. But these places and people appealed not merely to the snob, but also to the poet in Betjeman, not least because Ireland, really throughout his life – its changes only accelerated with grants from the EU and the coming of peace in the North – remained closer in touch with the old world than did England. The Village of Goldsmith was Deserted but there was still more here of the world Goldsmith lamented than could ever have been found in England. Here, too, was the world which had been loved by Edmund Spenser in that first generation of Anglo-Irish settlement during the sixteenth century. Spenser, one of the favourite poets of Betjeman's hated tutor Lewis, had loved Ireland. But Lewis had all but no visual sense, and as Betjeman once complained to his tutor, in a letter never posted, 'nowhere in [your] excellent book do you say anything appreciative or discerning of Spenser's amazing powers of topographical description, which are best appreciated when one has visited the neighbourhood of Clonmel, Waterford and Youghal'.

At home, when they were not all quarrelling the three of them, the Betjemans sat around listening to Bess talk of her ailments, or the latest cheap novel from the lending library. During schooldays, Betjeman had enjoyed conversations with soulmates about architecture or landscape. But it was only when he became an undergraduate, and began to mix, first with Bowra, and then in the country houses of Ireland, that he tasted the joy of talk among clever people. Cracky Clonmore took his brilliant young friend Betjeman on the rounds. They visited the Irish poet Katharine Tynan – she had known Gerard Manley Hopkins – they went to tea with 'A.E.' (G.W. Russell), where they had met Yeats 'divinely clothed . . . He talked very passionately, holding the floor the whole time about the Lane pictures, and was very polite to us.' When Betjeman left Naas to meet up with Ernest Betjemann, to travel back to England, he travelled as far as Galway with Yeats.

Colonel Kolkhorst

The taste for country-house life, and for its good talk, was greatly enhanced by that first summer visit to Ireland.

Social life was not a distraction from his education; it was his education, as a sympathetic tutor might have seen. A rival salon to Bowra's was that of Colonel Kolkhorst, which convened after church on Sunday mornings in rooms in Beaumont Street – now demolished to make way for the extension to the Taylor Institution. Kolkhorst was as unlike a colonel as it was possible to be, which was why the young bestowed this nickname upon him. He taught Spanish and Portuguese, but he was no scholar. His rented rooms (he was waiting to inherit Yarnton Manor, near Woodstock, from his father) were approached by a staircase reeking of gas and of his landlady's untrained dogs. His small apartments were crammed with clutter – suits of Japanese armour in which mice had nested, oriental figurines under dusty glass domes, Satsuma vases of questionable authenticity. A photograph of Walter Pater ('The Master') himself of confusingly military bearing – now he *could* have been a colonel – and dog-eared copies of the Yellow Book all attested to his Aesthetic Nineties credentials. 'Gug' – another of 'The Colonel's' nicknames – had been discovered by Cracky Clonmore, though Bowra, who in jealous mood claimed that Kolkhorst did not exist, maintained that he was Betjeman's invention. The parties, at which almost no dons ever appeared, consisted of groups of undergraduates, chiefly homosexual, drinking far too much sherry. Marsala was dispensed to those who had somehow 'blotted their copybook'. The Colonel held aloft a lump of sugar on a piece of cotton to sweeten the conversation, but, as at Bowra's parties, malice, particularly about other dons, was actively encouraged. Here, too, Betjeman encountered other lifelong friends – Alan Pryce-Jones, man of letters and future editor of the *Times Literary Supplement*; Osbert Lancaster, artist, cartoonist, wit; Colin Gill, immensely tall, immensely High Church priest, who composed some of the songs sung about the Colonel, which must have been funny once when sung with plenty of sherry inside you, but which always look a bit feeble when transcribed in *Summoned by Bells* and elsewhere.

In addition to the parties, and the churches, Betjeman spent his time at Oxford honing two skills which were to be his professional stocks in trade, and which enabled him to pay his bills more regularly than poetry ever could: journalism and public performing.

He was in several productions of the OUDS, and was an accomplished performer. He got sacked, however, when 'a cod photograph with a ribald caption' appeared in the *Cherwell*, the undergraduate magazine, claiming to be a picture of the OUDS rehearsing. At this time, they were in fact rehearsing *Lear*, with Harman Grisewood playing the King, and Betjeman the Fool. Since *Cherwell* that term was edited by Betjeman, and he, of course, had been the author of the spoof, Grisewood pompously, and successfully, demanded Betjeman's expulsion. 'For playing the fool, John has been prevented from playing the Fool', quipped Kolkhorst. If this is an example of Kolkhorst's wit at its best, one understands why the other dons preferred to pretend he did not exist.

In the world of student journalism, Betjeman made encounters among clever people who would not have wanted to spend their time either with the Smart Set or with the Kolkhorst brigade. The gangling, chain-smoking figure of Wystan Auden was one such, an early fan of Betjeman's poetry. The two were said to have had a fling, or perhaps a fumble, the legend being that Auden had to bribe his scout (college servant) £5 for keeping quiet when Betjeman was discovered in his bed. 'It wasn't worth the £5', he is quoted, by his brother, as saying. The incident might have happened, but the joke seems too unkind for the essentially benign Auden, who always took sex (a matter which interested him far less than it did Betjeman) in his stride. Betjeman denied the story.

All Betjeman's deepest emotional bonds were with those of the opposite sex; most of his friendships, and nearly all his loves, were with women. But this was a time when Oxford had almost no women. When Betjeman gave a party for Lord Alfred Douglas in his old rooms at Magdalen, then being inhabited by Harford Montgomery Hyde (later Wilde's biographer), there were a few women present. One of them, Elizabeth Harman (later Elizabeth Longford), asked Betjeman how she had come to be invited. 'Oh', he replied, 'you were one of the aesthetes' molls – you and Margaret Lane and Margaret Rawlings.' Later, in Ireland, after she had married Frank Pakenham, Harman was amazed by Betjeman's interest in women. It was not something for which her Oxford experience of him had prepared her. 'I remember going to a dance – one of those interminable Irish drives to some party forty miles away. And he was the life and soul of the party; he certainly flirted with every girl that he found himself with – to my amazement then, because this was *not* what I connected him with.'

Betjeman is not an overtly sexual poet. Very few poets ever have been – the author of *The Song of Solomon*, John Donne, or Rochester are far less usual than those who write about the emotional pains of being in love, rather than about the sensual pleasure of gratified desire. He carefully guarded his public image, especially during the period when the physical expression of the love which dares not speak its name was actually illegal. For example, when Humphrey Carpenter tried to repeat the story of the wasted £5 in his biography of Auden, Betjeman threatened to sue. In private, however, among gay male friends, he had the opposite tendency. With his chameleon-like desire to beguile his company, and show himself to be on his interlocutor's wavelength, he played up his sympathy. To James Lees-

Milne he spoke of wanting to kneel down and kiss the television when a certain male presenter came on. To John Guest, who compiled *The Best of Betjeman*, he claimed, in his late middle verging on old age, that he liked climbing on to the top of buses to rub himself against boys. All these claims have to be taken with the pinch of salt with which they were obviously delivered. He liked debating the percentage of homosexuality in male friends, and in conversation would always exaggerate the degree of it in himself, partly no doubt because he knew this was appealing to the sort of women, aesthetes' molls, to whom he was ardently attracted.

Undergraduate years are the time when such confusions become less confusing, and when the young have time to reflect upon their true emotional natures. Part of Betjeman's nature, both as a man and chiefly as a poet, was to yearn. Turgenev once confided in a woman that he could only write novels when he was in love. Betjeman was very nearly always in love, often unsuitably. Much of his best verse comes out of such experiences. One suspects that if he had had the sort of life which he claimed, from the wheelchair, to have wanted there would have been less poetry – no Joan Hunter Dunn, no Myfanwy, no Clemency the General's Daughter, all of whom owe their great strength as figures in poetry to the fact that they were not figures in his bed.

Hence the importance, though dismissed as a joke by Bowra in his *Memories*, of two women whom Betjeman loved during his undergraduate life.

> He picked up a waitress from an Oxford restaurant and took her out to look at churches, but gave her up when she did dance-steps up the aisle. At the other extreme was a very dutiful plain girl, the daughter of a clergyman, who appealed to his clerical tastes. She bicycled over to see him in Oxford and wore a strangely unbecoming raincoat.

The huge number of friends whom Betjeman made in such a short space of time at Oxford thought of both women as jokes,

Maurice Bowra

perhaps as jokes devised by Betjeman for their amusement. On one level, they were jokes. On another, they were Muses. Betjeman's inner *daimon*, the soul which made the poetry, feasted on such attachments. Surely the reason his poems make such a wide and deep appeal is because, contrary to what some of his friends supposed, such feelings of abject love and longing are the most cherished part of the lives of most of us?

One would not expect this to be wholly understood by sophisticates such as John Sparrow, of New College, a clever future lawyer, one day Warden of All Souls, nor by Tom Driberg of Christ Church, aesthete, prankster and, by the testimony of his posthumous memoir, erotomane *extraordinaire*. Such is the paradox of things, and of Betjeman's emotional make-up, that these two men, his undergraduate friends, were those to whom he invariably sent his poetry before publication to be checked and reworked.

If Betjeman had had a sympathetic tutor, his time at Oxford would have been an unspoilt triumph song. True, he would have been unlikely to get a very good degree, given the fact that he spent so much time acting, party-going, talking and doing undergraduate journalism. But these were days in which the more enlightened university teachers were able to see that 'higher education', as we now call it, consisted in more than passing exams.

Bowra, teaching Latin and Greek literature at Wadham College, and therefore having no influence at Betjeman's own college of Magdalen, could see how exceptional this young man was. He already had a prodigious knowledge of architecture, and of out-of-the-way literature. Few of his contemporaries were really attuned to the fact that Betjeman was already beginning to find his voice as a poet. Bowra knew this, though. He saw in such early poems as 'Death in Leamington' and 'The Arrest of Oscar Wilde at the Cadogan Hotel' 'how original they were and how much more they were than merely funny'. Unfortunately, Bowra was not his tutor. C.S. Lewis was. 'Heavy' Lewis, liked by some of his pupils over the years but more often feared for his bullying manner, drove away another of Betjeman's contemporaries, Henry Yorke, the novelist Henry Green, who was 'irritated and bored' by Lewis. Yorke positively wanted the experience which Betjeman was running away from. He was all too willing to go and work in the family 'works' – a beer-bottling factory in Birmingham, finding there rich material for his art, as well as a change from the rarefied, Etonian way in which his businessman father and upper-class mother had brought him up.

Betjeman fell foul of Lewis, and of the system, by failing an exam which in those days all Oxford undergraduates had to take – Divvers, or Divinity. Had he had a sensible tutor, such as Bowra, the man would have told him – 'Come on, Betj, you can pass this exam easily. It only consists of a few easy questions about the Acts of the Apostles and one book of the Old Testament.'

Bowra believed that at some level, frightened of a disgrace in the serious exams – the ones for his degree – Betjeman's psyche took the easy way out and failed an exam which, as a lifelong churchgoer he could have passed with ease. There may be some truth in this. For whatever reason, he failed Divinity, and was rusticated, that is, sent away from Oxford, and told to come back when he could pass the required exam. He got a job as a schoolteacher at Thorpe House, Gerrard's Cross, a private boarding school for boys. Even this post had been achieved with some difficulty because Lewis would not write him a kindly testimonial. It was only another don at Magdalen, the Rev. J.M. Thompson who taught history, who vouched for him.

Betjeman wrote to Lewis, asking him if he could return to Oxford in the following autumn to complete his degree course. He found that Lewis had in effect demoted him by recommending him to follow a course known as a pass degree. This would entitle any one who took it successfully to write the letters BA (Oxon.) after their name. But it was not an honours degree, and those sitting for it were not allowed to study a subject. It consisted of three papers – one elementary language paper, one of military history, and one other, equally elementary, of literature. It was a course really designed for the rowing blues and rugby hearties.

Lewis gave Betjeman absolutely minimal help, even with the application to do the pass degree.

> Dear Betjemann,
> You must write to the Secretary of the Tutorial Board at once, telling him your position, and asking to be allowed to take a pass degree.
>
> As to my being 'a stone', I take it we understand each other very well. You called the tune of irony from the first time you met me, and I have never heard you speak of any serious subject without a snigger. It would, therefore, be odd if you expected to find gushing fountains of emotional sympathy from me whenever you chose to *change* the tune. You can't have it both ways, and I am sure that a man of your shrewdness does not really demand that I should keep 'sob-stuff' (is that the right word in your vocabulary?) permanently on tap in order to qualify me for appearing alternately as butt and as fairy godmother in your comedy . . .

The Secretary of the Board was then required to ask Lewis why Betjeman was being put in for a pass degree, and to assess his chances of getting an honours degree if he returned to his original course. Lewis deemed that Betjeman's chance of an honours degree was 'none'.

'When I went in for the English group', Betjeman recalled

bitterly in 1939, 'I had a viva' (an oral exam) 'from Mr Brett Smith. My answers on eighteenth- and nineteenth-century writers were not, I suspect, bad, and Mr B-S asked me at the viva, "Why are you not in for the Honours School?" Lewis was sitting beside Brett-Smith at the time, and said nothing.'

Betjeman did his best to make life awkward for Lewis. For instance, in his language paper, he opted not to do Latin or French but Welsh 'in the knowledge', claimed Osbert Lancaster, 'that in order to gratify this strange ambition Magdalen had been put to all the trouble and expense of importing a don from Aberystwyth twice a week, first-class'.

The fun was not to last for long. The 27 October edition of *Cherwell* carried a cartoon of Betjeman – is it by the youthful Osbert Lancaster? – wearing a scholar's gown, with a lopsided smile. In the background, a biretta'd clergyman in a cassock, and another, possibly a bishop in a frock coat and top hat, scuttle about beneath the spires. The issue of 17 November announced the engagement of the former editor, Bryan Guinness, to the Hon. Diana Mitford. The 1 December issue had a special 'Divvers Number' with a mock-guide of how to pass the divinity exam. It contained the instructions – 'Don't be facetious. It never pays and it costs a pound a time. Remember JOHN BETJEMAN.'

By then, Betjeman's fate had been sealed, and in spite of Sir Herbert Warren's distaste for sacking undergraduates, Lewis had been harsh.

Betjeman felt not merely that a gross personal injustice had been done, but that Lewis had failed in more general terms. In his long diatribe written out eight years later, but never posted, he berated Lewis for his philistinism ('I don't see how anyone with visual sensibility can live in Magdalen and be unmoved by architecture if their job is partly that of teaching an appreciation of English literature'). He went on to say, 'I was a very usual type of undergraduate, caught up with the latest fashions in "art"; pretentious and superficial. But all that, I have since discovered, is quite right in this type' — that is, in a budding aesthete. 'Indeed it should be encouraged, for it argues an awareness of what is going on and an incipient sensibility which can easily be crushed or misdirected forever by an unsympathetic tutor.'

He urged Lewis that, should 'one of the Betjeman type' come his way in the future, he should be sent to a more sympathetic tutor in another college. It is a perfectly intelligible letter, and it is highly characteristic. Betjeman, from early infancy, had 'shown off merrily', and been extremely thin-skinned, hyper-sensitive to criticism and bullying of any kind. Both these characteristics of the infant Betjeman were carried through grown-up life into old age. But with the showing-off there also went humility. He was never as certain as his admirers were of his talents, partly because he was an intelligent person, and he could see that the verses he was beginning to write were so unlike those of other aspirant serious poets such as his friends Auden and MacNeice. Everyone who recollected Betjeman, either as a Marlborough boy or as an undergraduate, recollected something totally extraordinary. ('A sustained and successful effort to present a convincing impersonation of a rather down-at-heel Tractarian hymn-writer recently unfrocked' was Osbert Lancaster's description.) He was not 'a very usual type of undergraduate'. He was not a very usual type of man. But, thanks to his tutor's total lack of sympathy, he was now being thrown out into the world. Eventually, large numbers of his fellow countrymen would come to share the delight and fascination in his character which was felt during that delirious time at Oxford. But in the short term the prospects of earning his living were not promising.

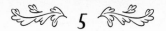

5

MAKING A MARK –
ARCHIE REV

In 1960, just after he had read *Summoned by Bells*, Evelyn Waugh
wrote in his diary:

> Betjeman's biography. John demonstrates how much more difficult it
> is to write blank verse than jingles and raises the question: *why* did he
> not go into his father's workshop? It would be far more honourable
> and useful to make expensive ashtrays than to appear on television and
> just as lucrative.

Waugh, three years older than Betjeman, had been introduced to
him at Biddesden by Diana Guinness. He moved in the same circles
of Bowra, Irish country houses, and upper-class Bohemia. By the
time Betjeman came down from Oxford, Waugh had published his
remarkable life of Dante Gabriel Rossetti and made a notable hit
with his hilarious first novel, *Decline and Fall*. The relationship
between the two men was edgy, perhaps best summarised by Waugh
himself in a letter to Betjeman's wife on 7 January 1950 – 'My love
to John. Though he doesn't love me as I love him.'

Anthony Powell, with his cool-eyed interest in the social-climbing
skills of his middle-class contemporaries, perhaps put a little of the
Waugh-Betjeman relationship into the friendship of Mark Members
and J.G. Quiggin in *A Dance to the Music of Time*. Both are destined
to become Men of Letters, but at the university have projected
very different self-images – Mark Members writing modernist verse
in the Day Lewis/Spender manner, and published in *Public School*

Verse, Quiggin liking to think of himself as a Marxist working-class intellectual. In neither respect is either character like Betjeman or Waugh. The detail which *is* like, comes when Sillery the don whose rooms provide the nursery for so many careers and encounters confronts Quiggin and Members with his knowledge that 'I had a suspicion that neither of you was aware of this . . . But you must live *practically* in the same street.' Waugh, the son of a well-known publisher and man of letters, was born and grew up in Golders Green, an unpretentious suburb not far from West Hill, Highgate. Neither of them was like Mark Members or Quiggin in character but in both cases there was a fairly dramatic exit from the social world of childhood into a set of rich and aristocratic young people who were dazzled by their genius.

Ernest Betjemann fixed his son up with a job in the City with a firm of marine insurers – Sedgwick Collins & Company. He loathed it, and it was not long before Basil Dufferin's mother persuaded Sir Horace Plunkett to take John Betjeman as his private secretary. Plunkett, then in his seventies, was obsessed by the idea of forming agricultural co-operatives. 'And being slightly off his head', as Betjeman told Patrick Balfour, 'has written the first chapter of a book of nine chapters no less than seventy-two times. He says the same thing over and over again and rarely completes one of his sentences which suits my style of thinking.'

This strange job lasted only a few months. Betjeman's old Marlborough friend John Bowle stole the job off him, rather as Quiggin 'takes over' the novelist St John Clarke, who had employed Mark Members as his secretary in Powell's *Dance*. There was the regulation spell as a prep-school master. Waugh had drawn on his teaching experiences to good effect and created the ludicrous Llanabba Castle in *Decline and Fall*. W.H. Auden was happy as a master at The Downs School, Colwall. He wrote a revue for the boys to perform and wanted Betjeman to come and hear his favourite boy sing one of the lyrics –

I've the face of an angel
  I've got round blue eyes
But if you knew the things I do
  It would cause you some surprise.
But where ignorance is bliss, my dears,
  'Tis folly to be wise.

Betjeman got a job as the cricket master at Heddon Court Preparatory School in Cockfosters. One of the masters remarked to him, after net practice, 'Do you know what Winters told me, Betjeman? *He didn't think you'd ever held a bat.*'

As an English teacher, he tried to interest the boys in Alexander Pope and in Dr Johnson, without much success. He encouraged the boys who were interested in poetry, and even took favourites out to the cinema, choosing as unsuitable a programme as possible – the German lesbian film *Mädchen in Uniform*. 'I think there are three types of schoolmaster', Betjeman said later in life.

(1) Those who are solely interested in getting pupils through examinations, who think in terms of marks and of clever dodges for learning dates and grammar. These people may be of no use to the soul or brain but they are useful in teaching how to qualify for Civil Service posts or to become a school master oneself. (2) People of very strong personality who are devoted to their subject and to implanting their enthusiasm for it in others. The disadvantage of this kind of teacher is that if one reacts unfavourably to his personality, he is hell. (3) Various sorts of people who go in for teaching and soon find that they are not qualified for the work, so that they become either inspectors or civil servants, or quietly take to drink.

Betjeman did not remain a teacher long enough, perhaps, to fall into any of these three categories himself. But as a personality he obviously belonged to the second category, though it was in the sphere of broadcasting, rather than of schooling, that he would

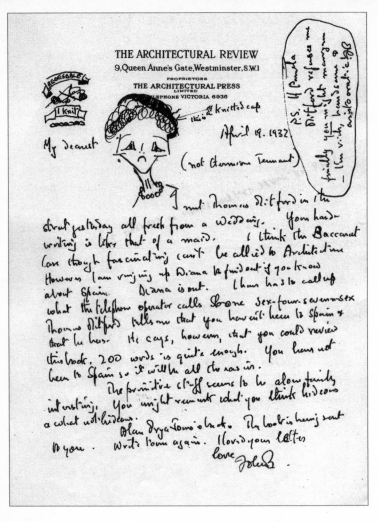

JB loved Nancy Mitford's triangular eyes

demonstrate both the enthusiasm for a subject, architecture, and the
strength of character. Though the more imaginative children at
Heddon Court found him entertaining, and though he made friends

with the headmaster – strangely enough, an Old Etonian communist, John Humphrey Hope – it was inevitable that he would be sacked.

His centre of interest was always with his Oxford friends. After only a month at Heddon Court, he was writing to Bryan Guinness – 'Now look here, old boy. I can get away to dinner any evening. What do you say to a little meal one day with you and your authoress wife? It would by [*sic*] such fun after the prunes and suet of this place. I long to see Miss Mitford.'

Guinness married, aged twenty-two, the eighteen-year-old daughter of Lord Redesdale, Diana Mitford, tall, blonde, impatient, clever. He read for the Bar, but was also a poet, and they were at the centre of a clever circle – Harold and William Acton, Roy Harrod, the Yorkes, Robert Byron, Evelyn Waugh, Randolph and Diana Churchill (Diana Mitford's cousins). When they acquired Biddesden, a beautiful brick house built in the early eighteenth century by General Webb (one of Marlborough's generals), Diana used her precocious skills to create interiors of stunning elegance. Their best friends in the country were Lytton Strachey and Dora Carrington, living nearby at Ham Spray.

Betjeman was happily adopted into the set. One of the Guinnesses' enthusiasms was for hymn-singing. Diana, as a teenager, had passed through a religious phase. Although belief left her, the religious temperament was never entirely shaken off, nor the memory of playing the organ in the tiny church at Swinbrook. ('Holy, holy, holy' was her favourite hymn – she chose it, seventy years later, for her funeral.) There was a piano in the dining room. Diana's teenaged sister Unity Valkyrie Mitford liked more evangelical hymns such as

> There were ninety-and-nine who safely lay
>   In the shelter of the fold,
> And one was out on the hills away,
>   Far off from the gates of gold.

Archibald and Jumbo

Betjeman's teddy bear, Archibald, shared this religious bent as he was later to share Unity's political views. In his letters to friends at this period, Betjeman often included drawings of the bear, sometimes mounted in a pulpit to say 'Praise the Lord'. 'Archibald, my bear, has accepted a call to the Congregational Church on Wansted Flats where he has been doing the duty of lay reader for some years . . .' 'Archibald looks like this and . . . is very interested in Temperance Work at Clacton-on-Sea . . .' 'Archibald has accepted the Incumbency of Raum's Episcopal Chapel, Homerton, E. 17. It is a proprietary chapel and in communion with a part of the Church of England. He has always been associated with the Evangelical Party and he will have to wear a black gown in the pulpit as the Surplice is considered ritualistic . . .'

This was just the sort of humour which had so enraged C.S. Lewis, the troubled atheist. The parlourmaid at Biddesden, May Amende, was a religious woman who objected to the mingling of hymns with social fun. They sang them all the time, after meals, or in the car, bowling along to visit neighbours or explore old churches. 'She thought we were scoffing', recalled another Mitford sister, Pamela, who had a cottage on the estate at Biddesden.

She and C.S. Lewis were both right and wrong. The essence of Betjeman's humour, running through so much of his best verse, is that it is impossible, when catching his tone, to disentangle the larkiness (different somehow from scoffing) from serious emotion. Often such seriousness had to come filtered through humour as a protective device. This was as true of profane, as of sacred love.

All his grown-up life, he was in love with people. He developed crushes and manias for beautiful faces. Many recollect his love poetry as comic verse, which of course it is —

> Is it distaste that makes her frown,
> So furious and freckled, down
> On an unhealthy worm like me?

But like sentimental songs, pop songs or music hall, Betjeman's poems, even these larky ones, stay in the head, and become associated with experiences and emotions which are themselves non-comic.

> Her sulky lips were shaped for sin,
> Her sturdy legs were flannel-slack'd,
> The strongest legs in Pontefract.

One of the girls he loved in his early twenties was Camilla Russell, daughter of the chief of the Cairo police, Sir John Russell. He met her at Sezincote and for a number of years bombarded her with light-hearted protestations of love. They were even engaged until her mother got to hear of it and put a stop to the matter. Their relationship, as far as physical love was concerned, had not gone beyond a few kisses. At Biddesden, he fell in love with Pamela Mitford. She ran the farm, and he picked up the farmworkers' habit of calling her 'Miss Pam'.

'I was very, very fond of him', she recalled,

> but I wasn't *in love* with him. He liked me to drive him to
> Marlborough so he could show me his classroom, and to drive up on
> to the Downs to the deserted village of Snap; you could see the
> remains of the cottages . . . Of course he was highly religious and
> always wanted to go to Matins in Appleshaw, so we'd bicycle there
> together. Sometimes when I was in London we'd go off to very
> peculiar churches south of the river, where they sang hymns like
> 'Shall we gather at the river' and then you had to be 'saved' at the

Pamela Mitford

end of the service. Those who wanted to be saved stayed on and the other people left. We stayed and were both saved. We had to go into a cubby-hole with this parson . . .

She remembered: 'He said he'd like to marry me but I rather declined. I think he would have been much too shy to have advanced on one. He wasn't like that at all.' Diana Mitford always maintained that 'Woman' (the family nickname for Pamela) would have made an ideal wife for Betjeman, and regretted not having him as a brother-in-law. The 'shyness', and the inability, quite, to shake free from the same-sex emotional preoccupations of Marlborough and Oxford, might have been unsatisfactory for the wife herself, however amusing it would have been to have him as a member of the family circle. As in profane, so in sacred love, there was also the disturbing sense of his spreading his favours. If not 'like that at all', in the sense of making physical advances, he was quite capable of having extreme crushes on several people at once. He was also able to go into a cubby-hole with a parson and be saved at the same time as being an agnostic, an Anglo-Catholic, and, for much of the 1930s, a Quaker.

From the late 1920s, he had begun to attend Meetings at the Society of Friends, and in 1931 he formally joined them in St Martin's Lane, London, only resigning in 1937. Sir Horace Plunkett had noted in his diary on 17 February 1929, that he had to fetch John Betjeman from his Meeting House of the Society of Friends at Esher.

'Four Quakers and he communed (mostly in silence). I have at any rate a good, honest, extremely clever secretary.'

There is nothing unusual about being afloat, emotionally and religiously, in one's twenties. What distinguished Betjeman's flightiness was the humour with which it was all presented, and the element of control. Friends did not merely observe his journey from afar, they were drawn into it — the Oxford waitress who was taken on 'church crawls' until she danced in the aisle; Sir Horace Plunkett in his late seventies going all the way from his house in Weybridge to Esher to collect Betjeman from the Meeting House; Pamela Mitford penetrating Balham or Tooting in search of salvation — all like Archibald the Bear, dancing Betjeman's tune.

In these years of young bachelordom, he spent almost every weekend at Biddesden. In London, he lodged with his Oxford contemporary Randolph Churchill. Osbert Lancaster remembered Betjeman shrieking with laughter at 3 Culross Street while Randolph Churchill telephoned a cabinet minister 'whose wife happened to be in bed with Randolph at the time'.

Culross Street, which leads from behind the American Embassy in Grosvenor Square to Park Lane, is a smart address by any standards on the Monopoly board, and certainly a surprising one for an impoverished poet with few prospects. Betjeman lived there because the house was owned by his Oxford friend Edward James.

A year younger than Betjeman (born August 1907) James was a definite exotic. Though he liked it to be thought that he was some kind of cousin of Henry James, the money in fact came from iron. It was a lot of money, made in the mid-nineteenth century. Edward James's mother was a Scottish aristocrat, a Forbes. Her husband, Willie James, one of three brothers to inherit the newly made fortune, was a noted sportsman and big-game hunter, who established her in West Dean Park, James Wyatt's fine neo-Gothic house five miles north of Chichester, rebuilt in the 1890s, and in two Lutyens houses, Gullane, near Muirfield in Scotland, and Monkton a few miles from West Dean, as well as the Mayfair house where Betjeman eventually lodged. Evie James, Edward's mother, was the natural daughter of the future Edward VII. Some believed her also, in later life, to have been his mistress – hence Belloc's scurrilous rhyme, 'And Mrs James shall entertain the King'. Although Edward James encouraged people to believe this story, it was without foundation, even though King Edward remained a friend of the family. Edward James had been to Eton with such fellow aesthetes as Brian Howard and Harold Acton, but he had steered clear of them. His mother's horror of homosexuality led him to be friends with clever heterosexual boys such as Christopher Sykes and Tom Mitford (brother of the Mitford sisters). At Oxford, his friends had been Randolph Churchill, Basil Dufferin, Tom Driberg. Though obviously preferring his own sex, these tastes did not really come to the fore until the end of a disastrous marriage with the ballet dancer Tilly Losch, whose footsteps were woven, in differing shades of green, into the stair carpet at West Dean. Salvador Dali is supposed to have said of Edward James, 'Of course, he is the most surrealist of us all.'

James's importance in the story of Betjeman is that he, together with Bowra, saw him primarily as a poet. Like Bryan Guinness, James wanted to be a poet himself.

'I dreamed of being remembered for being as great a poet as John Keats', he said. In 1930, James worked briefly as an honorary attaché at the British Embassy in Rome, with a job deciphering coded telegrams. He liked to claim, improbably, that one day he recorded that the Italian Navy was about to build 900,000 new submarines, when he meant nine – a mistake which caused Ramsay MacDonald to summon an emergency Cabinet Meeting.

The next year, 1931, he published Betjeman's *Mount Zion*. The poet himself had wanted a cover designed by Camilla Russell, but this was rejected by James. So too was the idea that each poem should be set in a different typeface.

The cover depicts an Edwardian woman holding a primitive

telephone or speaking tube to her mouth. The title above her is MOUNT ZION OR, and beneath her, it is IN TOUCH WITH THE INFINITE. It is a self-consciously surreal volume, especially the page illustrating 'A Seventeenth-Century Lyric' —

> The blewish eyeballs of my love
>   Are so enormous grown
> The muscles, which the pupils move
>   Won't twist 'em round alone

— lines which appear opposite a pink page adorned with the close-up drawings of over a dozen eyes, together with a few lips and nostrils. This poem was evidently thought to be too odd to be reprinted in any subsequent collections of Betjeman's verse. Nor, too, would he reprint 'The Garden City', with an illustration by himself —

> Hand-woven be my wefts, hand-made
>   My pottery for pottage
> And hoe and mattock, aye, and spade,
>   Hang up about my cottage.

In the light of his later feelings about the Roman Church, it is not surprising perhaps that 'St Aloysius Church, Oxford' should also be a poem which did not get included in his *Collected Poems*.

> Aloysius, rich and poor,
> Must enter by Thy grain'd oak door
> To realise with unreal eyes
> Reality and paradise.

There is a fatal irony, perhaps, in the fact that his wife would one day, to his deep grief, enter this very church in order to become a Roman Catholic.

Gathered here, however, there are also some of the distinctive Betjeman rhymes which would enter the canon of his well-known mature work — 'Death in Leamington' and 'The Flight from Bootle' being perhaps the best. The Bootle poem is especially original, and distinctive.

> Lonely in the Regent Palace,
>   Sipping her 'Banana Blush',
> Lilian lost sight of Alice
>   In the honey-coloured rush.
>
> Settled down at last from Bootle,
>   Alice whispered, 'Just a min,
> While I pop upstairs and rootle
>   For another safety pin' . . .

Lilian is left sitting a very long time, daydreaming while in the pavilion the band plays from the *Immortal Hour* and her friend Alice has done a runner, one presumes with a man. Strangely, one of the things which the poem conveys is not merely the loneliness of Lilian, but also – a novelistic ability this – the slight sense of menace which hovers over the fate of Alice who will not 'be quite the same again'. These two women are to be joined eventually by a whole array of characters brought to life in vivid Betjemanic vignettes – the overweight don's wife, dying at a bus stop, the anxious upper-middle-class woman praying in Westminster Abbey, fair Elaine, the bobby-soxer – that is, adolescent – or the 'thousand business women / Having baths in Camden Town'. There is an element of mockery in his perception of their lives, and a whiff of snobbery. But there is a much greater element of sympathy and empathy. Such women had never, quite, been hymned in English poetry. The whole book was dedicated to Mrs Arthur Dugdale of Sezincote 'under whose minarets I have been raised from the deepest depression and spent the happiest days of my life'.

After the statutory false start of school teaching, and the generalised sense, all but universal among creative people in their twenties, that they would never find anyone to pay them for what they wanted to do with their lives, rather than force them into uncongenial work for cash, Betjeman was lucky enough to find a job which was ideal. Bowra and a young man called Maurice Hastings were the catalysts. 'I can't teach. I can't get on with my father. If ever I earn two hundred a year I shall be extremely lucky. I'm absolutely sunk', Betjeman complained to them. Hastings felt sure that his brother Hubert de Cronin Hastings could get Betj a job on *The Architectural Review*, a periodical which de Cronin Hastings effectively controlled.

Patrick Leigh Fermor was a boy at King's School Canterbury in 1931 when Betjeman came there to give a lecture. Fifty-four years later in 1985, Leigh Fermor was himself a famous and distinguished war hero and travel writer who spoke at the unveiling of a memorial plaque to Betjeman the Poet Laureate in Westminster Abbey. He remembered a Betjeman very unlike the later laureate of the 'dim' — a young man of twenty-five, slim, smartly dressed in a dinner-jacket, dark-haired and pale. This was a figure unlike any previous lecturer those schoolboys had ever seen. He spoke lightly, spontaneously and urgently about modernism. He began by speaking of the clean classical lines of the Parthenon and this in turn led to an exegesis of the modernist creed, praising the spare uncluttered lines of Le Corbusier and the Bauhaus School. As Leigh Fermor told the affectionately-amused Abbey congregation half a century later, 'the merits of ferro-concrete and the simplicity of tubular steel furniture were rapturously extolled'.

'If anyone asks me who invented modern architecture', Betjeman himself wrote in 1974, 'I answer, "Obscurity Hastings".'

Obscurity Hastings was the nickname of Hubert de Cronin Hastings, 'not because he was indefinite but because he liked hiding in the background'. After Percy Hastings's death the *Architectural Review*, which he owned and which was edited by the architect to St Paul's Cathedral, Sir Mervyn Macartney, a pupil of Norman Shaw, changed direction. 'Mr Hubert felt it was a little old-fashioned and I don't think he thought that Christian Barman was modern enough for the new world of glass boxes and concrete which Mr Hubert foresaw as the future of England. And how right he was in his foresight' . . . 'Obscurity always thought that foreigners were better than English people at architecture. Why he employed me was because my name is foreign.'

Clearly, the Betjeman aged twenty-five, expounding the beauty of the new world of glass boxes, is a very different figure from the Betjeman who in later life would love the St Pancras Hotel and All Saints', Margaret Street, and campaign so ceaselessly not merely against the destruction of old buildings, but also against the construction of town centres which were directly inspired by those very architectural ideas which had so excited Obscurity Cronin and his friends. There is no law against changing one's mind in matters of taste, and there is no doubt that Betjeman fell under the spell of Obscurity Cronin. Some Betjeman admirers are shocked to discover that their idol admired Le Corbusier in 1931. It has been suggested that there is a link between the simple Quakerism embraced by Betjeman in the 1930s and his love of clean lines and architectural simplicities. (See Timothy Mowl's *Stylistic Cold Wars: Betjeman Versus Pevsner.*) It is not to be denied that Betjeman, while working for the modernist *Architectural Review* under the tutelage of Obscurity Cronin, was converted to modernism, and that this doctrinal approach to architecture was something which he subsequently abandoned. But on the other hand, unlike some of his younger groupies, Betjeman was never opposed to modern architecture *per se*. He was opposed to ugliness, and the aesthetic bad manners of erecting modern architecture out of scale with existing older buildings in its immediate vicinity, and against architecture which seemed to express enmity of the human race. The truth is, they were heady days in which to live, and anyone with an aesthetic awareness would be bound to be excited by modernism in its various forms, *simply as a form*. Where this form does not clash with an existing townscape, the effects of such innovatory work are still, eighty and more years on, thrilling. It has to be said that most of the *Archie Rev* writers of those clean-cut days who lived to see English towns dominated by blocks of flats and offices, modern road systems and multi-storey car parks changed the views which they had held in the early 1930s, so Betjeman was not alone. Most conspicuous, and articulate, of these was an extraordinary man called Philip Morton Shand, always known, and addressed, by friends as P. Morton Shand. By the strange tricks played on the whirligig of time, P. Morton Shand will probably be best known to history as the grandfather of Camilla Shand, destined, having been Mrs Parker-Bowles, to become the second wife of the Prince of Wales. In his day, P. Morton Shand was known, privately, as a womaniser on the heroic scale, with four marriages to his credit, and on the printed page as one of the most outspoken defenders of the Bauhaus, and of architectural modernism. It was P. Morton Shand who converted Betjeman to the British Arts and Crafts architects who were the pioneers or fore-runners of Le Corbusier and Gropius – an idea which made its appeal to a young German student of English architecture, one Nikolaus Pevsner. (Tim Mowl speculates interestingly that Pevsner actually derived this idea from reading Betjeman in the *Archie Rev*, and this fuelled Betjeman's subsequent dislike of Pevsner.) Shand's most distinctive characteristic was the certainty with which he attached value-judgements to his praise or denunciation of buildings. It is not unique to architectural historians to make such strident judgements, of course, but ever since Ruskin, it has been a feature of English architectural taste that it should have excited such passion that those who wrote about it – Betjeman included – should do so with rapture or vitriol. Shand described the Empire Theatre, Leicester Square, as 'one of the most supremely parvenu buildings in the world'. The Marble Arch Regal 'looks as if it had been dressed for the part as a flash gigolo by some Alexander the Great of the Edgware Road'.

Later, in the 1950s, Shand repented of his early love of the Bauhaus. Perhaps such 1930s tastes are comparable to the absolutist political doctrines which seduced so many intelligent minds during that turbulent decade and which, with hindsight, appeared danger-ous and grotesque. 'I have frightful nightmares', P. Morton Shand admitted in 1958,

> and no wonder, for I am haunted by a gnawing sense of guilt in having, in however minor and obscure degree, helped to bring about, anyhow encouraged and praised, the embryo searchings that have now materialized into a monster neither of us [i.e. neither Shand nor Betjeman] could have foreseen: Contemporary Architecture (= the piling up of gigantic children's toy bricks in utterly dehumanized and meaningless forms), 'Art' and all that. It is no longer funny; it is frightening, all-invading menace.

Even during this unlikely 'modernist' phase of Betjeman's taste at the *Archie Rev*, however, we can see Our Man being distinctively himself. In 1933, for example, he was sent by the magazine to report on the opening of E. Vincent Harris's Civic Hall at Leeds. To understand Leeds, he wrote, 'one must acquire a Leeds sense of proportion. And this is done by realising two things about Leeds. First, it is a Victorian city. Secondly it is parochial. These two qualities are far more blessed than is generally supposed.' Timothy Mowl is right to suggest that it was in this article that Betjeman discovered his distinctive voice. He had gone north predisposed to mock the neo-Georgian Civic Hall. But discovering the building's popularity among the people he spoke to in pubs, and walking about the centre of Leeds and getting a feel for the place, he realised that buildings can not be detached from topography, and that the most important part of a building's context is not just its physical locale, but its place in the lives of actual people who live and work in and around it.

Equally distinctive, and Betjemanic, in its different way, was his article in the *Architectural Review* on the old Arts and Crafts architect Charles Francis Annesley Voysey. Still spouting the P. Morton Shand

line about the Arts and Crafts school, Betjeman heralds Voysey as
the forerunner of modernism. But it is clear, even at the height of
his modernist enthusiasm, that what excites Betjeman about
Voysey is a whole cluster of things which have nothing whatever to
do with Gropius or Le Corbusier. There is the fact that here he was,
a survivor of the Victorian Age, one of those figures such as Bosie
Douglas or May Morris, William Morris's daughter, or Theodora
Bosanquet, Henry James's secretary, whom he enjoyed befriending
because they could provide a link with a past at once close in time
and imaginatively distant. Crossing St James's Park to meet him,
Betjeman found a small, bird-like, clean-shaven man. ('His jacket
had no lapels, as he considered those "non-functional survivals of
eighteenth century foppery".') Voysey, collaterally related to John
Wesley and to the Duke of Wellington, was a high old Tory. On the
very page in which Betjeman saluted him as an unconscious influence
on Le Corbusier, there was a short piece by Voysey himself, which
ended: 'When Gothic architecture ceased to be fashionable, away
went that lovely quality so often to be seen in the towns of Holland,
where all the houses are different, though sympathetically respecting
each other, like gentlemen. Now an angry rivalry, or a deadly dull
uniformity, is the dominant feature of our street Architecture.' This
last is far more in tune with the real Betjeman than the disciple of
P. Morton Shand trying to toe the *Archie Rev* line. And surely one
reason that he responded to Voysey had nothing to do with Shand, or
the modernists or his new colleagues? It was because Voysey, since his
boyhood, had been one of the architects whose work he had seen at
first hand overlooking Daymer Bay at Trebetherick. It was as much a
part of Betjeman's inner land- and seascape as the mountains of the
Lake District that stayed with Wordsworth all through his sojourns
in Cambridge, London and France.

If Betjeman at the *Architectural Review* allowed himself to be
influenced by P. Morton Shand, Obscurity Cronin and the
others, he was no less bumptious than he had been at Oxford. One

Penelope 'tastefully dressed'

colleague remem-bered how he would burst into rooms without knocking, 'just storming in when he wanted to'. If this failed to draw enough attention, there were the by now well-tried paths of exhibitionism. One lunchtime, he went out busking, singing music-hall songs outside a cinema until he had collected enough money to go in and see the film. On a hot summer's day, he wore the 'very briefest of swimming trunks' in the office. Peter Quennell, his old Oxford friend and contemporary, came into the office one day and found Betjeman's chair unoccupied, though heaped with papers. 'Among them I saw a huge blotting pad, evidently quite new, on which, using a sharp pencil and decorative Gothic script, he had inscribed the now familiar couplet:

> I sometimes think that I should like
> To be the saddle of a bike.'

Another visitor to the office, and one whose highly developed sense of herself as a 'character' was quite as strong as Betjeman's own, was a young woman called Penelope Chetwode. The daughter of the former Commander-in-Chief of the Indian Army, she had a deep, and serious, interest in Indian religion, art and architecture. The India of her childhood was something which, even when we read about it today, is difficult to reconstruct in the imagination. Figures such as the Chetwodes lived like princes, surrounded by servants. The Commander-in-Chief's house in Delhi was so big that 'it's like a pantomime palace and we live a kind of pantomime existence', she wrote. In India she had befriended Robert Byron, the Etonian traveller and aesthete later famed for his *Road to Oxiana*, and it was he who was responsible for her meeting Betjeman. She wrote an article on the cave temples of Ellora in the Deccan, and Byron suggested she took it to the *Architectural Review* to show it to Obscurity Hastings. True to form, Hastings made an excuse not to meet a 'new person'. Instead, she was shown into Betjeman's office. He was on the telephone talking to Pamela Mitford.

Eventually, the conversation came to an end, and she introduced herself, in her whining, cockneyfied voice which immediately enchanted him. She remembered,

> we both got down on our hands and knees and I showed him all the
> photographs I had taken of Ellora. He wasn't the least bit interested in
> Indian art. Anyway the long and short of it was that he did publish it,
> and that's how we met. And I was suddenly very attracted to him and
> started falling for him.

Not long after meeting her, he presented her with a copy of *Mount Zion*.

> Penelope Chetwode, I always think, is not only tastefully dressed
> despite the hours she wears out her clothes in the Reading Room of
> the British Museum, but is also the possessor of unique social charm
> that has made her the cynosure of all eyes – whether surrounded by
> the horn rims of Bloomsbury Spectacle frames or the paint & powder
> of a high class drawing room. So compelling is her character that I am
> obliged to write for her this facetious dedication. I am that clever
> chap John Betjeman.

'A down at heel Tractarian hymn-writer' and wife

6

MARRIAGE

This was not to be a marriage, like so many, which began in harmony, developed strains, and then fell apart. From the very beginning of the relationship between these strong personalities, there existed those tensions and difficulties which characterised the marriage until his death. There was his own jealously guarded sense of self, around which there existed, even in the days before his fame, something in the nature of a cult. There was also his ambivalence, his inability to commit wholly to one other person, his lack of a monogamous sense. For her part, there was an equally strong sense of self, an assumed or innate oddity. There was a need to be alone, and a need to travel, especially in India. And there was a resistance to the cult, a fierce resentment of it, and a desire to cut him down to size. For both of them, the tensions were part of the attraction, part of the love. So, this was never going to be an easy marriage.

Marriages are all ultimately secrets. More is known of this one than of most, because they spent a lot of time apart, and Penelope, in particular, articulated her feelings about what was going on between them in long letters. In the end, however, the secret remains, and it is certainly no part of this book's brief to pluck out a mystery. What is worth remembering, through a marriage which was by any standards extremely rocky, is that there is something palpably genuine in the love he expressed for her at its beginning, in its middle and in its last years. He always was, as he so often signed himself to her, 'Yours trewly Tewpie'. From an early stage, they had begun to write to one another in a peculiar lingo imitative of

Penelope's distinctive pronunciation of English and to address one another by nicknames. She was Plymmie, after the River Plym, a waterway which divides Devon from Cornwall, and with which she had no obvious connection. How she came to be associated with the Plym in his mind, I do not know. There is a psychological aptness in the name which he might or might not have intended. Once west of Plymouth he was in his own world, his world of childhood. She was the Guardian of the borderlands between his buried childhood self, with its teddy bear and its tantrums, and the grown-up world of friends and practicalities. He sometimes called her Philth or Propeller. He was Tewpie.

In later years, Penelope said that she didn't think herself pretty enough to marry an aristocrat so decided to settle for a member of the intelligentsia. There is a sulky eroticism in all the photographs of her at this age which belies any such protestation. She was gamine of feature, but large-breasted, and strong, fully aware of her charms. When she met Betjeman she had two other Johns in her sights – Johnnie Churchill, painter nephew of Sir Winston; and Sir John Marshall, an expert in Indian archaeology, married and in his fifties. Marshall was married with two children, and her love for Churchill waned.

> It was quite different with Johnnie, just young adolescents being in love with love & all mixed up with that awful Wagnerianism. Then Sir John was pure physical passion although I tried, at the time, to think it was archaeology. I was never in love with him after I returned from India & only sorry for him. But for you I have a love which can never exist for anyone else, I don't want it to & I know it cannot.

He for his part, while being overwhelmed by Penelope and obsessed by love for her, was perfectly able to fall in love with some-one else. When Penelope first told her parents of her feelings for Betjeman, they were appalled. 'We ask people like that to our houses, but we don't marry them', Lady Chetwode said – a remark which somehow parallels Randolph Churchill's explanation of why

he helped to elect Cyril Connolly
and Peter Quennell to White's Club
('We like them to see how we live').

The parents took Penelope to
India to get her out of Betjeman's
way. While she was away, Betjeman
went to stay at Sezincote and met
a childhood friend of Plymmie's
called Billa (short for Wilhelmine)
Cresswell, a glossy-eyed, dark-haired
young sensualist who, like Penelope,
was a soldier's daughter. Her father
had been killed in the First World
War; her stepfather, General Sir
Peter Strickland KCB, was at
Aldershot when Penelope's father
the field marshal was commanding there.

*Wilhelmine 'Billa' Cresswell
(later Harrod)*

'We didn't go all the way', Billa said coyly, 'we lay on the sofa and
kissed and cuddled.' Later, she was to object to the green slime with
which Betjeman's teeth always appeared to be coated. The intimacies
at Sezincote were enough for the young people to consider themselves
engaged. In a long letter written from the *Architectural Review* after the
Sezincote weekend to Billa, addressed as 'Darling East End girl' – East
End of England, that is, she was of old Norfolk gentry – he gleefully
spelt out the reasons why he would be so unsuitable a husband –

(a) Loose character, weak and self-indulgent and egocentric. Extravagant
     and selfish.

(b) No birth – parents estranged from me and one another – and not at
     all the right class for Generals. No hope whatever of their getting on.
     'After all she must marry a gentleman.'

(c) Contracted already to someone who undoubtedly loves me and to
     whom it is going to be horrible to have to be unkind.

(d) Income £400 a year. Suppose in the first year I make nothing extra (it
is all luck and highly probable) then this with your £100 makes £500.
£500 = £7.12.1 a week . . .

That is the short part of the letter, but there follow hundreds of words
protesting his love. As for Philth – 'Dishonesty is the best policy – and
the kindest at present. I love you, I love you, I love you.'

A month later, he was expressing his love for Mary St Clair
Erskine.

> It will annoy Philth very much as she is always inclined to be jealous
> of my affection for you. It will also console me as I am beginning to
> think I cannot afford to marry Philth, as she is really an expensive
> person like you, although, unlike you, she thinks she can live in
> squalor on my few hundred a year and enjoy it . . . Also I think I
> should soon become as dim as hell and be known as the common
> little man Penelope Chetwode married . . .

Penelope was always enraged by his vacillations, and by his
emotional infidelities. She was equally and insistently aware, given
the protective feelings of Betjeman's fans, that she needed some time
to herself, and she needed to be allowed to assert her own
independence and freedom, alongside her love for him. To be faced
with the possibility of one's fiancé becoming engaged to one's close
friends as soon as one is out of the country could only have been
troubling. But there was surely more to it than simple jealousy or
sexual insecurity. In shrewd diaries of old age, Anthony Powell
noted: 'Although admiring Betjeman as a poet, I always felt I was
regarded by him as not sufficiently captive to the Betjeman cult.' If
this was an element of friendship, how much more must this have
been the case in that of a potential marriage. After she had expressed
dismay at his engagement to Billa, and broken off her own engage-
ment to Betjeman, Penelope received a letter of protest from Bryan
Guinness:

I have no right to interfere in the lives of either yourself or John, and it would be proper for me to apologise before attempting to do so; but I shan't, as it can do you no harm to hear my views, and if they annoy you it will be easy for you to tear up this letter and no doubt, to forget what it says . . . Now there can only be two possible reasons for which you have broken off your engagement to him. One is that you do not love him any more . . . There is however the alternative possibility that you do care for John and that you have broken off your engagement as a result of parental pressure conscious or unconscious. If so, I cannot say how much I deprecate your cowardice. John is a very great person. He is eccentric and needs looking after: but he has a genius of a very unusual kind. (He is incidentally a very great and old friend of mine, as you know, or I should not be writing this.) Such a person endowed as he is for your service, with great emotional capacity, is not lightly to be cast on one side because your parents were not at the same public school as his. If you are soon to live a life of your own unhedged by the false barriers of snobbery you must stand fast. As for putting your fancy foreign travel before the course of your duty and the inclination of your heart, I would not have believed it possible that the shallowest nature could have urged so basely selfish and mundane an excuse . . . I can't bear to see John so unhappy – that is why I have been so impertinent.

Guinness conveniently overlooks, in this letter, Betjeman's capacity to hurt Penelope, and the fact that she adored her father (in many ways it was the deepest love of her life), and was in turn adored by him. She knew that her marriage to Betjeman would hurt the old man.

On 28 June, however, she wrote a hugely long letter from the South of France, where she had gone to stay with an aunt.

I love you all right, you needn't fear that, BUT just stop & think for a moment (think for a very long time) before you ultimately decide what it will mean for *you*. It is quite different for me, I shall be living in different countries I am very partial to, I shall be working at things

which really interest me among nothing but congenial people but you
will be living in London which you so rightly hate . . . Would you
really be happier if you had a nice domesticated wife to keep house for
you? A wife who liked the things you liked but had no strong opposing
instincts of her own? . . . If you marry me now I probably won't be
able to give you that for 4 or 5 years & even after that time I may go
off periodically for several months at a time. This means you've got
another few years ahead of noisy smelly London, & you'll get the
same nerves and headaches & sick feelings as you've had in the past –
and your extra money will go mostly in taxis and entertaining . . .
When you suggested living in Dorset my own county it wasn't from
dislike of the English that I objected – it was simply because I
suddenly realised that I'd get completely out of touch with all my
Injun things & consequently get unpleasantly irritable. But living in
London wouldn't have helped an atom.

For a twenty-three-year-old, addressing an emotional chaotic of
just less than twenty-eight, this manifesto seems remarkably clear-
headed. On the sixth page of the epistle, she turns to another aspect
of Betjeman which perhaps neither she, nor any of his friends, nor
his biographer, could ever quite determine – the extent to which
the superficiality and the jokes go all the way through like the name
of a seaside resort through a stick of rock. It is this, the possibility
that he was deeply superficial, which disturbs her about the various
'engagements' and infidelities of the year 1933.

I know you were annoyed when I first wrote & suggested marrying in
a few years, but when it comes to being engaged 5 *times* (actually it's
only once besides me, isn't it? And then only for 2 days to Billa) and
saying that you take everything as a joke and have no depth of feeling
it makes my blood boil.

This obviously refers to the judgement expressed by her mother who
has weighed in and offered her advice to Penelope, since she goes on,

I wrote to her and said, as a matter of fact, John is capable of far deeper and finer feelings than you have ever dreamed of or can hope to conceive – and surely I should know. If your friends, or rather semi-friends, your real pals like Cracky and Etchells would never do it, are really going about saying that you treat life entirely as a joke and never take anything seriously, then Nancy Mitford's novel *Christmas Pudding* was indeed prophetic – when you appear as a character who longs to be taken seriously but whose every action and production is taken as a joke and thought to be intended as such.

In the event, it was Nancy Mitford herself who urged Betjeman, if he was serious about Penelope, to go to the South of France and win her back.

A month after she wrote her long manifesto, Penelope Chetwode was married to John Betjeman, at the Edmonton Register Office. The venue was chosen because of its proximity to Heddon Court, the prep school where the groom had taught before he got his job on the *Archie Rev*. Present at the ceremony were Betjeman's parents, Hubert de Cronin Hastings and Isabel Hope, the headmaster's wife. After they were married, they went into London for a celebratory luncheon of roast beef and Yorkshire pudding at the Great Eastern Hotel, Liverpool Street, and the honeymoon was a few days at the Green Man, the village pub at Braxted, Essex. 'Ooooh, I did enjoy Essex', Penelope wrote to her husband, when she had returned to her parents' house to face the difficult business of telling them what she had done. Her father's reaction is very touching, as expressed in a letter to her that autumn, from Marseilles, en route to Inja –

I *just hated* saying goodbye to you my own darling. It would have been just the same whoever you had married. It is such a break when the young birds one has watched growing leave the nest.

I am happier now about you. I can never say I like your choice – but I feel that you are so quite sure you are right, & have mapped out your life so thoroughly, that it will be the worst luck if it is not a success . . . Remember always if you are unhappy or in trouble there are always your old daddy's arms to fly to, always open & always ready as long as I live.

It was a matter of course that the field-marshal and his wife should be subsumed into the Betjeman jokey mythos, becoming figures such as 'Colonel' Kolkhorst, or 'Father' Arber of Holy Trinity, Gas Street whose previous existence, pre-Betjeman, had probably been real enough to themselves, but who now found themselves re-invented as one of his private jokes. Betjeman, who had partly yearned to marry into the upper class, and partly through self-protection, partly through masochism, partly through a desire to subvert, had really longed to be known as the common little man Penelope Chetwode married, built up the Chetwodes, when describing them to his friends, as creatures of pure farce. Bowra was soon telling everyone that when the Chetwodes' butler had said, 'Yes, Miss Penelope', the field marshal had sharply stated, 'She's not Miss Penelope, she's Mrs Bargeman.' Searching around for how the young man should address him, Sir Philip had allegedly said, 'You can't call me Philip, that wouldn't do. You can't call me father – I'm not your father. You'd better call me Field Marshal.' Betjeman repeated this statement not only to old friends like Bowra but also to strangers he had barely met. In 1933, for example, he regaled a lunch-table of young clergy at St Alban's, Holborn, with the story.

On 20 November 1931, the field marshal wrote to his daughter:

Penelope, darling, Your John must be a very stupid man. We have had quite a lot of letters from people who are cross with him because he mimics and mocks me & mother – & imitates interviews with us. People all think it is in such bad taste. We have smothered our feelings & done all we can for both of you & it is so common & rude to mock at any older people let alone those who have done all they can for you. Several people have said they won't have you again because of it

. . . Even Roger [her brother] has heard of it in America. It is not only rude & common it is surely very foolish if nothing else, & leaves a nasty taste in the mouth, my dear, & makes us think we were right in our objection to the marriage. Try and stop him doing it.

The Chetwodes — Roger, Alice, Penelope, Philip

Betjeman wrote to the Chetwodes indignantly denying it, though his mother-in-law said, 'I believe it and always shall.' What Sir Philip Chetwode would probably never realise was that, as with his attitude to religious and aesthetic objects of devotion, laughter and mockery signalled in Betjeman a mixture of emotions which included admiration. 'All the things I love — and hate —': a comment by Alan Bennett at a military funeral comes to mind. Three years after Betjeman married, King George V died, and it inspired one of the best public poems of the twentieth century. Who can doubt that, in the final stanza, Betjeman is thinking of those ramrod-straight, decent figures who shored up the British Empire in its last phases, men, in short, like Sir Philip Chetwode? In twelve lines, he captures the dullness of the late king — his shooting, his stamps, his obsession with correct dress; and the momentous nature of the change, the final putting to sleep of the Victorian age as, at Croydon airport, the anarchic and 'unsuitable' figure of Edward VIII, with his flash clothes, divorced mistress and alleged fascistic leanings, arrives. None of these things is spelt out, they are all implied in the essential simplicity of the lyric form —

Spirits of well-shot woodcock, partridge, snipe
    Flutter and bear him up the Norfolk sky:
In that red house in a red mahogany book-case
    The stamp collection waits with mounts long dry.

The big blue eyes are shut which saw wrong clothing
    And favourite fields and coverts from a horse;
Old men in country houses hear clocks ticking
    Over thick carpets with a deadened force;

Old men who never cheated, never doubted,
    Communicated monthly, sit and stare
At the new suburb stretched beyond the run-way
    Where a young man lands hatless from the air.

For the first few months they were married, they lived apart. They had lodged in a succession of nasty one-room flats in London, and Penelope wanted to study Sanskrit. With this end in view, she went to Germany, to perfect her German at the same time, since much of the Indian scholarship which she needed to pursue for her work was written in the German language. Interestingly, in the light of what was to come, she wrote from Germany that she was toying with the idea of a conversion to Roman Catholicism. According to Waugh family gossip, it was either just before or just after her marriage that she either had an affair (Waugh's version) or resisted one (her version) with the novelist, who was himself a recent (1930) convert. 'There is no possible chance of my going over for *2 yrs at the very least*', she assured the Quaker husband on 8 November 1933. In Germany, she later admitted, she had fallen for one or two other people, but not gone beyond flirtations. She had gone to the opera which inspired Hitler to become both a Wagnerian and a populist political leader – *Rienzi* – and wondered whether the *Architectural Review* would like a review of the big exhibition on the history of photography –

There is a large room with larger than life size snaps of Nazi
Demonstrations at Nuremberg etc. There are snaps of the youth
movement, German trades, Architecture (mostly old world, all
ultra-modern Corbusier etc styles are Communist) peasant types
(terrifying faces) villages etc etc. One notices particularly the
absence of surrealist snaps because the Cubist and Surrealist
movements are of course communist. It is useless to write a review
of the Ex. for the A.R. without reproducing some of the snaps and
I don't know if it's possible to get hold of the prints, especially the
early ones. P'raps you have already got someone on to it? If not,
I'll do something for you if you like.

Meanwhile, in Penelope's absence, Betjeman looked for some-
where to set up the marital home when she returned. The editor of
Architectural Review was a man called Christian Barman, known by
Betjeman inevitably as Barmy. He lived in the Vale of the White
Horse in the unwrecked and beautiful village of Uffington below the
Berkshire Downs. Barmy found the Betjemans a house, Garrard's
Farm, which they took at a rent of £36 per annum. It was to be their
home for twelve years. The house needed to be got ready before it
was habitable – and it was always a place of austere comfort, lit by
oil lamps. A pretty, dark-haired young woman called Molly Higgins
was found who would help Betjeman, in Penelope's absence, to
prepare his marital home for habitation. 'An affair was inevitable',
wrote Betjeman's daughter. It did not last more than a few months.
Penelope, to whom Betjeman confessed at once, seems to have felt just
as guilty, in her letters, that she has neglected him, as he did about his
infidelity – if anything, slightly more guilty.

> Darling, I'm so relieved you say I can come back. I think you will
> find it will work alright, anyhow on my side now . . . I hope you'll be
> happy with me but if you aren't you can always go off with M.H. . . .
> It will be lovely if we can go down ter Bryan the first weekend as then
> we'll be able to motor over to Garrards straightaway.

Moti at Garrard's Farm, Uffington

He had jokingly feared that she would come back from Germany a Nazi. In fact, it was their intelligent, mercurial friend Diana Guinness who was fatefully to accompany her sister Unity Valkyrie to Germany that same summer. Diana would leave her liberal-minded poet husband, and their bohemian circle at Biddesden, for the aspirant fascist leader Sir Oswald Mosley, whom they had invited, with Winston Churchill, Augustus John, and crowds of others to Diana's twenty-second birthday ball. These dramas lay (just) ahead. At this distance in time, one is overwhelmed by how young they all were, and how fixed their destinies, by decisions taken often quite randomly.

In the case of the Betjemans, there was a third in the marriage from the start, of whom Betjeman himself had perhaps not been sufficiently aware during all the melodramas of courtship. On their last visit to India together, Penelope's father had bought her a wiry little grey, 14.2 hands high, imported from Mosul to race in Bombay. A 'grey' is what horsey people call a snow-white horse. She called him Moti which means Pearl in Hindi. She hunted with him for two seasons with the Delhi foxhounds, as well as putting him in for endless hunter trials. This was during the period of her affair with Sir John Marshall, when she was learning all about Indian art and archaeology and her father Sir Philip, Commander-in-Chief of the Indian Army, was undertaking the important task of 'indianising' the army. (Until 1932, all the officers in the Indian Army were British, and it was Chetwode's task to train up Indian officers to lead their own men.)

Moti came back from India at the first opportunity and was taken to live in Uffington with the newly-weds. Penelope knew nothing of stable management and she engaged a boy in the village, Jackie Goodenough, a school-leaver aged fourteen, for 10 shillings a week to groom the horse. She dressed Jackie in black breeches and gaiters, the traditional groom's uniform. She began slowly to teach herself how to groom and feed a horse, getting the information from a book. For the housekeeping, she brought with her a German cook-general, Paula Steinbrecher, who spoke no English and who for the first year believed that Betjeman's name was 'Shut up', since Penelope said this to him so often.

Her passion for horses did not confine itself to the stable. In all the houses of which she was the mistress, tack was brought indoors. Kitchens, corridors and staircases smelt of leather, mingled with the fruity aroma of Cochaline, a red oily polish which softens leather. Strewn over kitchen chairs, hanging from lamps and banisters, were bridles, girths, martingales, nosebands, breastplates and reins. She requisitioned one of the ground-floor rooms as a harness room.

Betjeman claimed to hate horses, and from the start he and Penelope quarrelled about almost everything. She claimed he was a bully who would not allow her friends to come and stay without

Faringdon: Penelope, Moti, Robert Heber-Percy
and Evelyn Waugh

making a row, or going away when they came to see her. 'I take all
your new friends to my bosom . . . and get to like them then
YOU get bored with them and play hell if I go on asking them to
meals.' Nevertheless, they had an enormous acquaintance, with
many friends, old and new, coming to Sunday luncheon or staying
for the night. Though the leathery Cochaline smell shocked the
more urban visitors, and though the house was very cold in the
winter, it is clear from surviving letters that Penelope kept house to
quite high standards. Wystan Auden came to stay shortly after they
had moved in, and they took him to a meet of the local hunt. 'I hope
no one killed themselves at that meet', he wrote, 'also that you
haven't discovered how much mud I brought into the sitting room.

I tried to brush it but there were ominous stains still on the carpet.'

One neighbour and friend who took a less tolerant view of hunting was Samuel Gurney who lived in the nearby village of Compton Regis. His family were Norwich Quakers, Betjeman's new religion, but Gurney himself was an advanced Anglo-Catholic. He was very rich, drove a Rolls-Royce, and paid to have the lovely little medieval church of Compton Beauchamp, perched on the edge of the Downs near the Ridgeway and Wayland's Smithy, turned into a luminous Baroque shrine. With the refurbishments to altar and lamps by Martin Travers, this whitewashed English medieval church takes on something of the feeling of a Spanish hermitage, and you feel as you step inside that perhaps Philip II's Armada had after all been successful and the English village churches had been adapted to the religion of El Greco and St John of the Cross.

Gurney was a serious churchman, who worried about the coarsening of the spirit which would result in pursuing the fox.

> The thing itself outrages conscience. Theologically, of course,
> every evil produces good results, and every pang and pain swells the
> treasury of the Passion; but nevertheless it is 'woe to that man by
> whom the offence cometh'. Its indefinite continuance is unthinkable.
> It won't really square with the faith. Put it another way. Picture the
> bright young thing, leaving the altar in the morning, her lips rosy
> with the Blood of Jesus: returning home at night, her finger dripping
> with the blood of vixen. Or Jesus, Mary and Joseph, all in at the
> death and blooded. Have I put it too strongly?

Another Anglo-Catholic who lived nearby and had his influence on Betjeman was Adrian Bishop, an Etonian friend of Bowra's, a brilliant linguist and talker, acerbic, homosexual, loud baritone-voiced. Having mocked and hated religion in the early years when Bowra knew him, he suddenly converted, and in the years before making up his mind to become an (Anglican) Benedictine monk of Nashdom Abbey, he went to live in Uffington.

Betjeman and Moti at Garrard's Farm

'Penelope is practising mysticism', he wrote to Bowra, 'but the Kingdom of Heaven is not taken by storm.'

For all the disruptions to his ego which marriage caused, and for all the tempestuousness of his relations with Penelope from the very beginning, Betjeman early in his marriage began a serious return to the Church, from which he never turned back. The fact that they had smart friends never prevented either Betjeman from forming bonds with their near neighbours, in any of the places they lived. They were friends with the Misses Molly and Edmee Butler, the bootfaced local squiresses. They made friends with the locals in the pub, the Craven Arms, where Betjeman fooled around playing darts underarm, to the amusement of other customers whom he would then stand drinks. And they naturally gravitated towards the big, damp, cruciform church, known as 'the Cathedral of the Vale'. The vicar, the Rev. George Bridle, accepted the new young couple who were eager to take an active role. Betjeman eventually became the people's warden and together with Penelope started the Uffington Parochial Youth Fellowship. The village young-sters felt that the Betjemans 'got things going', with entertainments, talks, tennis tournaments, concerts, fêtes.

'Summer is icumen in.'

Osbert Lancaster did a sub-lime drawing of the Betjemans and friends performing 'Summer is icumen in' for an audience in the village hall. Osbert Lancaster is playing the flute. Penelope is strumming a guitar. Karen Lancaster and Adrian Bishop are trilling in the back row, while in the fore-ground stand Betjeman and Bowra belting out the words, Bowra looking as if he is barking orders on a parade-ground and Betj, eyes aloft and wonky teeth bared, looking more as if he is warbling a sentimental love song from the Edwardian music hall. At the piano sits a bald, saturnine figure, with a bow tie and an eye-glass, and his fingers poised over the keys with the expertise of a serious concert performer.

The pianist was Lord Berners, who lived at the nearby Faringdon House. He has his followers, but even now it is remarkable that Berners is not more highly regarded. In *Who's Who*, Berners recorded: 'Recreations *none*'. He never made a public speech in his life, 'except for the three short sentences with which he opened the Faringdon cinema'. Unlike the self-advertising Sitwells, he was an example of an aristocrat of genuine accomplishment in at least three spheres. He was a talented painter in the manner of the early Corot, who was exhibited at the Lefevre Galleries. He was a witty, camp novelist – the best two are *Far from the Madding War* and *The Girls of Radcliff Hall*. And he was a seriously good composer who had studied with Stravinsky and Casella. He was a brilliant parodist and could do especially clever parodies of German lieder, French and English songs. But his real music deserves much wider recognition, especially the 'Three Pieces for Orchestra' of 1916, the 'Fantaisie espagnole' of 1918–19 and his ballet music – three scores for the Sadler's Wells Company.

He had been brought up as Gerald Tyrwhitt, in Bridgnorth at Apley Park. His parents intended him to have a sporting country life. His aesthetic soul rebelled. In 1918, when he was thirty-five, he inherited the barony of Berners and the Tyrwhitt baronetcy from an uncle, adding the name of Wilson. He was now Sir Gerald Hugh Tyrwhitt-Wilson, fourteenth Baron Berners. He sold his Berners estates and bought Faringdon House where he remained for the rest of his life. His custom of dyeing his doves in bright colours immediately signalled him as an 'eccentric' to the locals. He also owned a house in Rome overlooking the Forum, and watched the rise of Fascism with quiet admiration, never falling for its more brutal excesses, but not being drawn, either, to the more hysterical attacks upon it by his fellow countrymen.

Berners was one of those rare homosexuals who genuinely liked women. Penelope took to him instantly, and often had Moti harnessed to a four-wheeled dog-cart, which she had bought in the neighbouring village, Stanford in the Vale, for £12 and drove over to Faringdon. Berners painted them together: Penelope and Moti standing in his elegant drawing room. In the photographs, he sits at a low easel, wearing co-respondent shoes.

Penelope had time on her hands to develop friendship. For the first four years of her marriage, she did not become pregnant. Her husband was away during the week. Friendships with such multi-

Faringdon: Lady Mary Lygon, Robert Heber-Percy,
Penelope, Lord Berners

talented figures as Berners deserve and take time. During the
hunting season, she and Moti could be 'out' as much as they liked.
She enjoyed the almost surreal chance encounters she had with her
fellow riders. An elderly gentleman rode up and the following
exchange took place –

> E.G. Where did you get that nice horse?
> P. Inja.
> E.G. And what were you doing in India?
> P. Staying with my father.
> E.G. And what was he doing there?
> P. Commander-in-Chief.

Meanwhile, Betjeman had begun the routine which would be
the pattern, and the eventual undoing, of his marriage, either of

commuting to London each day – initially from Challow Station – or of staying up in town several days, and returning for weekends with his friends. The Vale of the White Horse was, as he recalled,

> the furthest place from London I could find which you could leave and get back to in a day. Fares were low. It was lovely getting beyond Reading in the train from London into what was true country. In Uffington people still spoke with Berkshire accents . . . Uffington had its own railway station then lit with oil lamps.

And his fortunes were distinctly looking up.

Since the end of 1933, Betjeman had supplemented his income on the *Archie Rev* by writing articles for the *Evening Standard*, then a Beaverbrook paper. Even more than the *Daily Express*, which in those days was an influential newspaper, the *Evening Standard* was a vehicle for its proprietor's whims. The 'Londoner's Diary' was a gossip column, but it was much more than this. Those who wrote for it – Harold Nicolson had just resigned as one of the writers before Betjeman arrived, Randolph Churchill was a regular, Malcolm Muggeridge joined the paper about this time – were employed as mouthpieces of their Master's Voice, able to interpret and give shape to his whims and prejudices. The 'Diary' was edited by a former diplomat and spy called Robert Bruce Lockhart with a natural spy's gift for putting two and two together. Once he saw in *The Times* personal column that a dog was missing near Churt. Could it belong to Lloyd George, wondered Lockhart. His underlings spent the day on the telephone and, yes, it turned out indeed to be the dog of the former Prime Minister, the very terrier which had once bitten the Prime Minister of Italy, Signor Orlando, at Rapallo. Beaverbrook, who credited himself with the rise of Lloyd George to the premiership in 1916, and his removal from office seven years later, would have been delighted by this story. The 'Diary' and its team of clever young writers were in a way his spies, sending out signals to the world about the trivial details of great, or celebrated, people, their wives, their dinner-parties, their pets. (Stories of love affairs were not mentioned in those days.) Betjeman's old house mate, Randolph Churchill, was a valued member of the team – as was, on occasion, his father, who edited the 'Diary' sometimes in Lockhart's absence. Randolph's colleagues would be impressed to hear him shouting into the telephone receiver to Cabinet ministers and courtiers: 'That you, Bobbity? Duff? Fruity? Rab?' It was Patrick Balfour and Randolph Churchill who got Betjeman to help them with an article called 'Peers without Tears'. Then they got Betjeman the unlikely assignment of interviewing Myrna Loy. He asked her if she liked Perpendicular architecture. On the strength of this achievement, Betjeman became a member of 'Londoner's Diary' with special responsibility for films. He was taken on by the editor of the paper, Percy Cudlipp, and paid the amazingly big salary of 16 guineas a week to write a regular film criticism. That meant that in only three weeks, he would have earned the entire annual rent on Garrard's Farm, and had money left over. The Betjemans had discovered the perhaps dangerous ease with which a clever person can make money as a journalist.

The writers on 'Londoner's Diary', in addition to Randolph Churchill and Patrick Balfour, were Betjeman's other aristocratic friends, Peter Fleming and Lady Mary Pakenham, sister of Frank. He made his mark on the paper, as he did in any new setting, by larking about. The talk of the office one day was the story of Betjeman passing the former Foreign Secretary, Sir John Simon, in the street, a severe stuffed-shirt sort of character, and pretending to have an epileptic fit on the pavement just in front of him. His film criticisms were hit and miss; he liked funny films, especially W.C. Fields, Laurel and Hardy and 'Schnozzle' Durante, but Bing Crosby crooning, or endless costume dramas, were not to his taste. Few, if any, of his office colleagues, except those who knew him already, had much inkling that this jokey young man was destined for fame as a poet.

It was in another area of work that Betjeman found his *métier*. When he was working on the *Architectural Review*, Betjeman was introduced to the publicity manager of Shell – Jack Beddington. He was thirteen years older than Betjeman, a jolly, Balliol man who had served in the First World War and was now employed to promote the image of the famous oil company. 'An old Rugbeian', Betjeman described him, 'very fat and full of laughter. I used to call him "the old filthy". He liked taking pictures of nude women covered in oil. He didn't like churches one bit.' Impressive amounts of posters, films and other artwork were commissioned by Beddington, using artists as distinguished and varied as Graham Sutherland, Ben Nicholson, Duncan Grant, Rex Whistler, Edward Bawden and Richard Guyatt. Posters of beauty spots cunningly became identified with the very thing which would wreck their beauty: the growth of motoring. Writers were also enlisted by Beddington, and in 1933, when the idea of writing a series of guide books to British counties, the *Shell Guides*, was adopted, Betjeman became the general editor.

In 1977, Betjeman recalled those days for his granddaughter, Endellion Lycett Green, in a very long letter. He described his railway journeys into London.

> The slowest part of the journey was the underground railway from Paddington to Farringdon Street, the nearest underground station to the *Evening Standard* office.
>
> . . . One morning I was travelling down on the Inner Circle underground from Paddington to Farringdon Street when the train did a very unusual thing. It waited for a long time at King's Cross Station. My father, your great-grandfather, had a factory, founded in 1820, on the Pentonville Road. (It is still there and owned by the Medici Society.) King's Cross Underground was the nearest station. I remember thinking as the train waited at King's Cross, 'Shall I go out and see my father?' A voice inside me seemed to say, 'Yes, do go and see him. It won't take you long and you won't be too late for the film.' The train went on waiting but I felt too lazy at that time of the morning to bother to get out and take a tram up the hill. Then we went on and with

JB's sketchbook: Berkshire landscape

other film writers I saw an American musical film called *George White's Scandals*.

When I got back to Uffington that evening the telephone rang. It was my father's managing clerk Mr H. V. Andrew, and he told me that my father had died that morning while talking to him. Do you think my father was trying to get through to me? Do you think he knew he was going to die so swiftly? I don't know. All I can tell you is that it happened and Gramelope [i.e. Penelope] will remember it.

She offered me a strawberry that we had grown in our garden at Uffington when I heard the news and I remember being too upset to want to eat it.

7

MR PAHPER – THE DEFINING FRIENDSHIP

Ernest Betjemann died on 22 June 1934. On 27 August of the same year, probate was complete, the sum of £1, 699 0s 3d had been paid in death duties to the Inland Revenue, and the will was legal. The bulk of his estate was left to his wife – namely the freehold of the two houses, 53 Church Street and 'Undertown', Trebetherick, all the furniture, plate and personal effects, and the sum of £2,000 – which converts to £315,923.44p in inflationary terms in 2002, using the index of average earnings. Two thousand five hundred fully paid ordinary shares apiece in G. Betjemann & Sons Limited (free of duty) were left to Philip Rolls Asprey, who sold so much Betjemann ware in Bond Street, and Horace Victor Andrew, the managing director of the firm. They were in effect to have control of the firm from now onwards. Ernie left his sporting guns to his godson Hugh Francis Macklin de Paula, and, rather mysteriously, he left 'to Miss Norah Kennedy of "Cappagh", Kilrush, Co. Clare, Ireland', the sum of £300.

Alan Pryce-Jones ('Bog') tells a remarkable story in his autobiography, *The Bonus of Laughter*, published in 1987. 'John's funeral', he wrote,

> was less sensational than that of his father, which took place in Chelsea Old Church. John was an only child, and while he and his mother were waiting for the ceremony to begin a scene occurred like that in the second act of *Der Rosenkavalier*. A second, unknown Mrs Betjeman suddenly erupted with a second family, and it turned out that for many years Mr Betjeman had lived a second and hitherto secret life.

It is hard to know what to make of this very striking claim. I have been through the registers of marriage for the period of Ernest Betjemann's life and it is simply not true that he was a bigamist in the legal sense of the term. He contracted no marriage either before or after his marriage to Bess, in Scotland, Ireland, England or Wales. (The marriage of Mabel Bessie Dawson is recorded in the Hendon registration district in the September quarter of 1902.) Nor do any of the registers of birth record Ernest Betjemann as the father. So there was no second Mrs Betjemann or second family in any sense which can be traced. This does not rule out the possibility that Ernie kept a common-law wife the paternity of whose children is unrecorded. There is no record in Ireland that he married Norah Kennedy, bigamously or otherwise, and indeed my pursuit of Norah Kennedy herself reached a dead end though I *think* her parents were probably John Kennedy, labourer, and Mary Partill, servant, who were married in the Roman Catholic chapel of Kilrush, Co. Clare on 12 July 1904. Whether this Norah had illegitimate issue, by Ernest Betjemann or by another, I have been unable to establish.

There is, however, some anecdotal evidence for Ernie's having had mistresses. Pierce Synnott, the Oxford friend who invited John Betjeman to stay in Ireland in the summer of 1926, told Billy Clonmore that Ernest Betjemann had spoilt the holiday by arriving in Ireland himself

> and is tearing the son to Galway to hold his [fishing] line while he jokes with Ranjitsinghji [a cricketer who had bought the 30,000-acre Ballynahinch estate]. Selfish and incongruous pursuits. He must be the vilest man who ever lived, v. rich, gives his son nothing, forbids him to read poetry, kicks his wife, brings mistresses into the house, spends all on keeping shoots and fishing, makes his son go with him, makes scenes in public, and spends his spare time in persecuting people.

It is safe to assume that this unflattering portrait of old Ernie comes from his son. It is presumably how Betjeman saw his father when, in his twenties, he was getting on badly with the old man. Some of it, we know to be untrue. This book began with a recollection by an older Betjeman, of Ernie reading Goldsmith's poem *The Deserted Village* to his son 'almost daily'. So much for his forbidding him to read poetry. That Ernie was coarse and bad-tempered, we need not doubt. If he brought mistresses to the house, then Alan Pryce-Jones's story loses some of its edge, since neither Bess nor John would have been much surprised by the appearance of 'another woman' at the funeral. Given the development of Betjeman's own life, an appalling relationship with his son, leading to all but total estrangement, and an all but bigamous life with two women, the death of Ernest Betjemann seems all the more poignant. Ernie left nothing directly to John Betjeman, his only son, though the will specifies that 'after the death of my wife my Trustees shall stand possessed of the Trust Fund in Trust for my son John Betjeman absolutely'. This fits with the testimony of *Summoned by Bells* about his relationship with the father –

> My dear deaf father, how I loved him then
> Before the years of our estrangement came!

He recalls his ham-fisted attempts at shooting and country sports:

> 'Shoot!' said my father, helping with my gun,
> And aiming at the rabbit – 'Quick, boy, fire!'
> But I had not released the safety-catch.
> I was a poet. That was why I failed.
> My faith in this chimera brought an end
> To all my father's hopes. In later years,
> Now old and ill, he asked me once again
> To carry on the firm, I still refused.

G. Betjemann & Sons continued as a working firm until the war, but Betjeman the poet had little or nothing to do with it, and the business was eventually wound up. In *Summoned by Bells*, Betjeman reproached himself for disappointing his father, and the workforce, by not taking over the running of the firm —

> I see
> His kind grey eyes look woundedly at mine,
> I see the workmen seeking other jobs.

The correspondence which he had with his mother in the aftermath of Ernest's death shows that he did not abandon the business in a hurry, nor was it sold off until Horace Anderson, the works manager, and the rest of the staff were at least offered the possibility of work by Asprey's, who had their own factory making goods similar to those sold by G. Betjemann & Sons Ltd. On 20 November 1937, for example, he wrote a long letter to 'Darling Bessie' — which was what he called his mother, not Mother or Mummy — explaining that he had had his own solicitor look over the terms of Ernie's will, and discovered that he was actually a shareholder of the company. The lawyer advised against going into liquidation, because the chief assets of the firm were the land on which the works stood, and the men who worked there. Horace Anderson was very pleased with this development. Betjeman shows himself throughout this long protracted business to have been much more conscientious and unselfish than his self-reproach in *Summoned by Bells* would warrant. He wants Bessie to get some capital to live on — and the sale of the company appears to have brought her in about £4,000, quite a lot of money pre-war. Nor was it done in a hurry. As late as 27 June 1938, Horace Anderson was still writing to 'Dear Mr John' about cocktail glasses. Betjeman suggested calling a new design 'The 19th Hole Cocktail Glass'. Anderson did not like the title and suggested that 'the Club House Glass would be a little better understood by the trade than Dormy Glass, the latter being appreciated by Golf Players only'. Perhaps, who knows, if war had not come, Betjeman might have warmed to the idea of taking some part in the firm. In August

1940, Bessie's solicitor told him that she alone had the power to wind up G. Betjemann & Sons, and this eventually happened without consulting Betjeman. Though a shareholder, he did not have shares which entitled him to a vote in the matter.

The death of Ernest Betjemann put a definite seal on his son's life as did the birth of John's son Paul Betjeman on 26 November 1937. The lives of father Ernest and son John were both intertwined at the deepest level, and fiercely at odds; they were both utterly different, and yet the younger man, formed by the elder, was destined to follow his patterns of life. Betjemann *père* had his life at the works, when he pursued his career as a businessman and manufacturer, and his rather grander life with shooting friends in Hertfordshire. Likewise, Betjeman the broadcaster and hack journalist also had higher-class aristocratic friends. Betjemann *père* had, in effect, two wives and two families. This too – though not yet – was to be the pattern of the mature Betjeman's emotional journey. Through the lives of both men ran Church of England piety (High) combined with irascibility and sensuality. But with the death of Ernest Betjemann, there had come the rounding-off of one end of the story.

With Ernie dead and the Islington works with all its history and emotional baggage now in other hands, Betjeman junior was now free to become Betjeman. The Guinnesses had seen he was 'a genius of a very unusual kind'. Bowra had admired his poems from the start. But, as the experience at the *Evening Standard* showed, there were still many who saw Betj primarily as a comic turn. And much of the time he was in danger of seeing himself entirely in this way.

In his poetry, and in the architectural writings and broadcasts of his maturity, there was always humour, but there was also something more to Betjeman. Penelope could see that 'you as it in yew ter wroite really good what is known as "worth whoile" books, probably about harchitecture and nointeenth cent harchitects and other alloied subjects'. He had it in him, too, to be one of the most astute poets of place. Nourished by his huge collection of topographical books, his watercolourist's eye would focus on 'Highgate Hill's thick elm-encrusted side', on 'grasses bending heavy with a shower', on ash trees in Cornwall 'bent landwards by the Western lash', on the 'after-storm-wet-sky' shining on the Avon estuary. He had it in him to write elegies for an England which was doomed and vanishing, to touch its spirit, capture its oddities and its echoes from the past. There is a vision which is pure 'Betjeman'. The early poems had been hit and miss. Was he going to dissipate all his talent in journalism, and conversation and social life?

For so gregarious a being, the Muse of Poetry needed to take flesh in human loves and friendships. His friendship with John Piper marked the new phase of Betjeman's life. The paintings of the one, the poems of the other, provide a highly comparable elegiac vision. There is no doubt that they were catalysts to one another and that their best work was stimulated by their friendship.

Jim Richards, Betjeman's colleague on the *Architectural Review*, was married to Peggy Angus, who was putting on a show of abstract paintings for the Artists' International exhibition, a group founded to help refugees from Nazi Germany. Piper contributed some pictures.

Born on 13 December 1903, and educated at Kingswood School, Epsom, and Epsom College, Piper had gone straight from school into his father's firm of solicitors. Only his father's early death in 1927 had released him from the boredom of office life. He went to Richmond School of Art, and joined London's Royal College of Art in 1928. A year later he married another art student, Eileen Holding, but this did not last.

Like most very young artists, Piper drew his inspiration from the most admired masters of his day – in his case, Matisse, Picasso and Braque. He experimented with a variety of abstract inspirations, cubism, paper collages, and also constructions in which rods and discs of differing textures and forms would be applied to boards.

Mr Pahper

With the dissolution of his marriage, Piper had fallen in love with one of his wife's friends, Myfanwy Evans, who shared his enthusiasm not only for modern art and for music, but also for topography. 'Send me some S. Devon lighthouses from Dartmoor and other intimations of your existence', he said to her on a postcard during the first summer of their relationship.

Piper was a gaunt-faced, hollow-eyed, eagle-nosed man of almost monkish appearance, with short hair *en brosse*. Myfanwy, with her sloping shoulders and floppy short hair, had the look of a schoolboy. They were to be devoted life-companions, marrying when the law allowed on 24 February 1937 at the Marylebone Register Office. By then they had become the Betjemans' dearest friends.

Jim Richards, at that exhibition in 1936, suggested that Piper might like to get involved in the *Shell Guides*. Not long afterwards Piper received a letter from Betjeman – 'Dear Artist, Marx Richards tells me that you are good at writing guidebooks. Would you like to do Oxfordshire?'

'We realised we liked the same things', Betjeman recollected.

Piper's abstract creations of the early to mid-1930s are imitations of continental giants. His desire for Myfanwy to send him postcards of South Devon lighthouses was an intimation of a much more personal desire to engage with English landscape, and architectural monuments. Still using collage to great effect, he

produced some wonderful sea-
scapes, notably in Dungeness
and in Aberaeron. Lighthouses
figured largely in these mid-
1930s works, but also did
Welsh chapels and medieval
ruins. In the October 1936 issue
of *Architectural Review*, Piper
wrote an article on 'England's
Early Sculptors'. He saw that the
relief-carvings on Northumbrian
and Cornish crosses, or the
strange faces carved on the font
at Toller Fratrum in Dorset,
were forebears of much that
he had admired in Picasso. The
medieval sculptors had 'immense

My silken Myfanwy

personal conviction'. In discovering the genius of these unnamed
English craftsmen-sculptors, Piper found his own style, his own
immense personal conviction.

Much of this was helped by working with Betjeman on the *Shell
Guides*, and by the journeys the two men made together, looking at
churches. On one such expedition, in Much Wenlock in Shropshire,
they had to wait in a hotel's side-room before being admitted for tea,
and a waitress came forward and said in a strong North Country
accent, 'Will you two men come forward please.' When they sat
down to tea, Betjeman had adopted the *persona* of a commercial
traveller, who spoke in the same strong accent as the waitress. His
'colleague' was therefore 'Mister Pahper', a nickname which stuck.

Wherever they went – and they collaborated on the Shropshire
volume of the *Shell Guides* – Piper photographed or sketched churches.
'He drew absolutely certainly with a quill pen', Betjeman recalled,
'and you could tell at once from the line whether it was decayed or

Greek revival in Reading: St Mary's, Castle Street

Victorian . . . I don't think I've ever felt so confident as I did with Mr Piper. I remember once in Salop I suddenly lost my temper and then I felt I had wounded a tame animal.' For Piper's part, it was directly through browsing in Betjeman's huge library of topographical books that he discovered his *métier*. The abstract phase had come to an inevitable end, and Piper had begun to ask himself, 'Where do we go from here? . . . I found I was English and Romantic, so I looked at Cotman, Turner, Blake, Palmer and painters in that tradition and tried to draw the things I seemed born to love.'

The friendship between Pipers and Betjemans was very much one of four, and not just of two people. Myfanwy had known Penelope Chetwode as a girl. They had been at school together for a short spell at Queen's College, Harley Street, though Myfanwy, more academic, transferred to North London Collegiate, and then went on to St Hugh's College, Oxford. (In the Betjeman poems about her, he makes her a student at St Hilda's, presumably for reasons of easier scansion.) Betjeman had no sooner met her than she had joined the reredos of his goddesses, 'Ringleader, tom-boy, and chum to the weak'. In 'Myfanwy', she is nanny ('Black-stockinged legs under navy-blue serge'), treating him to Fuller's angel-cake and Robertson's marmalade, and possessing a 'fortunate bicycle' which makes another appearance in 'Myfanwy at Oxford', this time laden with 'Kant on the handle-bars, Marx in the saddlebag' while the willowy figure of Myfanwy Evans blends in the incense-choked shrines of St Paul's and St Barnabas's with the Celtic Myfanwy of Arthur Machen's *The Secret Glory*. The 'Lonely Hearts' columns of newspapers sometimes advertise for companions who will offer 'Friendship at First'. Betjeman offered most of his women friends Courtly Love at first which cascaded through laughter into friendship.

Myfanwy was immensely impressed by her first visit to Garrard's Farm, and by the fact that Penelope had trained up two village girls to cook and serve excellent meals. Because she had known Penelope and been to her girlhood home in St John's Wood, the Pipers could also supply that not always easy category – friends who could help entertain family. The Betjemans brought the field marshal and Lady Chetwode over to the Pipers' house at Fawley Bottom (Fawley Bum)

Peter Quennell

near Henley. 'What's that?' asked the field marshal pointing at a custard marrow on the table. When told, he replied, 'Were you ever in Kashmir?'

Betjeman's friends, Osbert and Karen Lancaster, also took an instant liking to the Pipers, so there were many happy meals together. As his amusing memoirs show, Lancaster had been exposed to so much mumbo-jumbo throughout his childhood, when his mother tried out one branch of Hidden Wisdom after another, that he remained immune as an adult to the wilder reaches of religious enthusiasm but he was a practising Anglican. Both Betjemans as a married team had found a deep bond in the Church. It soon became clear that it was much more than a thing of hymn-singing round the harmonium, or wanting to join in with village life, and so offering to help at church. Visitors to Garrard's Farm would find themselves subject to various forms of persuasion, not always subtle. Peter Quennell, who had been engaged to write the volume on Somerset for the *Shell Guides*, went to stay at Uffington on a particularly cold winter weekend. After an excellent Sunday luncheon he retired to his bedroom in the hope of burrowing beneath the blankets for warmth. Half asleep, he realised that someone was joining him, and he turned his body to find Penelope Betjeman, well-swathed with cardies, snuggling down to join him. A keen amorist, Quennell had noted Penelope's charms and felt flattered by her directness of approach. But he had mistaken the reason for this visit. 'Naow, Peter', she said in her loud Cockney, 'what is orl this about not believing in the Divinity of Chroist? Woi don't yew believe?'

In 1937, while on holiday with Penelope in Rome, Betjeman had read a book called *Elements of the Spiritual Life*. He had felt his faith renewed as he absorbed its pages. Its author was the Rev. Francis Harton, vicar of Baulking only four miles from Uffington. Both Father Harton and his wife Sibyl became Betjeman friends. Indeed, it was through Sibyl that the Betjemans met the Hartons. Mrs Harton found herself on a train with a couple who were in the middle of a row. 'They were quite oblivious of being in public.'

Before long, Father Harton had become Betjeman's and Penelope's confessor. 'Thank you for making our marriage so happy again', Penelope once wrote to him.

Father Harton, as well as being vicar of Baulking, was a keen diner at the Mercers' Company in the City of London, of which he was the Master. When he became Dean of Wells in 1951, Betjeman exclaimed – 'We thought he was just a humble country priest, and all the time he was eating his way into the most comfortable Deanery in England.' When Harton died in 1958 'while walking near Wells Cathedral', Betjeman wrote:

> He was a much-loved parish priest in the little village of Baulking, where he is to be buried. He was a staunch Catholic but did not believe in putting country people off with too much ritual. By constant visiting, unruffled example, the effective use of the Book of Common Prayer, and by preaching plain doctrinal sermons, he built up a loyal following.

Father Harton was a boring man, and, much as they revered him, the Betjemans mocked him behind his back, calling him Father Folky and Mrs Harton the Abbess. Bowra treasured the letter he wrote to Penelope to dispense with her services as an organist at Evensong in Baulking. It is quoted in full both by Bowra and in subsequent studies, but it does deserve its immortality:

Baulking Vicarage

My dear Penelope,

I have been thinking over the question of playing the harmonium
on Sunday evenings here and have reached the conclusion that I must
now take it over myself.

I am very grateful to you for doing it for so long and hate to
have to ask you to give it up, but, to put it plainly, your playing has
got worse and worse and the disaccord between the harmonium and
the congregation is becoming destructive of devotion. People are not
very sensitive here, but even some of them have begun to complain,
and they are not usually given to doing that. I do not like writing
this, but I think you will understand that it is my business to see that
divine worship is as perfect as it can be made. Perhaps the crankiness
of the instrument has something to do with the trouble. I think it
does require a careful and experienced player to deal with it.

Thank you ever so much for stepping so generously into the
breach when Sibyl was ill; it was the greatest possible help to me and
your results were noticeably better then than now.

Yours ever, F.P. Harton

He gave her a copy of H.V. Morton's *In the Footsteps of the Master*
inscribed 'With grateful thanks from the Vicar and Churchwardens
of Baulking'.

Although the Pipers considered Father Folky 'a pompous old
trout', it was at his hands that they sought the sacrament of baptism,
followed by confirmation, by the Bishop of Oxford, in Uffington
Parish Church.

Am very annoyed with the folky's [sic] for thinking the atmosphere
in this house is not Holy enough for you to have lunch in before the
laying on of hands. You could easily bring Edware [sic] over for the day
and leave him with Betty but I suppose he would be miserable without
you. Anyway you must come and have tea afterwards. Much love to

St Paul's, Avenue Road, Swiss Cottage

you both and I am showing the Folkys J. Piper's *Listener* articles which should put them in their places about Georgian.

The Pipers were intimidated by the service partly because there were 'hundreds of kiddies' present. After Confirmation they received Holy Communion and then, in Piper's recollection, they were 'married'. Presumably, by 'married', Piper meant 'received a nuptial blessing' since their actual wedding had already taken place.

For the remaining few years of peacetime, the Betjemans and the Pipers were constantly in one another's company, quite often joined by the Lancasters ('What a service you did us the day you brought the Pipers into our lives', Osbert Lancaster was to write to Betjeman). Piper's enthusiasm for 'church crawls' was insatiable. He remembered Betjeman complaining, 'I can't do more than ten churches a day, old boy.'

As their friend David Cecil once remarked, 'it is only second-rate minds which reject the obvious'. The churches of England are its glory. This seems an obvious fact today, to unbelievers as well as to the faithful. But at the moment Piper and Betjeman became friends the German air force was being built up and would, after the out-break of war, bomb English cities, destroying many of the finest churches. A less obvious threat came from within. This was from the Church itself, the clergy who could not see, what was obvious to the rest of the population, that each parish church, even the duller ones, is a gospel in stone. Each tells us much more than most sermons or uplifting books. And it is also a link with our forebears, with the past. (The very reason why some of the more power-mad clergy hate church buildings.)

Pleasure, laughter, aesthetic delight led them on their ceaseless church crawls. But in its inexhaustible and encyclopaedic scope, their obsession would allow them to build up a huge store of personal knowledge and visual memories, which would be put, not only into the *Shell Guides*, but also into the *Collins Guide to English Parish Churches* (illustrated by Piper) as into hundreds of Piper pictures and dozens of Betjeman poems. Their journeys together also laid the ground-work for many of Betjeman's best topographical films. Just as John Ruskin with sketch-pad, pencil and brush (later, with camera) felt himself to be immortalising the last vestiges of

Gothic Europe before it was destroyed by industrialisation, there is a strong sense in both Piper and Betjeman, instinctual at first, and later taught by experience, that their love of churches had an elegiac tinge. But it also, without being solemn, had a serious purpose and effect. Most people in England would not choose to put into words what they 'believe', and few are regular churchgoers. But to the 75 per cent or more who always answer on censuses and questionnaires that they believe in God, as indeed to the 25 per cent who take a different view, the buildings, with their peculiar atmosphere, and encrustations of historical memories and associations, are deeply treasured. Betjeman's and Piper's much younger friend Richard Ingrams rightly observed that this was 'a partnership which did more to teach Englishmen to love their churches and their Church than anything or anyone in modern times'.

How profoundly seriously Betjeman regarded religious questions is shown in the remarkable letter he wrote on 25 March 1939 to Roy Harrod, the economist who had married Billa Cresswell. Evidently Harrod had written to Betjeman asking him whether he really seriously believed in 'all that'. Harrod had said that the theists he had met were all bores and that they did not tell us anything of interest. Religion leaves the problems of the world 'unsorted'. Betjeman replied by asking: 'What are the problems? For you, economic ones? That someone is worse off than someone else? . . . That people are tortured and unhappy mentally and physically . . . ?' Then he put into words why he went to church.

> I choose the Christian's way (and completely fail to live up to it) because I believe it is true and because I believe – for possibly a split second in six months, but that's enough – that Christ is really the incarnate Son of God and that Sacraments are a means of grace and that grace alone gives one the power to do what one ought to do. And once I have accepted that, the questions of atonement, the Trinity, Heaven and Hell become logical and correct. Of course my attitude to

them is different from that of an Italian peasant, but that is because words can never explain mysteries, my *knowledge* of them is the same as that of the peasant. By knowledge I mean knowing with more than the intellect. You would not hold this possible. You believe that the intellect is our highest faculty and that mind and body are all we have. If you throw in spirit, then even a thing like positive, tangible evil becomes possible. Then one's spiritual life becomes the activist of one and we are racing in an arena of witnesses living, dead and unborn into the world.

I feel this will shock you, you dear Liberal intellectual old thing . . . I know that you are a negative force but may even do some service by immunising people against worse creeds such as Fascism. I believe it is positive and that can alone save the world, not from Fascism, or Nazism, but from evil. If I did not believe that I should live in the present and squeal at death all the time, instead of most of the time.

Even before the bombs began to fall, the destruction of England was well under way. Betjeman became a preservationist by instinct. So many good buildings, of whose history and architecture he had built up an intimate knowledge, were the victims of human greed and stupidity. An obvious example was All Hallows' Church, Lombard Street, in the City of London, which the ecclesiastical commissioners proposed to remove, so that the site could be sold to a stock bank. Betjeman wrote to *The Times* reminding readers of the fate of St Katherine Coleman, 'one of the few unspoiled Georgian interiors in the Country', demolished in 1919, its magnificent fittings distributed here and there to quite inappropriate settings. C.R. Ashbee, the Arts and Crafts designer (and erotomaniac) wrote congratulating Betjeman on his letter. 'Till we all get a unified & intelligent constructive policy on which there is agreement between (a) Architects and Engineers, (b) The L.C.C., (c) The Church, (d) The City, (e) The Crown Estates in London, I place them in this order of importance, we shall have no chance for any *London Plan* that

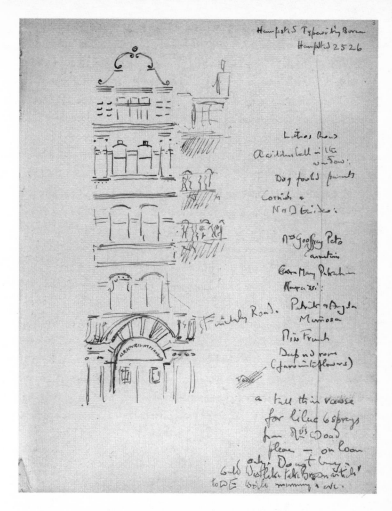

Arkwright Mansions, flats on the Finchley Road

is worth the name.' Only the post-war scene would demonstrate quite how true this was. Ashbee, like Comper, became one of those older designers, craftsmen and artists whom Betjeman befriended, fairly often making a visit to Godden Green, Sevenoaks, to see him.

Already, in the late 1930s, people were beginning to look to Betjeman as the man who would voice their dismay at the vandalistic destruction of good architecture. A letter from R.L.P. Jowitt, secretary of the Georgian Group, written to Garrard's Farm after the outbreak of war, tries to enlist his support to save the Old Town Hall in Devizes, and speaks of a threat to demolish the Clarendon Hotel in Oxford and replace it with a Woolworth's shop. Already, at thirty-three years old Betjeman had become a figure to whom people were beginning to look as a natural saviour of threatened architecture. In 1938, he published *An Oxford University Chest*, an impassioned mishmash of a book, which lambasts the heedless manner in which the university, as landlords, allowed their property to be developed. Graham Greene, in his review of the book, singles out for especial praise, Betjeman's evocation of St Ebbe's, with its Georgian alleyways and little shops with 'their painted firescreens, writhing vases, cumbersome clocks such as might deck the parlour of some small farm among the elms ten or twenty miles away'. It is almost as if both men could foresee that this fascinating bit of old Oxford would be gouged out in the fullness of time, and in the late 1960s replaced with the 'Westgate Centre' with its supermarkets and multi-storey car park. The blend of humour, whimsy and anger in Betjeman's writing was becoming an acquired taste for a wider public.

8

BETJEMAN AT WAR

etjeman never entirely threw off the pacifist convictions which are required of Quakers. A month after the outbreak of war, he made a retreat at the Cowley Fathers' monastery in Oxford, and was still agonising about the morality of warfare. 'At present fighting in a war seems to me to be committing a new sin in defence of an old one.' Nor did he ever enter entirely into the 'wartime spirit'. 'Archie is very well and pro-Hitler I am sorry to say', Betjeman confided to Gerard Irvine, a schoolboy pen-pal ('Dearest little chum') whom he had come to know in the late 1930s after accepting the boy's invitation to give a talk at Haileybury. Perhaps the bear had succumbed to the conversational charms of Lady Mosley, something which was very easily done. Obviously Betjeman did not share his teddy bear's Hitlerite political beliefs, any more than his religious ones. (Archie was a strict Baptist.) Nevertheless, one wonders what Nancy Mitford made of his remark, made in May 1944, 'I'd like to see Diana and Co. Give them my love. One form of state control is as bad as another.'

His pacifist doubts about committing a new sin in defence of an old one, were confided to one of his heroes, the architect Ninian Comper. Betjeman's mind, even in the opening months of the war, was still focused on the things which were its perpetual concern.

There is no doubt that you have transformed church architecture in England and you stand on your own as the only creative genius in that sphere – with F.C. Eden a little lower down the scale. That is something which is its own reward and a greater reward than is

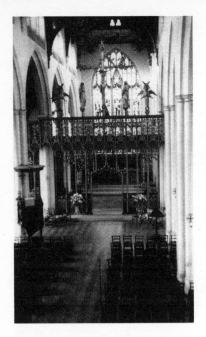

St Cyprian's,
a Comper masterpiece

given to other people in your art because your work has all been to the Glory of God.

The letter, which is a long one, is in the nature of an aesthetic manifesto, in which he thanks Comper for opening his eyes, and his heart, to how architecture affects the human spirit. How could it be, he asks himself, that he could appreciate the design of Greenwich Hospital, and of a really well-made underground train? The doctrinal modernism of the *Archie Rev* had been missing something. It was while he was sitting in the back of Comper's masterpiece near Baker Street Station, St Cyprian the Martyr, Clarence Gate (built 1903), that the truth dawned. 'I saw as I sat in St Cyprian's, proportion, attention to detail, colour, texture, and chiefly the purpose – the tabernacle as the centre of it all. This is as much of the present age as the aeroplane. It is not aping a past age, that is bad; or what pretends to be modern, and is not; that is worse.' As his copious wartime correspondence shows, Betjeman never stopped absorbing the messages given him by great architecture. His eye and feeling for place found new objects on which to focus, but his preoccupations were unshaken by the war. Nevertheless, a lurking dread hovered.

If he had any doubts about the sinfulness of fighting and killing, there was also another horror to be faced by those volunteering for service, namely the prospect of going abroad. 'What a joke about your being a Captain, if it is really true', he wrote to Alan Pryce-Jones. 'But how distasteful for you, having to go to France. Abroad is so nasty. I would rather die in Wolverhampton than Aix-la-Chapelle.' Becoming a captain, or indeed entering any of the services, was more difficult than Betjeman at first imagined.

One of the surprising things about the Second World War, for those living afterwards and reading accounts of its beginnings, is the difficulty encountered by so many men in getting enlisted in any sort of military service or war work. Evelyn Waugh's *Sword of Honour* trilogy fictionalizes his difficulties in finding

Ninian Comper

a regiment. The wartime novels in Anthony Powell's *Dance to the Music of Time* sequence reflect a similar failure to get suitable work on the part of a writer willing to do his bit.

Since 1938, Betjeman had been a volunteer in 'a silly thing called the Observer Corps'. Its members were given an instrument, known jocularly as a 'Heath Robinson', which consisted of a flat circular map table and a spindly tripod. It supposedly enabled the observer, before radar had been fully pioneered, to plot the movement of enemy aircraft in the skies above Britain. Such occasional work hardly qualified as full-time. Betjeman wrote to Kenneth Clark, director of the National Gallery, and asked what chance there was of getting a job in the Ministry of Information.

Dear Betjeman,

I do not know the origin of this deplorable idea that I have anything to do with the Ministry of Information and can get people jobs there. On the contrary I am trying hard to get a job there myself, without the least success. If I get there before you do I will try to wangle you in and hope you will do the same for me.

Sir Kenneth Clark and his wife were to become quite close friends of both the Betjemans and the Pipers, prompting Bowra's inevitable joke, when he felt that he had met Sir K and Jane Clark wherever he went – 'Jane and Sir K in all around I see'.

When Betjeman turned to the field marshal for help in finding a post, he received some characteristically brisk responses.

'My dear John', wrote Philip Chetwode on 3 October 1939,

I don't quite understand what part of the Air Force you want to get into. You are I suppose over age to join the regular Air Force, but perhaps you have heard of some job as Observer where they take men over 30. Do you know of any specific job you are qualified for which they are taking men of your age? [*sic*]

The officers round you at Uffington would know. I might then write to people in the air ministry but one can't just write to say please get so and so a job. They have probably got 5000 names asking for them.

Three months later, the field marshal was writing with equal exasperation,

I cannot understand what you want me to do. Your letters are so vague. It is no use saying you want a job in a thing. What job are you looking for?

You say your friend Evelyn Waugh is an officer in the R.M. Why not find out from him first how people get in? I imagine you would have to go through the ranks like everybody else does nowadays. I have not the remotest idea how the Marines are organised, and

St John's Wood — the Chetwodes' London house

whether there is any section dealing with maps, photographs, etc.
Waugh could tell you so.

Tell me any particular department or anything in which there
are vacancies and I will certainly write to Winston Churchill.

Betjeman was supposedly turned down for the RAF on health
grounds, though it has never been specified what these were. The
thought of him flying a Spitfire during the summer of 1940 would

[139]

have added a new dimension to the Battle of Britain. In the event, Kenneth Clark did fix Betjeman up with a job in the Ministry of Information, where he worked for about a year. It was based in the University of London's Senate House at the bottom of Malet Street, the newly completed building by Charles Holden, an architect whom, especially as a designer of London Underground stations, Betjeman greatly admired.

He lived with his mother-in-law in St John's Wood during the week and returned to Uffington at weekends. The 'war work' consisted in advising the Government about the use of film as a propaganda tool. Betjeman was required to read scripts of short films designed to promote such ideas as Digging for Victory or economising on water and fuel. Probably had he stayed there throughout the war his natural talent for film-making would have been used. As it is, posterity remembers Betjeman's time at the Ministry of Information not because of the work he did there, but because of the crush he formed on the bossy young woman who ran the canteen. Her name, to Betjeman's ears, had already become a line of poetry. 'Gosh', he remarked to Osbert Lancaster, 'you know I bet she is a doctor's daughter and I bet she comes from Surrey and by Jove do you know, I was right?'

If he got this slightly wrong (she was from Farnborough not from Aldershot) he had nevertheless seen, and immortalised, a young woman who spiritually lived in Surrey. The poem he wrote is his best known, and, together with the letter to Comper, written at about the same time, encapsulates the other side of his vision. If Comper enshrined his religious and aesthetic vision, Joan Hunter Dunn, whom he hardly knew, represented not only a picture of the athletic young womanhood he found so erotically alluring, but also a vision of his England. Nobody else could have written this poem. He wrote over two hundred poems, some very good and some not so good, but in this one he achieved perfection.

Miss J. Hunter Dunn, Miss J. Hunter Dunn,
Furnish'd and burnish'd by Aldershot sun,
What strenuous singles we played after tea,
We in the tournament – you against me!

Love-thirty, love-forty, oh! weakness of joy,
The speed of a swallow, the grace of a boy,
With carefullest carelessness, gaily you won,
I am weak from your loveliness, Joan Hunter Dunn.

Miss Joan Hunter Dunn, Miss Joan Hunter Dunn,
How mad I am, sad I am, glad that you won.
The warm-handled racket is back in its press,
But my shock-headed victor, she loves me no less . . .

Every word is right. It contains his lower-middle-class love of his
social superior, his bisexual love of 'The speed of a swallow, the grace
of a boy', his unfit love of the sporty; his feeling for her father's house
and garden, the shiny euonymus in the garden, the six-o'clock news
and the lime-juice and gin, the dance at the golf club, the car park –
'Around us are Rovers and Austins afar', the love. The poem is the
most triumphant bit of war work. 'We must all do our bit . . . *There's
a war on you know*', as he wrote to Cyril Connolly, who published the
poem in his magazine *Horizon*.

In the spring of 1940, Murray published *Old Lights for New
Chancels*. If, in that crucial year of European conflict, Britain had
somehow been obliterated, and this volume of verse had survived, it
would have left an unforgettable set of snapshots of England; of the
'leathery limbs of Upper Lambourne [*sic*]', of Pam, the Surrey girl,
'you great big mountainous sports girl', of Captain Webb from
Dawley, the man who swam the Channel, and whose image used to
appear on the old England's Glory matches, rising rigid and dead
from the old canal which brought the bricks from Coalbrookdale to
Lawley; of Cheltenham; of the Arts and Crafts church Holy Trinity,

Sloane Street; of an old poet who remembers Oscar and Bosie in the Café Royal – no doubt pronouncing it, as Max Beerbohm did, as if it were French; of a don's wife dying at an Oxford bus stop near the Dragon School; of Trebetherick ('Sand in the sandwiches, wasps in the tea') and of the Lake District, which is very decidedly not that of Wordsworth or of Ruskin, but that of the ramblers from Manchester – 'I pledge her in non-alcoholic wine / And give the H.P. Sauce another shake'. If the Nazis had won during that summer, as they easily might, and if England as everyone had known it had vanished, would not these poems in a strange sort of way have preserved a picture more accurate than the propaganda films whose scripts he was editing at the Ministry of Information?

The least successful poem in the book (in a way) is one of the most popular, often finding its way into anthologies and recitations, namely the Lady of 'In Westminster Abbey'. After the woman has prayed for the Germans to be bombed, she reminds The Management,

> Think of what our Nation stands for,
> Books from Boots' and country lanes,
> Free speech, free passes, class distinction,
> Democracy and proper drains.

What makes Betjeman such a delightful writer for his admirers and so irritating for those who do not subscribe to the cult is that he both thought these sentiments ridiculous and subscribed to them wholeheartedly.

Old Lights for New Chancels is a great advance on the previous two volumes. Whereas they had only contained a handful of good verses, mixed with many more duds, this one was largely dud-free. He was discovering his voice . . . Or was he? What is that voice? It is impossible to get to grips with it if you try to judge Betjeman by the standards which you would bring to the study of any of his contemporaries. The successful poems home in with disconcerting directness on such emotions as lust mingled with piety. They suck

the reader into experience whereas the modernistic mode devel-
oped by Eliot and Pound and imitated to a certain extent by all the
English rising hopefuls – Spender, Auden and Co. – was not to write
about yourself directly. Yeats pioneered a special kind of romantic
egotism in which his experiences, his friendships, his loves, are
mythologised in the reader's mind, so that Maude Gonne and Lady
Gregory become as familiar to us as characters in Greek myth. But
Yeats's prayer in Byzantium was answered, his bodily forms are not
natural, they are fashioned like things formed by Grecian goldsmiths,
'of hammered gold and gold enamelling'.

Betjeman steps into this tradition, behaving as if it did not exist,
and draws on two traditions, popular song and hymns, to resurrect
the notion of poetry which actually draws directly on experience.
The fact that these experiences might seem odd, or alien, to some
readers does not matter because the direct effect of them is so
strong. In any case, although many readers might not share his
fondness for Cornish saints or Arts and Crafts London churches,
there are very many who would, did, and do respond to his frank
depictions of sexual and emotional chaos.

I think one can take 'Senex', his kinkiest published poem to date,
to be a candid description of experience. It is basically a poem about
'cruising', about the mad, lustful moments which occur in most
young male lives, when more or less anything would satisfy the
craving, when almost any depravity could be imagined or indeed
committed. He wants to subdue the flesh, he enjoys the sights of
the bicycles in the hedge, he knows what they signify, he hopes that
religion will somehow or another subdue these chaotic and in some
way painful, because uncontrollable, emotions. When he published
this poem, 'Senex', he was just thirty-four years old. They are not
the thoughts of an old man but of a sex-troubled youngish man. The
book also contains two of the best poems he ever wrote, 'Myfanwy'
and 'Myfanwy at Oxford'. Here lust/love mingle with as well as
clashing with his religious impulses. Gold Myfanwy was not his

contemporary at Oxford, nor was she, as in the poem, at St Hilda's; she was at St Hugh's College, Oxford. But she was the star of the book, and, with her husband, the dedicatee of the volume. Given this fact, her letter of response, dated 19 March 1940, might strike some readers as a little graceless.

Having told 'my darling Poet' that the dedication is 'a source of great pride and pleasure', she continued,

> You will think it rude and not a little unkind of me to write in this vein but I have your career so much at heart that I must tell you what I feel – I know you can do anything you want if you give your mind to it. And if only that talent, that brilliant observation, could be turned towards things of *real* worth and employed in the service of that beauty of which there is only too little in this modern life. You could do so much good, and would, I sincerely believe, be so much happier.

Penelope was to make similar pleas to him over the next fifteen to twenty years – to produce something more 'worth-whoile', either serious poetry, or an architectural monograph. The fact is that, while he obviously saw what they meant, hence his constant self-reproach and self-deprecation as a fraud, an *arriviste*, a 'pop poet', he had, obviously, a very vivid awareness of his particular territory and talents. There was always going to be a tight-rope walk between frivolity and seriousness, between doggerel and poetry. The kinship he felt with showbiz people, either the old music-hall artistes who had delighted the early half of his life, or the telly celebrities whose ranks he would join in later life, was telling. He was as much at home with them, as with the poets. His popular appeal sprang from the fact that he was doing something very different from some of the more run-of-the-mill of his poetic contemporaries.

At the end of 1940, Betjeman learned that his life at the Ministry of Information, its shared office jokes, its love-fantasy in the canteen with Miss J. Hunter Dunn, and its regular returns to Uffington, was to come to an end. The British Ambassador in Dublin was looking for a press attaché who could launch a charm offensive on the Irish. The Irish Republic was neutral in the war. There was a press attaché at the German Embassy in Dublin, Karl Peterson, and, according to Sir John Maffey, 'a damn nice chap he was too'. This was not a view universally held. When Betjeman got to Dublin, he found out that Peterson was sleeping with Sally Travers, the pro-German daughter of the Anglo-Catholic architect Martin Travers. According to Betjeman, Peterson was 'unpopular . . . except among politically minded tarts and stockbroking and lawyer place-hunters'; Betjeman concluded that he 'does his cause more harm than good'. It was Maffey's daughter, Penelope Aitken, who first went to the MoI to sound Betjeman out. (He told her afterwards that she was so beautiful that after she had left the office he had to go and lie down.) 'I met John Betjeman, who is arriving over as your Press Attaché', she wrote to her father,

> I think he should be very good . . . The couple have a big reputation here, both rather eccentric and intellectual; he has written poetry and books on architecture and was also film critic on the *Standard*. He should be the sort of whimsical person the Irish will like and he likes them. I think he's a good choice.

Garrard's Farm was shut up. The Misses Butler took the keys and undertook to look after it for the Betjemans in their absence, which they wrongly imagined would not last more than three months. 'I wish I cared more about the war, then I would care more about my job', he told the Pipers. They did not come home again until the autumn of 1943.

While they were away, England, and especially London, would be subject to repeated air raids, with many of Betjeman's favourite old buildings being destroyed. In May 1941, John Summerson wrote to him,

> As you probably know, the last big raid was a knock-out as regards
> church architecture. St George's-in-the-East (well-photographed by us
> the day before), St Alban, Holborn, St John, Kennington, St Agnes,
> Kennington, St John, Red Lion Square, St George's Cathedral,
> Southwark, and I fear many others – Chelsea, St Olave, Hart Street,
> St Mildred, Bread Street, O, Lor', what a massacre!

Away from the bombs and horrors of London at war, the Betjemans were living first as paying guests at Dunsinea House, Castleknock, near Dublin. Later they (John, Penelope and their infant Paul) moved to a house called Collinstown near Clondalkin. Moti the horse came over, and in that land of horses, Penelope had plenty of opportunity to ride him. When Laurence Olivier came over to Ireland to film *Henry V*, Moti was nearly used as the king's charger at Agincourt, but in the event it was decided that 'it wasn't correct as Arabs hadn't been imported to England at that date'.

Sean O'Betjeman, as he inevitably became in his letters home to English friends, was highly successful at his work, which chiefly consisted in dining out and going to parties and being out and about among the Irish, with the aim of lessening anti-English prejudice. 'They are all very fearful of British propaganda here. I don't blame them.'

> I have to see pro-Germans, pro-Italians, pro-British, and most of all,
> anti-British people. The German Legation here is pretty dim and
> repulsive. I have to see journalists, writers, artists, poets. I have to go
> round stating, 'Britain will win in the end' and I have to be charming
> to everyone, and I am getting eaten up with hate of my fellow-beings
> as a result,

he confessed to Oliver Stonor.

So worried were the IRA by the Betjeman charm offensive that

Mother and child: Penelope and Candida

they considered assassinating him. In 1967, Betjeman received a letter from Diarmuid Brennan, of Stevenage, Hertfordshire, who said that he was responsible for civilian intelligence for the Army Council of the IRA. 'Oddly . . . you became a source of much anxiety to the Army Council of the IRA. I got communications describing you as "dangerous" and a *person of menace* to all of us. In short, you were depicted in the blackest of colours.' Brennan was told to tail Betjeman and give daily reports on his movements. Brennan claimed in his letter that gangsters in the Second Battalion of the Dublin Brigade wanted to shoot a British diplomat in order to take the spotlight off the IRA's internal difficulties. These gunmen asked for photographs of Betjeman, but, claimed Brennan, having read some of Betjeman's poetry, he decided he 'couldn't be much of a secret agent'. He also claims that he gave the gunmen photographs of a different person, a cousin of his who was a Special Branch officer, and told them that they were under police surveillance and had no chance of being able to carry out an assassination unobserved.

It is impossible to know at this distance of time how much of this letter reflects the truth. Betjeman on a number of occasions described his function as that of a 'spy' in Dublin, and he probably was involved with collecting secret information. Eamon de Valera, President of the Republic, made Irish neutrality (as his biographer Lord Longford said) 'highly benevolent to the Allies'. This lanky scholar, who had taken part in the Easter Rising of 1916, was feared by English politicians, though not by the Betjemans, who loved his old-fashionedness. Many Irish volunteered to fight in the British forces, but had de Valera brought Ireland into the war on the side of Britain (Churchill offered him Northern Ireland if he did so) it would have restarted the Irish Civil War. 'Dev', a Spanish American born in New York of a Irish mother, had the outsider's love of all that old Ireland stood for. This passionately Catholic and Celtic twilight lover of the past would have been impressed by Betjeman's having taken the trouble to learn Gaelic, and he would have responded to the things which both Betjemans liked about Ireland, 'where everyone – Roman, Anglican, Non-conformist – believes in another world and where everyone goes to church'. He would also probably have responded kindly to Penelope's plea to him, when they met for the last time, not to tarmac the Irish roads. 'I spent a lot of time defending Dev here for his consistency, if not his tact', Betjeman wrote to his friend Geoffrey Taylor when they had come back to England.

Taylor's was the friendship which meant most to him in Dublin. Geoffrey Taylor was a quiet, gentle poet who shared Betjeman's passionate love of creepy-crawlies. Betjeman loved lice, wasps, daddy-long-legs, and would spend hours staring at them. Taylor was an expert on beetles and on plant life. He was a conscientious objector, which Betjeman also found appealing. The outbreak of war had caused him to leave England and return to his native Ireland, renting his brother's house, Airton House, Tallaght, a few miles from Collinstown. Penelope and John would come over in a horse-drawn cart and Taylor and Betjeman spent hours together reading and reciting poetry. From their shared enthusiasm sprang the edited anthology *English, Scottish and Welsh Landscape* which the two chose together, and which John Piper illustrated, an undervalued book.

Their friends in England missed them too. The Lancasters stayed for long periods with the Pipers. 'We've had a happy time with them with no rancours or squabbles', Myfanwy reported. 'They are funny. But in the end they are a bit of a spiritual burden. Osbert so sophisticatedly helpless & Karen so enervated. But they are the nicest possible evacuees if you must have them except quarrelsome old geniuses like you.'

Both Pipers wrote to Betjeman often, to 'my dearest Exile', 'Dearest Plymouth Brother', 'Dear Sean', keeping the jokes and the friendship alive across the estranging Irish Sea. 'Oh how I miss you',

Myfanwy wrote. 'It's really awfull [*sic*], I do hope to goodness you don't get to like Ireland and stay there.'

Betjeman replied to her that 'I think a good deal about your hair & eyes & about your figure. These Colleens here have too big heads and too thin legs & are too twilit.' He complained, 'I cannot believe that such an expense of spirit as this job is will not bring a reward of some kind. No time to myself at all . . . no peace at the office and Politics day and night.' While Betjeman wrote to Mr Pahper, sending 'my fondest love to luscious bubble-breasted, golden-haired, blue-eyed, strapping, milky Goldilox', Penelope characteristically enquired after the Pipers' religious life.

'Did you go to Confession at the Folkies before Easter?' she asked.

> We find ourselves spiritually quite dead. St John's . . . the only
> really Catholic Church [she means, of course, Church of Ireland, i.e.
> Anglican Church with the sort of ethos to which the High Church
> Betjemans were accustomed in England] is 7 miles away so it is
> impossible to get there for early Mass except by car and the petrol
> is so short. Father Colquoun, the Vicar, is an excellent confessor, but
> we hate not having any proper Parish life. One must undoubtedly be
> Roman over here if one really wants to enter into the life of the
> country, but as we want to return to England as soon as possible
> we cannot 'go over' just for a few months, tho' it would be very
> convenient if we could.

In the light of Penelope's subsequent conversion to Rome, and its calamitous consequence for her marriage, this letter sounds an unconscious but solemn chord.

When friends came over, it served as an almost painful reminder of how much they missed the carefree, pre-war days of church-crawling, conversation and shared jokes. 'What a week!' Osbert Lancaster wrote in 1942:

I think I can safely say that I have not enjoyed myself so intensely and so uninterruptedly since the war started. You, I know, are sick to death of the whole atmosphere but to me it was all wonderful. I am prepared to take your word for it that the charm soon palls but I cannot recollect ever having been so immediately impressed with a place at first sight before. The architecture was a revelation, the Whites [Terence de Vere White and his wife] I found charming and my bowels worked with wonderful smoothness. I now discover Bedford Square to be drab in colour and appallingly inadequate in size; the Ministry a sordid burden and the water as hard as tintacks . . .

'Much love – don't quarrel with Propeller', had been Myfanwy Piper's sign-off to a letter when the Betjemans set out for Ireland. The quarrels were part of the inevitable texture of the Betjemans' married life, as was Betjeman's constant falling in love with other women. In Ireland, this tendency remained on the level of crushes, and, as with Miss J. Hunter Dunn at the Ministry of Information in London, it provided some memorable verse. In Tulira in County Galway, Betjeman met Lord Hemphill and his beautiful American wife Emily. She had met her husband while riding in the Borghese Gardens in Rome in 1926. Though a brilliant horsewoman, she had taken a fall. Lord Hemphill, riding by, had instantly leapt from his horse and run to her assistance. A year later they married in New York and moved into Tulira, the Victorian house built by Edward Martyn and immortalised in George Moore's *Hail and Farewell*.

Emily was in love with a man not her husband when she met Betjeman – and she subsequently married him – Ion Villiers-Stuart. Betjeman was obliged to worship from afar, but on one afternoon he went for a bicycle ride with her through the strange primeval-look- ing landscape of the Burren in County Clare. It produced one of the best evocations of Irish landscape, and of the 'feel' of rural Ireland ever written – 'Ireland with Emily'.

. . . Stony seaboard, far and foreign,
   Stony hills poured over space,
Stony outcrop of the Burren,
   Stones in every fertile place,
Little fields with boulders dotted,
Grey-stone shoulders saffron-spotted,
Stone-walled cabins thatched with reeds,
Where a Stone Age people breeds
   The last of Europe's stone age race.

Has it held, the warm June weather?
   Draining shallow sea-pools dry,
When we bicycled together
   Down the bohreens fuchsia-high.
Till there rose, abrupt and lonely,
A ruined abbey, chancel only,
Lichen-crusted, time-befriended,
Soared the arches, splayed and splendid,
   Romanesque against the sky . . .

When the Betjemans left Ireland, Betj continued to write to Emily, saying he would cross the water for her, but this was a dream, and in England he found other, more available female company.

In his farewell speech, Frank Gallagher, UK Representative at Dublin Castle, said,

> Sure the Betjemans will, across the water, carry on their work of levelling out the peaks and valleys in the estimation of us into one sweet and pleasant plain. We shall remember them. One thing they will carry with them as proof of Irish hospitality is that they came three and went four . . . To the four of them we wish the Irish blessing, *Dia go deo libh*, God be with you.

Candida Rose Betjeman had been born at the Rotunda Hospital, Dublin, in September 1942.

The ceaseless activity expected of Betjeman, the endless round of parties with people the Betjemans did not know, had exhausted both of them, and they were glad to return to England. By the end of 1943, Betjeman had been posted to the 'P' branch of the Admiralty in Bath, arriving in March 1944. The department was stationed in the Empire Hotel, and Betjeman – whose immediate superior was Richard Hughes, author of *High Wind in Jamaica* – was supposedly in charge of producing two publications, *The Green 'Un*, which supplied current bulletins about the best places to find supplies of labour, steel, wood, etc., and *The Pink 'Un*, which was top secret and gave bulletins about recent damage from bombardment. Those who shared the office with Betjeman, who included the future Lord Weinstock, remembered him chain-smoking and writing book-reviews for the *Daily Herald* in office time. As he told Nancy Mitford in a letter, life was 'wonderfully boring'.

He was away from his wife, who had returned to Garrard's Farm and was preoccupied with her young children. Some love affairs were presumably inevitable and this time he found women who were willing, unlike Emily in Ireland, to go the whole way.

Alice Jennings was working for the BBC in Bristol when she met Betjeman. She was married, but her husband was away. Betjeman came to make a programme with Geoffrey Grigson.

> I came to the Listening Room in order to put him on the air,
> being the Programme Engineer, now called Studio Manageress, and
> John said, 'Who's that girl?' And Griggers from a great height said,
> 'That's your PE'. At that time everybody in the BBC and probably
> elsewhere too was bristling with initials, and coming upon this latest
> one, John burst into a great chortle of enchantment, so infectious
> that I joined in too, and that's how our friendship started up, and
> how henceforth I was called PE.

They kept their affair a secret, and it was not long-lasting, even though they wrote to one another annually until he died. The affair provoked a poem which annoyed Alice, 'the shortest I ever wrote', according to Betj. She wrote to him, 'You may be a thumping crook, but I'm *not* an ordinary little woman'. But it is one of his best.

In a Bath Tea-shop

'Let us not speak, for the love we bear one another –
  Let us hold hands and look.'
She, such a very ordinary little woman;
  He, such a thumping crook;
But both, for a moment, little lower than the angels
  In the teashop's ingle-nook.

An affair which did not inspire any poetry was with a colleague at the Admiralty, the writer Honor Tracy, a boozy Catholic convert who, in spite of English origins, made her name as an Irish writer, with such amusing tales of Irish life as *The Straight and Narrow Path* and *Mind You, I've Said Nothing*. (Incidentally, she could be seen as the missing link between Iris Murdoch and John Betjeman, having slept with them both.)

The celebrated regret, expressed when beyond his last legs and in a wheelchair, that he had not had enough sex in his life did not mean that there was *none*. He was not 'all talk', but talk was perhaps more fun than the actuality for Betjeman. As a very young man, he had enjoyed writing erotic poetry for the delectation of his Marlborough chum John Bowle. But Betjeman was no John Donne or Byron who could be inspired to write his best verse by a day in his mistress's (or wife's) arms. It is as easy to say that men are religious because they have morbid guilt about sex, as it is to put the sentence the other way around. My own hunch, having done all the research for this biography, is that Betjeman, like many depressives, was low-sexed and that the televised regret was true: he had very little sex in his life. But who can tell. One thing is conspicuous on the printed page. Sex was nearly always associated in his poetry with death.

The mouth that opens for a kiss
Has got no tongue inside.

The two little affairs in Bath made all but no impact on his imagination. If there was anything to survive from that sojourn in the West Country, it was his friendship with the novelist Anthony Powell, whose house (The Chantry, Frome, Somerset) usually provided a stopping-off point for Betjeman and family as they made their slow progress each year from Berkshire to Cornwall, stopping at what felt (to the children) like every church on the way.

9

THE PATH TO ROME

Many people found it difficult to readjust to peacetime life. Soldiers returned from years away to find children who barely knew them. Humdrum civilian jobs which had felt tolerable, in 1939, now, after six years in armed combat, seemed very different. 'Oh, I have been happy here!' Queen Mary said as she left Badminton House, her wartime billet. 'Here I've been anybody to everybody, and back in London I shall have to begin being Queen Mary all over again.'

Betjeman, as so often, was an unusual case. His war, after the initial semi-farcical attempts to get into the RAF, had been, especially in Ireland, a continuation of peacetime incarnations. He had been hired, whether as a broadcaster, or as a propagandist-cum-diplomat, to go on being Betjeman. But he was approaching his fortieth birthday, and the decisions he made now, about the division of his time, would determine the remainder of his creative life. Some old friendships, too, could never be resumed. Basil Dufferin (known to his family as Ava) had been killed in Burma. Only once, some ten years after 'Little Bloody's' death, did Betjeman meet the daughter, Lady Caroline Blackwood. He felt so overpowered that he resolved never to meet her again. Though the eyes were a different colour, Little Bloody's large and brown, Caroline's a searching steel blue, he felt again the magic of that person with whom he had 'been more in love . . . than with any human being he had ever met in the world' and from whom he had 'never received so much as the touch of a hand on the shoulder'. His poetic tribute to Ava – 'Friend of my youth, you are dead!' – reads like an amateur attempt at threnody, and not particularly competent at that. Whereas he could soar to heights of prosodic ingenuity, inspired by a bicycle ride with a pretty American woman he barely knew, or the glimpse of a general's daughter rowing her sharpie, he was seldom capable of writing poetry when his feelings were most deeply engaged. In the poem about Little Bloody, he wanders about the quads of Oxford and remembers the Hooray Henrys of the late 1920s roaring back from Thame in their borrowed Bugattis. As the victory bells peal out over the city, he cries,

> Stop, oh many bells, stop
> > pouring on roses and creeper
> Your unremembering peal
> > this hollow, unhallowed V.E. Day, –
> I am deaf to your notes and dead
> > by a soldier's body in Burma.

The clumsiness of bells 'pouring' on roses does not mean anything and lacks any of the pinpoint accuracy of

> Evening light will bring the water,
> > Day-long sun will burst the bud,
> Clemency, the General's daughter,
> > Will return upon the flood . . .

Imagine what Housman, or Yeats, would have done with the premature death of a young Irish aristocrat.

Betjeman had a natural gift for consoling the bereaved, and it was to him, outside the family, more than any other friend, that Ava's widow Maureen turned. He went to Hove, former residence of his old friend Bosie who had also died in the war, and where Maureen was staying in a hotel, to comfort her. Later they exchanged long letters of memories. It was to Betjeman that she turned to get the wording right on Ava's memorial tablet. 'You know the heavenly Campo Santo at Clandeboye, don't you? Where Ava's father and grandfather and grandmother are buried? Well I thought I'd have a similar one put – just as if he was buried there – but with an inscription on it saying "This in memory of etc. etc.".'

Johnson, in Boswell's pages, is often called upon to think of epitaphs for his friends. Betjeman got Ninian Comper to design the memorial at Clandeboye which commemorated 'a man of brilliance and of many friends' who had been killed in action at the age of thirty-five, 'recapturing Burma the country which his grandfather annexed to the British Crown'.

Those friends who lived on to remember Ava, such as Bowra and Sparrow and Kolkhorst, now seemed even dearer. Regular visits to the Pahpers at Fawley Bum could be resumed, as could the familiar routines of marital rows, and earning a living. Betjeman worked for the British Council in Oxford, continuing work he had begun at the end of the war. This required a car, and a brand-new Vauxhall 14 hp saloon (grey) was bought from J. Coxeter & Co. of Park End Street, Oxford. Betjeman's children remembered that he used to drive it 'like the clappers'.

But Uffington life was over, and this was the first huge change which peacetime brought to the Betjeman ménage.

John Wheeler, their landlord in Uffington, said that he wanted Garrard's Farm for his son Peter to live in. House-hunting began. It was Robert Heber-Percy, Lord Berners's boyfriend, who found them the beautiful Old Rectory at Farnborough, the highest village in Berkshire. It was for sale at £3,500. '1730ish. Red brick seven hundred feet up on the downs. No water, no light, no heat', Betjeman wrote to Evelyn Waugh.

Having already settled £5,000 upon Penelope on her wedding (she tied it up in trust for any children who might be born to her), Field Marshal, now Lord, Chetwode (the barony was created for him in 1945) not only did buy her the house, but also settled a further £14,000 on her, with the promise of a further £38,000 (subject to death duties) upon his own death, which happened in 1950. As was observed when assessing the value of her marriage settlement, there are many different ways of judging the equivalent values or purchasing-powers of sums of money at different periods of British history. It has to be borne in mind, for example, that far fewer British people, proportionately, owned their homes and that property was there-fore, in inflationary terms, much, much cheaper. The cost of the rectory, £3,500, judged by the standards of the retail price index, would be £92,325, or by the standards of average national earnings, £359,302 39p in 2002 – in either case, this would seem prodigiously cheap by modern standards. Penelope's capital of £14,000 in 1945 would have been worth the equivalent of £1,128,516 19p in 2002 when measured by the standard of average earnings. This reflects a common pattern among the capital-owning or rentier class until the 1970s, namely that their capital far exceeded the value of their house, whereas nowadays, with a much larger property-owning class, property tends to be a middle-class family's largest asset.

The heavy taxes imposed by the post-war Labour Government on capital, and on inheritance, did not endear it to the Betjemans. Established in their big, cold rectory, they took a view of Major Attlee's socialist policies which was not unlike Evelyn Waugh's. Waugh, on giving a copy of Betjeman's poems to Deborah Cavendish (later Duchess of Devonshire), slipped a typed Betjeman poem between its leaves. This samizdat document was evidently considered too hostile to the great British worker to be publishable in Attlee's Britain.

> When father went out on his basic [petrol ration]
> With Muriel, Shirley and me
> We drove up to somebody's mansion
> And asked *them* to give us some tea.
> 'Get out of there, we're the workers;
> This mansion is ours, so to speak;
> For Dad turns a handle at Sidcup

For twenty-five guineas a week.
I'm paid by the buffet at Didcot
For insultin' the passengers there.
The way they keeps rattlin' the doorknob
Disturbs me in doin' my hair.
And Shirley does crosswords at Dolcis.
She's ever so clever at clues,
Plus twelve quid a week and her dinner
For refusing the customers shoes.
And Muriel *slaved* at the laundry
From ten forty five until four;
But the overtime rates was enormous
So she don't *have* to work any more.
So get the 'ell out of that mansion
We workers have got all the tin,
And Dad has been promised a peerage
When the Communist party gets in.

However we judge the matter, though, the Betjemans were the reverse of poor. They usually felt poor, partly because neither of them was good at handling money, and partly because they sometimes enjoyed the company of those who were much richer than themselves. But they were in fact very much more comfortably placed than most people in that bleak, post-war austerity England.

The fact that they did not install electricity or running water was not because they were unable to afford these luxuries. Penelope at least enjoyed the discomfort and Betjeman probably enjoyed the thought of the house itself not being aesthetically spoilt by mod cons. The villagers in Farnborough were very amused that the first 'improvement' which the Betjemans made to the property was to remove a bathroom. The field marshal spent a week with them over their first Christmas and according to Penelope found it like living in the dark ages. He cannot see by lamp light and the lav. plugs don't pull and the bath water keeps running out. He is also very cross because he says that I have carved the ham wrong, he started it straight down then I sliced it across thus exposing a large surface to the atmosphere to dry. However as we all eat several slices three times a day it won't get the chance to dry right off.

The Betjemans fetched their water every day from a communal village pump. Every night Betjeman filled paraffin lamps, trimmed wicks and lit fires. In the winter, the whole family huddled round a coke stove in the huge inner hall which had been a village schoolroom. In the summer months, however, the large airy rectory was filled with light, and though surrounded by beech trees, it commanded marvellous views across Watership Down.

For the growing children, who made friends with the children in the village and adopted their accents ('grossly proletarian' noted Evelyn Waugh, whose own mother – his wife once alleged – spoke with a Bristol accent), Farnborough was a paradise. Betjeman's story *Archie and the Strict Baptists* reflects the bear's sense of distraction when he is uprooted from his favourite chapel in the Vale, to live in Farnborough. Though only a few miles from Uffington as the crow flies, Farnborough itself was a place which added to the strains on the Betjemans' marriage. For a start, the village itself was smaller and much less friendly than Uffington. Betjeman always enjoyed pub life, and at Uffington he derived real pleasure from going to bell-ringing and getting drunk afterwards in the pub. At Farnborough, there was no pub. It had been removed decades since by a puritanical squire. Church life was also the reverse of consoling. 'My experience', Betjeman wrote to Gerard Irvine, 'is that there is no faith in English villages at all, only convention.' The flinty little church of All Saints', ashlar-faced, and with a Norman nave, is perched on the hill on the very edge of the downs, with a spectacular prospect. Inside it is small; its box pews are damp-feeling, and the vicar, Father

Railings in West Hampstead

Steele, not especially high, was unlikely to appeal to someone used to the glories of High Mass, and sanctuaries designed by Comper. It is surely of some significance that Farnborough does not receive a mention in the *Collins Guide to English Parish Churches* (ed. John Betjeman) and that anyone wishing to find out architectural details about Farnborough must turn to the despised Herr Doktor Pevsner. 'C of E village religion is no pleasure', Betjeman told Evelyn Waugh. 'In this village which has no Nonconformist Chapel, the only bulwark against complete paganism is the church and its chief supporters are Propeller and me. ' This was almost literally the case, and their daughter Candida remembers how very churchy both parents were *together* when they first came to Farnborough. There was shock, for example, when they called on a local farmer one Friday and found him eating meat for his lunch.

'If we were to desert it', Betjeman told Waugh,

> there would be no one to whip up people to attend the services, to run the church organisations, to keep the dilatory and woolly-minded incumbent (who lives in another village) to the celebration of Communion services any Sunday. It is just because it is so disheartening and so difficult and so easy to betray that we must keep this Christian witness going.

He wrote this letter while in the midst of the worst crisis of his marriage. The rift between the Betjemans after this crisis would become, according to their wise priest-friend Gerard Irvine, fundamentally unbridge-able – namely Penelope's decision to become a Roman Catholic.

When two strong-minded people come together and then drift apart, it is far too simple to attribute it all to one cause, and it should never be forgotten that part of the villain in this story was not the Pope (or Evelyn Waugh), it was Farnborough itself. Betjeman, from his schooldays onwards, was an

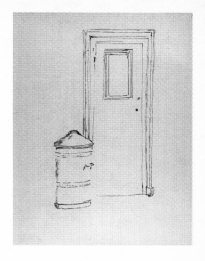

A well-placed dustbin

architecturally obsessed solitary, and he would always be that until the cruelties of Parkinson's disease in old age stopped him from wandering about England looking at buildings. Whether he was doing so with a bicycle and a sketch-book aged fifteen, or as an old man with a television crew, he was always on the move, looking for new architectural delights, noticing details which the untrained eye would take for granted or fail altogether to spot. In addition, he was compulsively sociable and he never stopped being a Londoner, who thought of London as the natural and normal place in which to make money. Uffington allowed for this peripatetic and confusing existence. In spite of the marital rows and, on Betjeman's side, the deep and ever-worsening depressions, it was all manageable at Uffington, because he could catch the train at Challow or Deedcoate – as he and the Propeller liked to pronounce Didcot in imitation of a genteel railway announcer they'd once heard – and usually be home by evening. Farnborough was too far from the nearest station for this – hence his purchase of the Ford. But although he could 'drive like the clappers' into Wantage or Oxford, he was never keen on long drives, and for his visits to far-flung friends and his journeys into London, overnight stops were now essential. The result was that Penelope became more and more isolated with the children, more and more resentful of his absences, and more and more the companion of her own religious thoughts and broodings.

As long ago as November 1933, Penelope had warned Betjeman of her fascination with the Church of Rome. At that time, he was a Quaker, and she was more in the nature of a seeker, who would go through a Zen Buddhist phase. But in the intervening years the Church of England had become a great shared bond. This was the Church of Father Folky, the Church of Uffington life, the Church which had tightened their bond with the Pipers. As well as a religious conviction, the Anglicanism of the Betjemans was something they did together, a form of marital glue.

It is clear from the very beginning of the marriage between these two very strong and eccentric characters, that both needed to assert their independence as well as their shared life and love. There were constant rows, and in spite of confessing them to Father Folky, neither of them seemed able to hold back from the fuming egotism which fuels such life-poisoning self-indulgence, this giving in to wrath. Some bad-tempered people justify their irascibility by claiming that rows clear the air. The self-inflicted suffering of the Betjemans who could not stop themselves rowing was a casebook example of how false is this idea. Betjeman, as his cult status developed through poems, and through the ever-increasing circle of admirers, was defined as an Anglican. His faith was central to his life, and it was not merely Christian, it was decidedly that of the Church of England. 'His Kingdom stretch from See to See', as he once wrote on a postcard to his fellow Anglican Sir Brian Batsford, 'Till all the world is C of E.' When, in 1963, an Anglican priest expressed his doubts about reunion with the Methodists, Betjeman wrote to him, 'I absolutely agree with you about fucking about with Methodists . . .

— another waste of time. No, the C of E is The Catholic Church, tempting though it is to think it isn't — and English Romanism is sectarian.' There was an inevitability, perhaps, that his wife, in trying to maintain and assert her own independence while married to such an overwhelmingly developed 'character', should have chosen to cut the tie which bound them closest. Her quest for God was different from his. He knew how to live with doubt, she didn't. She wanted certainties, and there was one Church, particularly in those days, which offered them. On a visit to Assisi, she had experienced, as must many visitors to that electrically charged spiritual powerhouse, something like a vision of the heavenly host. In Ireland she had missed the 'Catholic privileges' (as they are called by High Church devotees) on offer to Anglo-Catholics in England — meaning, frequent Mass, priests who are used to hearing confessions. So it was, in the post-war years, as the quarrels between the two of them got worse, and as her spiritual hungers became more aching, she turned to the spiritual path which he was least likely to follow.

Some time in 1947, she made the decision, not merely to dabble with Roman Catholicism, but to receive formal instruction in that faith. She went to the Dominicans (Order of Preachers) in Oxford, intellectual, and in some cases Bohemian figures who suited her inquiring spirit. Some of the Blackfriars, as Dominicans are called, after the black hoods and scapulars which they used to wear, were a match for Penelope's own eccentricities. Her best friends were Archbishop Mathew and his brother, Gervase Mathew, OP, who walked round Oxford hand in hand. The archbishop was usually dressed in a frock coat covered in spilt food; his brother was a gentle, clever expert on Byzantine art and on the court art of Richard II in England about which he wrote a delightful book. To discover a whole house, at Blackfriars, full of eccentric intellectual celibate priests was for Penelope like Hansel and Gretel's discovery of a house made of candies. ('This pensione', she once wrote from Florence, 'is simply lovely for me: there is no less than 8 priests

German Pietà

stayin at it & oi've troied by various means tew get into conversation with oone oroother of Them.')

The man who instructed her was called Father Conrad Pepler. Betjeman was devastated by the turn which she had taken. It was not simply that she was doubting the Church of England which he loved. At one point she airily wondered whether their marriage itself was 'valid' in the eyes of the Roman Church. Heedless to the tactlessness of discussing such a matter with a clergyman whom she scarcely knew, and who had never met her husband, Penelope wrote to Betjeman.

I went to see Rev Pepler yesterday morning at 10 a.m. About RC
Marriage Law. He said that before 1918 the R.C. Church claimed to
exercise jurisdiction over all marriages both Roman and non-Roman
but in that year the law was changed & from then on they only claimed
jurisdiction over Roman marriages & insisted on the ceremony being
performed before a priest. But they do recognize non-Roman
marriages as absolutely valid & with regard to the Pauline privilege he
has only known that used *once* in all his experience & that was in the
case of a woman married to a jew [*sic*] who started to persecute her
after she became a Roman. He says the R.C. Church *never* regards a
marriage as being rendered invalid if one of the parties turn Roman &
that the P.P. can only be used if you can prove continual persecution
which might endanger the faith of the convert: as when the non-
Roman party (and you would also have to PROVE him unbaptized
which Rev Pepler says is extremely difficult if he is middle-aged or
more) physically prevents his wife (or vice versa) from going to mass.

So you see the Roman Church including His Holiness regards our
marriage as indissoluble just as the Anglican Church does . . .

The Rev Pepler said just what the Rev Naish said: that my first
duty was to keep my family as united as possible & that I must always
make that my first concern˙

This was meant to be reassuring but it could not fail to have the
opposite effect. A marriage is a bond between two persons, not a
contract effected by the supernatural operation of a Church or a
clergyman. Even in Catholic theology, it is the man and the woman,
and not the priest, who are the ministers of the 'sacrament'. Outside
the Roman Church marriage is not regarded as a sacrament anyway.

Betjeman, always a mixture of overconfidence and terror,
suffered something akin to a nervous collapse and the prospect of his
wife deserting their shared Church was an infidelity quite as painful
as, probably more so than, any adultery.

Members of the younger generation, that is, of their children's generation, have speculated whether the two betrayals, of the marriage bed as well as of the Anglican altar, were not in some mysterious manner connected. Undoubtedly the strongest character to bombard the Betjemans with arguments for Roman conversion was Evelyn Waugh. Waugh's son Auberon (Bron), reviewing a biography of his father in *The Literary Review*, December 1986, wrote:

> Penelope Betjeman was most alarmed when, both before and after her marriage, Waugh made advances on her. 'I remember being very shocked' [she said] 'as he was a practising Roman Catholic . . . he never attracted me in the very least'. Evelyn Waugh's memory, at any rate in his later years, was different. On one of the last occasions I saw him, I happened to ask – apropos something he had said – whether he had ever been to bed with Lady Betjeman. The term he used was coarser and rather more explicit. 'Since you ask', he said after a pause, 'yes.'

This looks conclusive, but isn't. Bron's widow Teresa told me a slightly different version of the story. She was present, at the end of lunch at Combe Florey, when this conversation took place. No one had asked Evelyn Waugh whether or not he had been Penelope Betjeman's lover. He remarked, out of the blue – 'Are you asking me if I slept with her?' Bron had supplied the answer, 'Since you ask, yes.' In subsequent conversation about the exchange, neither Bron nor Teresa could ever remember what Evelyn Waugh's reply had been.

In the issue following of *The Literary Review*, however, Bron's friend Richard Ingrams recalled that the libel lawyer employed by Weidenfeld & Nicolson to vet the publication of Waugh's letters deleted a request from Waugh to Penelope for 'a fine fuck when I get back'. Ingrams also recalls Osbert Lancaster's claim that Waugh complained, 'She always laughs when I come.'

If there had been some amorous link between Waugh and Penelope, it was surely long in the past by 1947. This was not like Graham Greene and Catherine Woolston fornicating as they discussed the moral theology of St Thomas Aquinas. (Greene even claimed they had done it on the altar of a church.) Yet it is hard to banish from one's mind entirely the hearsay evidence of an erotic link between Waugh and Penelope, as one reads Waugh's assaults not merely on the Betjemans' faith but on their marriage. Certainly the letters confirm Anthony Powell's judgement of Waugh as a 'sadist', pronounced by Powell 'Sar-deest'. Waugh poured his feelings about Penelope into his novel, which he admitted is a portrait of her, about the Empress Helena. 'Isn't it nice that Penelope should be immortalised as St Helena?' asked Bowra. 'There are one or two points of difference, eg St H is very lacking in culture (notably in her inattention to the Latin translation of Homer) and rather indifferent to Oriental Mysticism.' In January 1946, Waugh wrote pruriently to Penelope for detailed comments on the 'hipporastic' passages in *Helena*. 'The Empress loses interest in such things when she is married. I describe her as hunting in the morning after her wedding night feeling the saddle as comforting her wounded maidenhead. Is that OK? After that she has no interest in sex.'

But it was at the end of that year, thanking Betjeman for a Christmas card, that Waugh let fire the first of several lengthy theological salvoes at his old friend.

> I have been painfully shocked by a brochure named 'Five Sermons by Laymen'. Last time I met you you told me you did not believe in the Resurrection. Now I find you expounding Protestant devotional practices from the pulpit. This WILL NOT DO . . .
>
> Your ecclesiastical position is entirely without reason. You cannot possibly be right. Zealous protestants may be (i.e. it is possible to say from the word go the Church was all wrong & had misunderstood everything Our Lord told them & that it required a new Divine Dispensation in the sixteenth century to put people on the right track again. That is just possible.) What is inconceivable is that Christ was made flesh in order to found a church, that He canalized His Grace in

the sacraments, that He gave His promise to abide in the Church to the end of time, that He saw the Church as a human corporation, part of His mystical body, one with the Saints triumphant – and then to point to a handful of homosexual curates and say, 'That is the true Church'.

There was much, much more of the same.

> You must not suppose that there is anything more than the most superficial resemblance between Catholics & Anglo-Catholics. They may look alike to you. An Australian, however well-informed, simply cannot distinguish between a piece of Trust House timbering and a genuine Tudor building; an Englishman however uncultured knows at once . . .

This provoked one of Betjeman's best responses. 'I am beginning to find that there is a lot to be said for sham half-timber. I have been visiting during the recent fine weather, some rich specimens in Metroland at Chesham and Amersham, sunk deep in bird baths and macrocarpa down lanterned drives.' That itself is a Betjeman poem. Did Evelyn Waugh, a sharp but not a subtle mind, understand what Betjeman was trying to tell him, not just about Trust House timbering, but about the poor stabs human beings make at 'authenticity' and truth?

The gentleness of Betjeman's responses to the apoplectic Catholic apologist, never once asking Waugh to mind his own business, could be seen by a psychologist as classic examples of 'passive aggression'. He wrote urging Waugh to come to Farnborough and enjoy a Ford Madox Brown window at the nearby church of Brightwalton. He consistently praised Waugh's writing – on the biography of the Catholic convert Ronald Knox, of all things, 'Just my subject and just my writer'. He even praised *Helena*. 'What a wonderful book HELENA is . . . Congratulations too on the typography – it looks like Charlotte M Yonge.' And in general – 'I must write to tell you what I find myself doing after each publication you make that your last thing is the BEST THING YOU HAVE WRITTEN.' But these torrents of praise were not all buried aggression. They sprang from a genuine admiration for Waugh's writing, and a genuine shared sympathy and aesthetic vision. Over theology, they would never see eye to eye; and Betjeman knew his wife well enough to recognise that Penelope's journey to Rome, though perhaps helped along by Waugh's strange letters, was very much her own journey. It would almost certainly have happened even if she had not met Evelyn Waugh.

'It would be a pity to go to HELL because you prefer Henry Moore to Michelangelo. THIS GOES FOR PENELOPE TOO.'

Presumably, the point of that particular letter, written, one imagines, under the influence of alcohol, is to be found in these last capitalised words. 'What I cannot believe – this is a far more important carbuncle (you would call it)', Betjeman wrote back gently, 'than my occasional doubts about the Resurrection – is that the C of E is not part of the Catholic Church.'

For Betjeman this was not merely *a*, it was *the*, serious matter. It runs through all his poetry and much of his best poetry at that. Christ was found on the Highbury altar which fed Ernie and Bess in their early married days. Willesden 'glows with the present immanence of God'. Recalling his days at Pusey House, with Freddy Hood seated at the harmonium on a Saturday night, singing 'Sweet Sah – crament Divine!' during a service of 'Devotions' to prepare communicants for receiving Holy Communion the next morning, he could write:

> Those were the days when that divine baroque
> Transformed our English altars and our ways.
> Fiddle-back chasuble in mid-Lent pink
> Scandalized Rome and Protestants alike:
> 'Why do you try to ape the Holy See?'

> 'Why do you sojourn in a half-way house?'
> And if this doubt had ever troubled me
> (Praise God, they don't) I would have made the move.
> What seemed to me a greater question then
> Tugged and still tugs: Is Christ the son of God?
> Despite my frequent lapses into lust,
> Despite hypocrisy, revenge and hate,
> I learned at Pusey House the Catholic Faith.

This is such a powerful statement of a personal religious position that it is hard to know whether it is good poetry or not. It certainly seems deeper, and truer, than Waugh's childish simplifications, funny as those were. Betjeman's existential experience of Christ was in the sacraments of his own church. In so far as he had known Jesus, it was in Holy Communion in Highgate, Oxford, Uffington and Wantage. To turn his back on that was not just a disloyalty to the Church of England, much as he loved that institution. It would have been turning his back on Christ Himself as experienced in those places.

'If you accept an absurdity, as you do in pretending the Church of Wantage is the Catholic Church, and luxuriate in sentimental raptures', Waugh had spluttered, 'you will naturally break out in boils & carbuncles and question the authenticity of the Incarnation.'

By April 1947, Penelope felt she had to write,

Dearest Evelyn, I am very grateful to you for writing those letters to John tho' it is very disloyal of me to write to you and say that I still hope you will pray very hard indeed during the next few weeks for him because he is in a dreadful state he thinks you are the devil and wakes up in the middle of the night and raves and says he will leave me at once if I go over . . . However put yourself in his position: sup-pose Laura were to wake up and say to you tomorrow morning 'I have had a revelation of the TRUTH it is only to be found in A. Huxley's Yogibogi sect, I shall join it'. You would not unnaturally be a little put out. You might even threaten to leave the old girl should she persist.

Well John feels just like that. He thinks ROMAN Catholicism is a foreign religion which has no right to set up in this country, let alone try to make converts from what he regards as the true catholic church of the country. Your letters have brought it out in a remarkable way.

That divine baroque

Waugh was to reply, 'Dearest Penelope, I am by nature a bully and a scold and John's pertinacity in error brings out all that is worst in me. I am very sorry. I will lay off him in future', but the damage had somehow been done. Penelope herself, now aged thirty-eight, the 'Empress' – in Waugh's fantasy comforting her wounded maiden-head and having no interest in sex – evidently *was* persuaded by the force of Waugh's apologetics.

At Christmas 1947, Waugh complained to Nancy Mitford –

Betjeman delivered a Christmas Message on the wireless. First he said that as a little boy he had been a coward and a liar. Then he said he was sure all his listeners had been the same. Then he said he had been convinced of the truth of the Incarnation the other day by hearing a choir boy sing 'Once in Royal David's City' . . .

To Betjeman himself, Waugh – so much for his promise to 'lay off' – wrote:

One listener at least deeply resented the insinuation . . . that your listeners had all been cowards and liars in childhood. Properly brought up little boys are fantastically chivalrous. Later they deteriorate. How

would you have felt if instead of a choir boy at Cambridge you had
heard a muezzin in Isfahan?

The latter squib surely fails to hit the target. Betjeman in his Christmas
thoughts was, once again, keeping his eye on the mainstream question –

> And is it true? And is it true,
>   This most tremendous tale of all,
> Seen in a stained-glass window's hue,
>   A Baby in an ox's stall?
> The Maker of the stars and sea
> Become a Child on earth for me?
>
> And is it true? For if it is,
>   No loving fingers tying strings
> Around those tissued fripperies,
>   The sweet and silly Christmas things,
> Bath salts and inexpensive scent
> And hideous tie so kindly meant,
>
> No love that in a family dwells,
>   No carolling in frosty air,
> Nor all the steeple-shaking bells
>   Can with this single Truth compare –
> That God was Man in Palestine
> And lives to-day in Bread and Wine.

The love which in the Betjeman family dwelt was put under severe
strain that cold Christmas of 1947. It was the last Christmas when
they all went to the same Church.

For some days before she was 'received' into the RC Church,
Penelope made a retreat at Cherwell Edge, a large red house on the
edge of the University Parks, formerly the home of the historian
James Anthony Froude, but now used as a hostel for Roman Catholic
female students, especially nuns. It was not a silent retreat. 'Oi as

meals with the students ere and talk all ther toime', she told her husband. He went off to Cornwall to escape the pain of it, and then on to Denmark for a series of public talks and readings.

Penelope was conditionally rebaptised, another detail which upset Betjeman, in spite of her reassurance that 'it takes 10 seconds in the *vestry*'. Then, on 9 March 1948 in St Aloysius Church, Oxford, a small group of Oxford friends, including Maurice Bowra — no Catholic he — turned up to hear her announce that she 'hated and abjured' her former heresies, before being officially admitted to her new denomination.

To Geoffrey Taylor, Betjeman sent a version of a sonnet:

> In the Perspective of Eternity
>   The pain is nothing, now you go away
>   Above the stealing thatch now silvery-grey
> Our chiming church tower, calling 'Come to me
>
> My Sunday-sleeping villagers!' And she,
>   Still half my life, kneels now with those who say
>   'Take courage, daughter. Never cease to pray
> God's grace will break him of his heresy.'
>
> I, present with our Church of England few
>   At the dear words of Consecration see
>   The chalice lifted, hear the sanctus chime
> And glance across at that familiar pew.
>
> In the Perspective of Eternity
> The pain is nothing — but ah, God, in time.

Betjeman included the poem in *A Few Late Chrysanthemums*, but Jock Murray decided it was 'too personal', and at the last minute it was pulled out and never published until his daughter included it in Volume One of the *Letters*.

Personal it is indeed, and Father Pepler's hope that Penelope would be able at all times to make the united family her first concern was not one, given the very different personalities of husband and wife, which showed much sign of being fulfilled.

Nine days after becoming a Catholic, she wrote:

> Darlin Tewpie . . . Oi know oi was ysterical on Tuesday morning. Oi oped and oi thought oi would be mooch calmer about everythin after moi reception into the arms of the scarlet Woman (Archie is dictatin this) boot oi serpose it cannot appen all at oonce. It as been a year of great strain and tension for both of oos and as given me indergestion since January boot oi think it is clearin oop now . . .

Eighteen months later, Bowra, by being abrasively jokey, found words which must have been consoling to Betjeman.

> Dear Evelyn was never very high-brow. Perhaps it is just that which took him to Rome, which seems rapidly becoming a haven for those who have a natural aversion to thought. Poor Bog [Alan Pryce-Jones who became a Catholic for a very short period and then reverted to Anglicanism] seems to have made rather a b..ls of it, hasn't he?

One of the first things Paul Betjeman said to me when I met him in New York in November 2005 was – 'Before 1948 everything was all right. You realise that? 1948 was the year when everything came apart.' Osbert Lancaster spoke wittily, as always, but truly, when he said that, for Betjeman, going to church with a woman mattered more than going to bed.

The bitter blow of Penelope's defection drove Betjeman more and more into the consolations of friendship, and of love. Without any doubt the most crucial figure in Betjeman's professional life during this period was George Barnes, 'the Commander'. Barnes disliked the nickname. He had tried to get into the navy during the First World War and been turned down on health grounds. It became even more embarrassing to Barnes when Independent Television started, since there was a real commander, Commander Brownrigg, at Associated Rediffusion, which somehow added to the absurdity when Betjeman asked people, 'Do you know my friend Commander George Barnes, who has made himself a little niche in television?'

They had met when Barnes was head of the Talks Department in 1930, and he had early seen Betjeman's extraordinary potential for broadcasting, using him for wireless talks and learning to control his frivolities. Instead of reciting verses such as 'It isn't the same at St Winifred's now Monica's left the school', Betjeman was urged by Barnes to give informative and well-turned talks such as one on Parson Hawker of Morwenstow. Barnes was always urging him to do a programme, or perhaps a series, on the Oxford Movement. Like Jack Beddington at Shell, Barnes could see that Betjeman's unique combination of showmanship and topographical-cum-architectural knowledge made him the ideal broadcaster. George Barnes and his wife Anne became close friends, and Betjeman often retreated to their house near Tenterden in Kent – Prawls – as well as taking summer holidays with them in France. Like Penelope Betjeman, Anne Barnes was a lover of good food, and an excellent cook. Unlike Penelope, she enjoyed the occasional extravagance. On one occasion at Prawls, thinking to give Betjeman a treat, she bought a jar of caviare and hid it in the larder, intending to bring it out at dinner. She and a few guests stood on the lawn with drinks in their hands when Betjeman emerged from the house with a 'Cat-who's-got-the cream' expression on his face. He had found the caviare and eaten the lot. Their young son Anthony, known by Betjeman as Little Prawls, was also a close friend from the beginning. Anne Barnes was a good listener, and was soon the recipient of Betjeman's confidences. From 1944 onwards, Betjeman became a frequent guest at Prawls, even though Anne regretted never being able to persuade him to have a bath. Anthony, the first few times he met the poet, was overwhelmed by the pong.

His two obsessive crushes at this time were Margaret Wintringham, whom he had met at a poetry reading in Swindon, and a young South African poet, Patrick Cullinan. Margaret was married to a wine expert called Edmund Penning-Rowsell and because she and her husband were communists, she became the Party Member, or the Stakhanovite. She was put through the usual Betjeman routine of worship, but unlike many of the boys and girls whom he adored, she assumed that this would lead to some reciprocal lovemaking. When he visited her, for what she supposed would be adultery, however,

> with priggishness and self-righteousness, with fear and love, I insisted on doing nothing. She – oh God I can't put it down in ink or pencil or charcoal or anything – she [put up with] my priggishness. And now what have I? Remorse, internal writhings, detestation of everything here [Farnborough], inability to concentrate, fear of her revenge on me and the prospect of several more deliciously wonderful visits each with its sad ending.

She got her revenge with a bad poem –

For J.B.

> Remember when in your philosophy
> Human relationships take second place
> Your chastity is founded on my charity
> And through my grief you reach your State of Grace.

'Of course she's quite right', he told Anne Barnes, but the reader fifty years on wonders if he understood what she was saying.

Patrick Cullinan was an easier idol to adore. A South African boy at Charterhouse, with a blond lock of hair falling constantly over his bright blue eyes, he became a pen-pal of Betjeman's in the late 1940s and was asked to stay at Farnborough in 1950. 'John seems very fond of that South African boy, Penelope', said the field marshal to Betjeman's delight. He quoted the remark in a letter to Piper, and added,

He attracted Robert H-P so much that he called with 4 other queers to take a 2nd look and Gavin and his little American friend laid themselves out to be nice & would not let go when we called at Buscot . . . I fell in love so much that I felt no physical sensations at all beyond being drained of all power of limbs . . . Of course I am imagining things – a mere David Horner I am or Oliver Messel – but I think – that he looks at me with all his eyes and loves me or at any rate is very *fond* of me . . . I believe that my chief function is like the Colonel's – drawing out the young.

Unhappy, or rather luxuriating masochistically in unhappy love, as a distraction from real unhappiness in his marriage – Betjeman during these years in Farnborough has been made to seem a wretched person in the last few pages. That was only part of the picture. He continued to go into Oxford to work at the Oxford Preservation Trust. For his children, and their village friends, there were endless jokes, and larks. And Penelope continued to be a generous hostess and a good cook, entertaining every weekend.

The Mosleys, Sir Oswald and his wife Diana, were now living at Crowood, near Ramsbury, and often came over for Sunday luncheon. Betjeman had loved Diana since Biddesden days when she was married to Bryan Guinness, and the two had a deep bond of humour. Since she and her husband had been imprisoned during the war under the 18B regulation, which suspended habeas corpus, and entitled the Government to lock up citizens without trial, both Mosleys had become social pariahs in many circles. It was supposed that they had been to prison for treason, or that they had wanted Hitler to win the war. Neither thing was true, but the fact that Sir Oswald had been the leader of the British Union of Fascists led to very understandable confusions, not least because he hoped in these post-war years to re-form some kind of populist party from the rem-nant of the old Blackshirt movement. Betjeman felt a natural sympathy with those who were in disgrace, whether it was Lord

Lovely Diana

Alfred Douglas and Oscar, or clergymen who had in Freddy Hood's phrase 'stepped aside'. The Mosleys came into this category. Betjeman tried hard to get Alexander and Max Mosley, the two sons of Oswald and Diana, into English schools, though their parents eventually decided to educate them abroad. 'You really are an angel to have found a school which might accept Alexander and Max as pupils – or perhaps I should say a genius', wrote Diana in May 1946, 'Mr Tootill sounds as blissful as his name . . . I was beginning to despair as I had had so many furious refusals. Isn't it odd in a way; if I had a school I should welcome reds, in the hope of converting them.'

Mosley himself turned to Betjeman for help with the layout of his political newsletter, 'Action'. 'The public seem very willing to buy it when given an opportunity', he added optimistically. Betjeman gave advice about typography, but the times were not auspicious. A book printed by 'Mosley Publications Limited' was of 'vile appearance' because it 'was set up, in secret, at night, by one small printer, and was then completed when another broke down completely under the stress'.

A lost cause with which Betjeman was to have more success was in persuading the Prime Minister to put forward the name of the great Ninian Comper for a knighthood for his 'Wark'. T.S. Eliot, John Piper, Lord Shaftesbury, the Bishop of Chichester, the Reverend Mother of the Wantage Convent and many others were written to by Betjeman and asked to write individually to the PM. It was doubly challenging since as Charles Peers pointed out, 'old Comper has certainly not gone out of his way to make friends of his professional brethren during a long and distinguished career'. In the New Year's Honours of 1950, however, Betjeman's dream came true. P. Morton Shand was 'lost in admiration at your getting a knighthood for Comper. Obviously it is entirely your own work and was also intended as one straight between the eyes for the RIBA.' Not only was this the case. Even more satisfy-ingly – like the confusion caused at Magdalen by Betjeman's insistence upon studying medieval Welsh – it actually threw the anti-Comper architects into administrative confusion. John Summerson went into the RIBA canteen and enjoyed the unhappy faces there.

> Spragg said, I suppose you know. Comper's not an architect. Not
> an architect I said. No, he's not an architect. HE'S NOT ON THE
> REGISTER . . . J.N.C. is not on the register [Architects Registration
> Council of the United Kingdom] and does not pay a pound a year. If he
> styles himself 'architect' he is liable to prosecution and a heavy fine.
> BUT THE KING HAS KNIGHTED HIM AS AN ARCHITECT. Well,
> make of this what you like. Some will say it is a great blow for freedom.

And so it was.

The king held Garden Parties that summer as usual, and Lord Chetwode took his daughter along to one of them. It was to be the last summer of the field marshal's life. When he died, Betjeman said,

> very sad it will be for Penelope. Losing one parent is bad enough. When
> you lose both, you suddenly know you have stepped out into loneliness,
> there's no one to back you up or even to quarrel with, except other
> lonely people like yourself. I suppose husband and children are some
> consolation. But not much and they can't lessen the change.

Some people believe that once you have children yourself, you cease to be a child and become primarily a parent. This frank letter shows that psychologically Betjeman had never made that leap. A parent, or better still, a nanny, would alone comfort him in *his* loneliness.

Hop skip and jump in coltish ecstasy

Probably Penelope was very different. It was nice for her, however, that she went to a Buckingham Palace garden party with her aged father in the last weeks of his life. And after that experience, she wrote a letter to her husband which, in the light of Betjeman's subsequent career, seems prophetic:

> Woad was very please [*sic*] oi went ter the garden party with im
> boot it was very cold so we only stayed an hour. We saw the Roogby's
> [i.e. the former Sir John Maffey and wife, now Lord and Lady Rugby]
> and ee says as ow ee is troin ter get yew made poet laureate when
> Masefield kciks [*sic*] the boocket but that ow as yew moost wroite a
> poem about Prince Charles first.

She adds that she now has 'dia[rrhoea] . . . boot thqt [*sic*] was from eating too many of the King's cakes'.

10

DEFECTIONS

'I have the most beautiful secretary in the world & *yet* remain a faithful husband. Praise God for strength received', Betjeman wrote to his old schoolmaster T.S. Eliot on 14 May 1951. The manias for Patrick Cullinan, and for the Stakhanovite, Margaret Wintringham, faded in the bright rays of a new passion. Jill Menzies 'is very pure and blue-eyed and freckled and covered with gold fur and has a degree (2nd) in French at Oxford and she has a quietly dominating personality', he told another friend. To yet another, he rhapsodised, 'She is a very clever girl and looks like a ruined choirboy, with turned-up nose, wide apart grey eyes, freckles and golden down on her arms and legs. SHE IS VERY BEAUTIFUL AND GOOD AND CALM AND FUNNY.' Such passions punctuated his emotional life: they always had and always would. They fed his poetry. After an evening at one of his London clubs, at which he had entertained 'Freckly Jill', he wrote one of his worst gush-poems:'I could not speak for amazement at your beauty'. Jill Menzies was twenty-two when she came to work for him. He interviewed her in his office at *Time and Tide* and for his part it was love at first sight. From May 1951, she moved in with the Betjemans and lived *en famille*, helping with correspondence and typing until May 1953, when, as she said, 'I think I was getting too fond of him. I thought it would upset Penelope if I stayed.'

Penelope, the mother of two children aged eleven and nine, had probably never in her Anglican days practised birth control. As a fervent convert to Roman Catholicism, she certainly did not do so and made no secret of the fact that she saw sex 'only as a means of procreation, not interested at all as an amusement'.

In his thanksgiving for 'strength received' which enabled him to be a faithful husband Betjeman might have been speaking slightly too soon. Between his claim to Eliot in May 1951 that he was still a faithful husband, and his rapturous description of Freckly Jill in the second of the two letters quoted above, to Anne Barnes, a momentous meeting had occurred, one which would change Betjeman's marriage, and indeed redirect

'Freckly' Jill Menzies

the course of his life. On 15 May 1951, Betjeman accepted an invitation to dinner with Lady Pamela Berry, the wife of the proprietor of the *Daily Telegraph*. She was a connection by marriage of Penelope's and Betjeman had known her for over twenty years, having been at Oxford with her brother, Freddy Birkenhead. The daughter of F.E. Smith, the first Lord Birkenhead, and (from 1953 for over a decade) the mistress of Malcolm Muggeridge, this lively flirtatious socialite was the embodiment of everything Penelope detested about London. The little dinner which Lady Pamela had arranged had a missing guest. Guy Burgess, who had been exposed as a Soviet agent, had left the country that night and gone to live in Moscow. No one at the time read anything of significance in the face of one of the guests who did turn up at Lady Pamela's table, Betjeman's old Marlborough contemporary, Anthony Blunt, himself a Soviet agent who must have known as his hostess fussed and looked at the clock, and as they sat down late, with an empty place at the table, that his comrade was already on the way to Moscow.

Betjeman took less notice of Blunt than he did of another guest, a conspicuously tall, shy young woman named Lady Elizabeth Cavendish, who sat in almost total silence throughout the meal. Next day, the irrepressible Pamela telephoned everyone to tell them the sensational news that her missing dinner guest had been unmasked as a spy for the Russians. It would be amusing to read a typescript of her conversation with Blunt, assuming, as would be quite likely by this stage, that his telephone had been bugged by the KGB, if not

Lucian Freud's portrait of Elizabeth Cavendish, hanging at Chatsworth, was painted at about the period she met Betjeman

by British Intelligence. When she rang Betjeman, she asked him if he would be prepared to come on a cruise to Copenhagen in her husband's yacht. Rather surprisingly for someone who hated abroad, he said that he would do so only on condition that she also invited Elizabeth.

When Pamela rang Elizabeth, she invited her, adding the devastatingly tempting information that Betjeman was unhappy and that his marriage was going wrong.

Both Betjeman and Elizabeth Cavendish felt that they had fallen in love at that dinner, and they accepted the invitation to go on the cruise knowing what this might entail. Freckly Jill remembered, 'JB was very flattered. Elizabeth was mad about him and he was mad about her. Penelope didn't mind about Elizabeth any more than she

Elizabeth

minded about anyone else. After all, John was always falling in love.'

Some of his friends, especially his gay friends, felt that the constant succession of 'loves' was becoming tiresome. Colonel Kolkhorst asked him, 'Is it not time you gave your heart a rest, for a little while anyway? You have been at it non stop now for I don't know how many donkey's years, it isn't good for you.'

The Cavendish affair was to be very different from what had gone before. Previous loves had either been airy and Platonic, turning into poems and then into laughing friendships, as in the case of Gold Myfanwy; or, as with the 'ordinary little woman' in the Bath teashop, they were short flings, during which a full sexual relationship happened, only to be hastily and guiltily put behind him, with confession to a priest putting an end to the matter. Betjeman's lyrics about sex beg God to make him indifferent to the objects of his desire. He prays to see the 'wholly to my liking girl, / To see and not to care', which is not especially flattering to the girl.

Elizabeth Cavendish was a determined young woman who was not prepared to be treated in this way. She fell very much in love with Betjeman, and probably, for his part, his feelings were more closely engaged than they had been with some of the others, though quite how one judges these matters it is difficult to say. One of his fellow guests on the cruise to Copenhagen was Bog, his old Oxford friend Alan Pryce-Jones, and his wife Poppy, who was to die of cancer not long afterwards. By the time Cavendish came back from the cruise, she had acquired a nickname – Feeble – always a sign that you had entered the inner circle of Betjeman's imagination. She was also his lover.

The fact that she was the daughter of the tenth and sister of the eleventh dukes of Devonshire would not have diminished her attractions for the ever-aspirant Betjeman. When a friend, who always took Penelope's side in the matter, unkindly dismissed Elizabeth as 'just an upper-class nanny' she had, of course, managed to define in one short phrase Betjeman's ideal woman. From boyhood onwards, he had been attracted to nanny-figures. His poem about Myfanwy pictures her leaning over a *kinderbank* with himself as the kiddie inside. 'You will protect me, my silken Myfanwy, / Ringleader, tom-boy and chum to the weak.'

Elizabeth, still grieving for her father, who had died the previous year, would grow into being Betjeman's protectress, but when they first met, the boot was on the other foot. Betjeman felt her vulnerability (hence the nickname he gave her – Feeble). She was everything Penelope was not. She seemed emotionally needy and dependent upon him. She was quiet and gentle. Her humour was subtle. She was a committed and serious communicant of the Church of England.

What Elizabeth found in him was equally transparent to all who saw them together. They had a shared sense of humour. From the

Public life: Jill Balcon, Christopher Fry, David Cecil, JB

first, there was laughter between them, and laughter defined their relationship. They also had the Church, with all the complications which that devotion brought with it. Elizabeth to a large extent had reacted against the irreligion of her delightful brother the eleventh Duke who, in spite of a nominal allegiance to the Church of England, was no churchgoer. He was charming to women, and he followed what was in effect the code of his class when it came to adultery – as did his wife's brother-in-law Sir Oswald Mosley.

The world from which Elizabeth came took adultery for granted, though it followed certain codes and it tried not to divorce. She did not want an existence which was limited to hunting, country sports, entertaining or the Season. Belonging as she did to one of the most eminent of aristocratic lineages, her father one of the grandest dukes in the kingdom, her mother a Cecil, sister of Lord David the writer, and daughter of the fourth Marquess of Salisbury, Elizabeth came from two notably intelligent families. But she had no wish to lead the conventional upper-class life, and was naturally drawn to a Bohemian life in London, combined with what Penelope Betjeman would have called something 'worth whoile'. She was to become a magistrate and to work especially with young offenders. Like her uncle David Cecil and unlike her brother Andrew, she was naturally pious, and the complicated situation into which she fell when she found that she loved John Betjeman was not one which she would ideally have chosen. She wanted a 'normal' life, marriage and children, of whom she was especially fond. It did, however, suit her on several levels to fall in love with Betjeman since, while not being an aristocrat, he loved mixing with those who were, and understood her world.

The dinner table where they first met seems, as we think of it from this perspective in time, to have something of the quality of the Le Carré thrillers, those marvellous Cold War stories in which Smiley the agent unskeins the delicate strands of betrayal not only in the political but also in the marital life, his own wife's compulsive need to betray him in his bed being matched by his colleague Bill Haydon's compulsion to betray his country. By falling in love with one another, Betjeman and Cavendish, precisely because they had so much in common, put at risk all they cared for most, especially family life and the Church.

One of the things which Feeble and John Betjeman had in common, and one of the things which now separated him from his wife, was that they were both serious Anglicans. (Feeble's family nickname, coined by her sister-in-law Deborah Devonshire, is Deacon.) Alan Pryce-Jones, the witness to their burgeoning love on the cruise, was also a devout man. A year after the cruise, Pryce-Jones, the editor of the *Times Literary Supplement*, followed Penelope's path. 'He made a brief plunge to Rome . . . but didn't like what he found and swam out quickly', wrote his fellow Anglican Rose Macaulay in triumph.

Betjeman too rejoiced in Bog's return from Rome, and the two men loved going to High churches in London together, such as Grosvenor Chapel (sanctuary adorned by Comper) in South Audley Street, or St Cyprian's, Clarence Gate, the marvellous Comper masterpiece near Baker Street Station where the white interior is divided by a blaze of gold rood-screen, adorned with angels.

> I love the Bog villa and also the people
> Whose elegant brogues have the gravel to crunch on
> As sedately the bells from St Cyprian's steeple
> Will summon them northward to share the bog luncheon.

When Poppy Pryce-Jones died of cancer, in February 1953, Elizabeth Cavendish proposed marriage to the mainly gay Bog within a few months. By then, the strain and guilt of her affair with Betjeman had made her feel that she must find someone else. Pryce-Jones himself explained her motives as 'just an escape from JB whom she loved but didn't want to complicate his life'.

On his way down to have his annual family holiday in Cornwall in August 1953, Betjeman asked Bog, 'Do I stand between you and our loved Elizabeth? I sometimes feel I do. And by doing that I stand away from you and am no use to us and I would like to be of use. For I love you, my dear old Bog, and your little house and its trim garden and your interest in electric razors and Rilke. Don't give up the *TLS*. It really is frightfully good. The *only* interesting paper. And it is you that makes it so.'

As so often when Betjeman's emotions were deeply engaged, he made a joke of the situation and spoke of it openly. Since Oxford days, he had made his loves the subject of general conversation, so that anyone who met him would be told of his love, now for Little Bloody, now for Billa, now for Woman, now for Propeller, now for Freckly Jill. Antonia Pakenham, daughter of Betjeman's old friends Frank and Elizabeth, was at Alan Pryce-Jones's flat in the Albany in the early-to-mid-1950s when Betjeman seized her arm. 'Isn't

Elizabeth, too tall for an Irish train

she beautiful?' he said, pointing to Elizabeth Cavendish, and began reciting a poem he had made up about Bog and Paddy Leigh Fermor fighting a duel for Feeble's sake.

Being the secret consort of a married man had not been Elizabeth Cavendish's prime ambition in life. She was still a very young woman, with all her life before her, and she could have had no idea at this stage quite what a momentous thing had happened to her when she fell in love with Betjeman.

Her grandmother Alice, Marchioness of Salisbury (by birth a member of the Gore family, who produced Bishop Gore, founder of the Community of the Resurrection at Mirfield, and a Christian pastor committed to the Social Gospel) had advised Elizabeth that she must see how other people in England were living. From the age of 'eighteen or so', Elizabeth had spent most of each week in the East End of London in Poplar and Stepney as a social worker. She would go on to become a frequent prison-visitor, becoming chairman of the Board of Visitors at HM Prison, Wandsworth.

Finding herself in love with a married man, and in the midst of what was turning out to be not simply an affair but something much more serious, overturned her entire existence. Having lived with her mother in Cheyne Walk, she now bought the small house in Radnor Walk, Chelsea, which was to be her home for the rest of her life. Betjeman visited when he could, never staying at that address much more than once a week in the first ten years. Elizabeth recalls,

> At the beginning when John stayed at Patrick Kinross' house he was probably only up for a night or two a week, but that was only for a fairly short time until he moved to Cloth Fair when he was around a lot more, and of course as well we stayed a lot with the Pipers at Fawley Bottom and with Osbert and Karen [Lancaster] in Henley and others, and went just the two of us for two, three or four days looking at houses and churches all over England and staying in hotels

or sometimes with friends of John's. We also stayed a lot with Peggy and Lynam Thomas in their nice house on the cliff at Trebetherick, sometimes with them and other times they lent us the house. We also travelled abroad quite a bit.

From 1951 onwards, there was another, quite different element in her life. She accompanied Princess Margaret on her first official visit abroad, to Jamaica. The princess was a friend, but when she asked Elizabeth to accompany her she had said that since it was an official trip, she could come as her Lady-in-Waiting. She maintained this role until the Princess's death, following her on official visits, making sure that the Princess was kept comfortable on her journeys, and not monopolised by the over-talkative at receptions, official openings, and the like. 'The job involved answering queries, writing thank you letters and all sorts of other letters on her behalf, and generally being a background of commonsense to whom Princess Margaret could turn for friendship and advice.'

A number of people, including close members of Elizabeth's family, have found the friendship between the two women puzzling, but it was a deep one. It was forged at a house party of Lord Glenconner's. Those who knew both women at this period could see that one very obvious thing which they had in common was the love for men who, in the eyes of the church at least, were married to someone else – in Princess Margaret's case her father's former equerry Group Captain Peter Townsend.

Betjeman, in many ways a natural courtier, took to the friendship with the Princess and became part of it. Inevitably, given the difference in height between 'Feeble' and Princess Margaret, the Princess became 'Little Friend'.

An early outing, one of many walks, church-crawls, holidays and expeditions which Betjeman shared with his new love, was spiritually far from royalty. He took her to Willesden Churchyard, and wrote,

> Come walk with me, my love, to Neasden Lane.
> The chemicals from various factories
> Have bitten deep into the Portland Stone
> And streaked the white Carrara of the graves . . .

In this spot, so deeply 'Betjeman', he showed Elizabeth the grave of Laura Seymour, 'So long the loyal counsellor and friend' of Charles Reade, the Victorian writer who is buried with her. Reade, author of the long fifteenth-century historical romance *The Cloister and the Hearth*, was a prolific writer in his day and he was also, what Betjeman would have loved to have been, a Fellow of Magdalen College, Oxford. The relationship between him and his life-long companion remains mysterious, which is one of the subjects of Betjeman's poem 'In Willesden Churchyard'.

> Did Laura gently stroke her lover's head?
> And did her Charles look up into her eyes
> For loyal counsel there? I do not know.
> Doubtless some pedant for his Ph. D.
> Has ascertained the facts . . .

In this sometimes neglected, and very fine poem, which is both witty and moving, it is almost as if Betjeman in the 1950s saw the whole story – his long companionship with Elizabeth stretching forward through the future to his death, and the prurient curiosity which their friends, and posterity, would show in the relationship. It does not end with pedants, nor intrusive biographers. Very characteristically, he imagines himself dissolving, as Laura Seymour and Charles Reade have dissolved in the Willesden churchyard, and he feels, ever close, but not always consoling, the sacramental presence of Christ –

> I only know that as we see her grave
> My flesh, to dissolution nearer now
> Than yours, which is so milky white and soft,
> Frightens me, though the Blessed Sacrament

Not ten yards off in Willesden parish church
Glows with the present immanence of God.

Osbert Lancaster, one of Betjeman's closest friends in the second half of his life, used to say that he was the only person he knew who managed to be married, have a mistress and live the life of a bachelor all at once. From the year 1951, this needs to be borne in mind. Home life went on in Berkshire. His gregarious social life in London, and his travelling around England, partly for broadcasts, partly in search of architectural delight, continued as if he were a young unmarried man.

It was obvious to both Betjemans, after a particularly cold winter, when the boiler broke in the Rectory, that they would move. In October 1951, Penelope wrote to him at length about their shared hopes and plans.

Darlin Tewpie, oi AVE got confidence in yer earnin and writin powers, oi thinks yew earns a tremendous lot boot oi know it is in er soul-destroyin way and that nearly arf is removed in taxes. Oi also KNOW and ave always known that you as it in yew ter wroite really good what is known as 'worth whoile' books, probably about harchitecture and nointeenth cent harchitects and oother alloied soobjects. The point about mee is oi henjoy teaching catechism more than anything else at all and oi looves livin ere where oi can indoolge that whim fairly fully and also roide and ave paonies fer the children BOOT QUOIT HAPART from yer disloike of ther place oi KNAOW it is mad ter continue ere naow Woad is dead as hapart from the clear £1250 per year PLOOS overead expenses for repairs required per year the kiddies hexpense apart from school fees will HINCREASE as ther years go boi saow we joost mooost not live in sooch an hextravagant wa. There seem to me ter be two alternatives: oone ter live in tartish stiole [sic] in er mooch smaller oause with toini garden and no land and sell er lot of our furnityre. Then we would ave quoite er lot of cash ter spare for hentertaining and travelling haboaut and when both kiddies is at school oi could go abroad soomtoimes which would make oop fer los of paonies and caows. HOR, TWOOOOO ter ave er small dairy farm. I honestly ave confidence that I could make this pay well, doozens hof hinexperienced people ave sooceeded [*sic*] since the war and the chief qualification required is er real interest in cowns [*sic*] and er willingness ter spend toime hon their proper care. This would mean yew would ave ter continue yer reviewing fer one year after we sells this and goes tew er farm hafter which I am pretty certain yew could give it oop and do more serious wroitin sooch as oi KNOW and ave habselute confidence yew is still capable hof. Personally oi thinks we should go AWAY from so many friends fer a bit till we is both settled into our new way of loife oi am sure it would be easier ter get down ter work that way, boot if yew is bent on being near Hoxferd we will certainly gaow there. There poi t [*sic*] is hoi know we is both on each oothers nerves very badly and at the same toime hoi quoite hagree that we moost keep ther family tergether BOOT hoi am sure that when we AS faound her property hit woyld bee MOOCH better hif yew remove and stay with eg ther Colonel fer a month as hoi quoite honestly could not stand ther move with yew in er continueal state of nerves, whereas if yew soopervoises ther packing hof yer best books and pictures, then gaows off and wrtoites [*sic*] somewhere I n [*sic*] soom friends aouse oi can easily tackle ther move hom me hown and settle in with ther cows and get heverything goin and get the place coasy ready ter reeceeeveyew [*sic*] . . . Then when all is settled and heaps of gold is pourin into their milk pails we can all reunite in our noice little loove nest and be appy. It seems ter me idiotic not to dew more with moi capital than leave it in Himperial tobacco shares etc. Hoi know oi is er very bad woifie boot oi looves yew very mooch hoonderneath and oi know we can get hon very noicly when we loikes as we ave many friends hin common.

In the event, she cleverly found something which was a good compromise between tartish stoile and a dairy farm. Some Roman

Catholics met by Penelope at church offered to sell her their house in Wantage. Betjeman went to see it, and said, 'We must have this.' The Mead, set in seven acres, was a seventeenth-century farmhouse to which had been added a tile-hung, red-brick Victorian villa. It looked across fields to the middle of the old market-town of Wantage, and the parish church of St Peter and St Paul, whose bells chimed the quarters and played a hymn every third hour.

Wantage was a great centre of Victorian Anglo-Catholicism. The church had been one of the first in England to move to the ritualistic ceremonials which so shocked nineteenth-century Protestants. There was a daily recitation of Morning and Evening Prayer, and a daily Mass. In the inter-war years, there were over half a dozen curates attached to the church, and even in 1951 it was a lively concern. There was also a convent in the town, the Community of St Mary the Virgin, with nearly a hundred nuns, which ran a girls' boarding school. It was the ideal place for Betjeman, pillar of the Church, to have taken up residence. For all the chaos of his emotional life, his public persona was certainly that of Defender of the Faith. T.S. Eliot, himself a churchwarden of St Stephen's, Gloucester Road, one of the Highest churches in London, had been unwilling to sign a protest, centred around the Church of the Annunciation, Bryanston Street, Marble Arch, against the Christian rally in Hyde Park accompanying the opening of the Festival of Britain in the summer of that year, 1951. These purists objected to the rally on the grounds that it was ecumenical, and that Church of England bishops would share the platform with Nonconformist ministers. They objected to 'the mis-leading identification of the Church of England with those bodies which do not accept the traditional Faith of the Church'. The Roman Catholics were not taking part, 'and we feel that such an act can but give the non-Christian spectator a false idea of the religious life of this country. We also think that the participation of the Church of England may give the additional impression that Roman Catholics

Fellow churchman T.S. Eliot

are the only religious body which defends the full Catholic Faith.' Betjeman admitted to Eliot that he found the tone of the protest somewhat 'extreme'. 'But I have nailed my colours to the mast & cannot let down my co-signatories.'

He accepted huge numbers of speaking engagements in different parts of the country, sometimes at schools, sometimes in settings where he could rally support for the causes of architectural conservation or for the Church, if possible both. The patronal festival of the church at Staunton Harold in the autumn of 1953 provoked a typical response from the patron of the living, Earl Ferrers. The letter speaks of the attractions which drew the crowds –

The Archbishop – Ice creams – John Betjeman. In this part of the world few of us are Church of England, some of us are R.C. And the rest of us, Baptist, Anabaptist, Wesleyans, Utilitarians, Unitarians, Hot Gospellers, Blue Domers, or even of the Lady Huntingdon Persuasion. So, you see, even an Archbishop has his limitations. And that is why, in the first instance, I asked you to come down, and address us. I was both amused and amazed by your prompt reply, combining as it did, extreme humility with an unusual capacity for human friendship. Those are qualities we love and admire. 'And behold we were not disappointed'. I know that that lecture cost you a pint of blood. You would feel, I fancy, somewhat rewarded had you heard some of the comments upon it. 'Mr Betjeman was inspired' . . . 'John Betjeman's brilliance' etc. Fair comment? Anyhow freely given.

It was one of two visits to Derbyshire that autumn – Derbyshire being the county of Chatsworth, and the dukes of Devonshire, and Hardwick Hall, the great Elizabethan house, at present being occupied by Elizabeth's grandmother, the Dowager Duchess of Devonshire. 'When I asked the Dowager Duchess', Betjeman told Patrick Kinross, 'whether she had ever used Chiswick House she said, "Only for breakfasts. But people don't have them now. We went there by barouche. In those days *everyone* had a villa – there was Syon, Osterley and the Buccleuchs had that place at Richmond." When I asked whether she used Compton Place, Eastbourne, she said, "*Always* at Whitsun".'

Nooni nooni nooni noewke

wrote Betjeman to Penelope,

Er ooby went off to stay with a duke
Nibberly Nobberly nibberly nob
Er ooby was clearly a bit of a snob.

While David Cecil's friends such as Rowse or Evelyn Waugh, who did not really know Elizabeth's mother, 'Mowcher', could see her almost as a symbol of the vanishing aristocratic caste they idolised, for Betjeman, she was to become a real friend. True, she was of the old school, who called her servants, male or female, simply by their surnames. She was through and through an aristocrat. Like her brother Lord David Cecil, however, she was one of those unusual people who was equally at ease in the company of anyone. According to Rowse, meeting her had inspired him to change his manly working-class West-Country voice into that of a flutey dowager. Rowse had been at Christ Church at exactly the same time as David Cecil. When Lord David introduced his friend to his sister, she had impressed the young

'Mowcher' — portrait by
Lucian Freud at Chatsworth

Cornish socialist by saying, 'When I'm depressed, Mr Rowse, I plant an *avenue*.'

Despite Rowse's apocryphal story about planting an avenue, Mowcher was not especially addicted to living in grand houses. As they gathered round the wireless to hear the news of the outbreak of war at Chatsworth, the duke said, 'Well, one good thing about this news. It gives us the excuse to move out of here.' This, the tenth Duke, Eddy, had succeeded his father in 1938, and he and Mowcher had only ever lived in Chatsworth for a few months. (It became a school, attended by Elizabeth Cavendish.) Their firstborn, who would have succeeded as the eleventh Duke, was killed in action in 1944 and thereafter Eddy Devonshire never entered Chatsworth. When the tenth Duke died, in 1950, he was succeeded by his second son, Andrew, married to the Hon. Deborah Mitford, youngest sister of Nancy, Diana and Co. Mowcher eventually moved in to Moor View, Edensor. It had been the head gardener's house. As any visitor to Chatsworth knows, the gardens are spectacularly large, and head gardeners did well for themselves – it has six bedrooms. Nevertheless, Moor View is probably less 'grand' than Combe Florey (Waugh's last house) or Trenarren, where Rowse lived for the last forty years of his life. Admittedly, it was only her holiday house, and she lived for most of the year in London.

Mowcher took to Betjeman immediately, and not merely as a friend. If it is true that Lord David Cecil and his wife expressed misgivings about their niece's liaison with their old friend, Mowcher, churchgoer as she was, embraced Betjeman as if he were her son-in-law. To those in the family it was clear that she was all but in love with him herself. She was destined to live into deep old age, and to outlive Betjeman himself. In the first stages of his love for Elizabeth, it was for much of the time a threesome. There was never, as far as Elizabeth's family was concerned, anything furtive about her life with Betjeman. He was taken whole-heartedly into that family and loved by all of them until death.

The contrast between life with Penelope and life with Elizabeth could not have been greater. Whereas life in the Old Rectory, Farnborough, and the Mead had been one of discomfort, punctuated by rows, Betjeman's time at Moor View seemed like a fulfilment of the wish expressed by the *Book of Common Prayer* – 'to pass our time in rest and quietness'. He wrote in 1958 a letter to Deborah Devonshire in which he spoke of

> dear, feeble, pale, freckled, soft-spoken Elizabeth. She and I and her Mum are engaged in reading Jane Austen out loud. She and I for the first time, owing to having been talked to about Jane Austen in the past and being put off by being told how much we would like her. But we do. She is terrifically funny & her theme, throughout, I'm happy to say, is class. We've read Emma, Mansfield Park, P&P since Christmas are nearly through Sense & Sensibility & have still Persuasion and Northanger Abbey. I absolutely understand people's keenness on her & so does f.P.F.s-s Elizabeth. I am off to retreat in Nashdom Abbey (C of E) taking 'Sons and Lovers' as a counterblast to remind me of Notts . . .

To give some idea of how *mouvementé*, perhaps in all senses, Betjeman's life had become, that summer and autumn of 1953, as well as his annual fortnight in Cornwall with the family and his new friend Rowse, and two visits to Derbyshire, Betjeman had also made a pilgrimage to the West Country to Powderham Castle, and to Exmouth where, with Elizabeth's sister Lady Anne Tree, he had offered advice about the Georgian shell-work at La Ronde. He visited Hertfordshire, which was less pleasant –

> Stevenage New Town in the rainy afternoon . . . Three miles of Lionel Brett-style prefabs interrupted by Hugh Casson blocks of flats and two shopping arcades and concrete roads and lampposts throughout and no trees, only muddy Hertfordshire inclines. I saw through the vast, unprivate ground-floor window of a house, a grey-faced woman washing up. My goodness, it was terrifying. And kiddies' scooters lying out in the rain on the streets and a big vita-glass school on stilts.

As the 1950s wore on, the old days at the *Archie Rev*, when modernist architects such as Lionel Brett might have appealed to Betjeman, seemed very remote.

As he travelled around England and saw such places as Stevenage New Town, his anger grew. He saw old market towns everywhere being wrecked, and London, instead of being rebuilt well after the war, being shared out among spivs and speculators. A large share of the blame for this he attributed to those academic architectural historians who had lent their theoretical expertise and their good names to endorsing the modernist programmes which were uglifying towns and spoiling lives. Chief villain was 'Professor Doktor Nikolaus Pevsner'. When Betjeman discovered that Bog employed Pevsner to write for the *TLS* he said he was

> HORRIFIED . . . This is not a personal matter with me. I don't
> know him. I only know that if he writes about anything one really
> knows about, his work is inaccurate while purporting to be
> encyclopaedic, ostentatious and his aesthetic judgements are absurd.
> He has no eye at all. If you regard him as an ambitious impresario,
> you can be charitable about that side of him and his desire to establish
> himself as an Englishman.

Throughout this busy period, Betjeman was earning money as a journalist, writing a weekly book review for the *Daily Telegraph*, and continuing to be the literary adviser for *Time and Tide*. From 1952 onwards, he also wrote a 'Men and Buildings' column for the *Telegraph*. In addition to serving on the Diocesan Advisory Committee for the dioceses of London and Oxford, he was also enlisted to the Royal Fine Art Commission. Much the most popular poet alive, he was now a public man, and what he stood for was something which was almost instantly recognisable. The hectic, over-crowded existence established after his move to Wantage was to set a pattern he would follow for the rest of his life, until illness and old age wrought another change. That pattern was, that he would spend the weekends, most of them, and holidays, with his family, and the rest of his time with Elizabeth Cavendish, or leading a bachelor existence either travelling round Britain or in London.

Photo by Anne Barnes of Betj in France

His popularity and fame grew with his skills as a broadcaster. In terms of his career, and the shape which it was to take, perhaps the most significant thing to happen at the beginning of the 1950s was the appointment of George Barnes as the Director of Television at the BBC. Until the Coronation in 1953, television was not really going to become a popular medium. After that, people gradually began to buy or to hire television sets and families would gather round, like fair Elaine the bobby-soxer, for 'sandwich supper and the television screen'. Even in 1951, Barnes and his colleagues could see its huge potential. Popular culture was transformed by it during the 1950s, and Betjeman's star potential was something which Barnes saw, and nurtured, from the first.

A very long letter written by Barnes in July 1951 outlined some of Betjeman's ideas for a series of weekly or fortnightly films. One such idea involved a programme lasting thirty or sixty minutes in which he examined the history of just one church. He would look at the monuments in the church, and then take the camera out into the surrounding district to see the sort of people who had been commemorated, and the houses they lived in. He would examine old prints and see how the church interior had changed over the years. Anyone whose architectural education began by watching Betjeman on television – and that includes a whole generation growing up in the 1950s and 1960s – will remember his preternatural eye for detail. He early established such a good relationship with cameramen and such a clear idea of what he wanted them to look at, that his best programmes were in effect directed by himself, though of course his name did not appear as the director's.

A second type of programme would be to visit the homes of famous English poets by helicopter swooping down over the landscape which had helped to form their imagination – Shakespeare's Warwickshire, Cowper's North Bucks, Crabbe's Suffolk coast, Tennyson's Lincolnshire and the Isle of Wight. Again, anyone remembering the later films of Betjeman's maturity – for instance, the staggering opening shots of his film about Parson Kilvert, with a camera playing over the huge green lushness of the Clyro Valley – will see that from the very beginning as a television broadcaster, Betjeman knew exactly what he was up to, and what effects he

*On holiday in France — Elizabeth, Anne Barnes,
George Barnes, Betjeman*

wished to achieve. A third idea, which as far as I know was never
followed up, was for a film, or series of films, about transport, again
using helicopters and aerial photography to follow Roman roads,
coaching roads, canals and railways. The excitement in Barnes's
account of his conversations with Betjeman is palpable long before
any of these programmes had been made; Betjeman had helped him
see the potential of the new medium. The shared passion for making
a success of television was something which deepened the bond
between Betjeman and the Barneses; but also the fact that Anne and
the Commander accepted Elizabeth as part of his life. (The Barneses
took Elizabeth and Betjeman on holiday to France together in 1952.)
Though Anne Barnes was Betjeman's *confidante*, and though she
always gave Betjeman and Elizabeth a shared bed when they stayed at
Prawls, even to her there was an element of mystery in the Babes

in the Wood style relationship, and she feared Betjeman's religious guilt sometimes marred the happiness. Not normally much given to strong language, Anne Barnes once exclaimed – 'I *do* hope he's fucking her!' after one of Betj and Feeble's visits.

Both the women in the triangle, Elizabeth and Penelope, assumed that he was going to choose between them. Programmed perhaps by a father who, if not an actual bigamist, had a number of extra-marital liaisons, Betjeman was never going to do this – though of course none of them knew this at the time. He dithered, and agonised, and the situation from the start took its toll on his temper and his health. Nevertheless, beneath his dithering was the 'whim of iron', and at some deep level he had no intention of breaking up his family for the sake of the new love. Life at the Mead, Wantage, there-fore followed a frequently merry pattern, with friends old and new. Candida's best schoolfriend was Anne Baring (Betjeman pronounced her name Arne, partly because she liked Arne's 'Rule Britannia'). During the move from Farnborough, Candida lodged with the Barings, who lived at Ardington House, near Wantage, and thereafter the families became firm friends, and holidays, Christmases and Sunday luncheons would be spent together, and with a group of other local families. Betjeman did not drop friends, so that the cumulative growth of his circle was immense, with Pipers and Lancasters continuing to see the Betjemans, and old friends from Oxford days such as Sparrow, Driberg and Kolkhorst still keeping in regular touch.

In the friendship with Evelyn Waugh, the power-balance very distinctly shifted. The attempts to make Betjeman into a Roman Catholic had signally failed. 'Oi habsolutely realise naow that the Anglican Church is yewer church and that Rome would be quoite alien and distasteful ter yew', Penelope acknowledged though she continued to make wholly unsuccessful bids to have Candida brought up as RC while 'the Powlie' was allowed to be Church of England. Moreover, Waugh, who had in the late 1940s nearly sent Betjeman mad with his theological crusades, was now himself, under the influence of the combination of alcohol and chloral, suffering from those delusions which he would work up into the masterpiece *The Ordeal of Gilbert Pinfold*. Readers of that extraordinary book will recollect that Mr Pinfold is given a washstand designed by the Victorian architect and designer William Burges. This incident was all true, and the donor in real life was Betjeman. Burges was perhaps the most technicoloured artist-designer of the Gothic revival. In a BBC talk about Burges's Cardiff Castle, Betjeman had said, 'A great brain has made this place. I don't see how anyone could fail to be impressed by its weird beauty . . . You see people coming out and blinking their eyes, awed into silence, punch-drunk as it were, from the force of this Victorian dream of the Middle Ages.'

There is something on the verge of grotesque about Burges's work. 'Punch-drunk' is just right. Betjeman loved Burges's own house in Kensington, Tower House, and befriended the owners, E.R.B. Graham and his wife. It was their hope that Betjeman would take over the Tower House, something which in the event – Mrs Graham died in 1962 – he felt he could not afford to do. (She left him the remaining two-year lease on the house, but on the expiry of the lease, he would have been liable for £10,000-worth of dilapidations.)

Early in the 1950s, the Grahams gave Betjeman the famous washstand. He would have liked to install it in the Mead, having decorated the house with rich wallpapers from Watts & Co., the ecclesiastical furnishers – the Gothic 'Kinnersley' in terracotta for the hall, and a blue tendrilly design for the drawing room. Having decided he did not want the washstand himself, he offered it to Waugh on the understanding that when Waugh died, or if he chose to dispose of it, it should be given to the Victoria and Albert Museum.

Given the heat of their exchanges only two years before over the subject of Roman Catholicism, Waugh was winded with this act of generosity.

Well, my dear fellow, all I can say is I am bowled over. What a present! I will see it never falls into the hands of the V&A. Did you know there is a note on Burges's painted furniture in Waring's Catalogue of 1862 Exhibition, with a plate of a cabinet which looks contemporary with Magnum Opus?

It was an early symptom of his mental imbalance that Mr Pinfold clearly 'remembers' that the washstand had a serpentine bronze pipe which led from the mouth of the dragon into the basin. When the removal-men brought the washstand to Piers Court, Stinchcombe, near Dursley, Glos, Waugh remonstrated with them, accusing them of having lost this vital tap in transit. He then wrote to the haulage firm to complain and finally drew Betjeman into the controversy, only to receive the rather chilling put-down, 'Oh no, old boy. There never was a pipe from the tap to the basin such as you envisaged.'

In the novel, Betjeman is described as 'a poet and artist by nature who had let himself become popularised'. Among the paranoid fantasies which Pinfold endures on his long voyage to Ceylon, overhearing the captain torturing and killing a Lascar steward, hearing voices in his cabin which accuse him of being a Jewish homosexual *arriviste*, and so on, he also 'hears' a BBC broadcast in which the Betjeman figure, Jimmy Lance, is reading out private letters from him, Pinfold, to a riot of studio laughter. Someone called June Cumberleigh is also joining in the laughter. 'She was a wholly respectable, clever, funny-faced girl who had got drawn into Bohemia through her friendship with James Lance.'

There was something a little wistful, too, in Waugh's observation of the ease with which Betjeman had charmed his way into the Chatsworth circle. Whatever misgivings they all had about Elizabeth's liaison with a married man twice her age, they all loved him and accepted him as semi-court-jester semi-family. Far more painful even than the madness in *Pinfold* is Waugh's clear and sane recognition that he has made himself so unamiable. 'He had made no new friends in late years. Sometimes he thought he detected a slight coldness among his old cronies. It was always he, it seemed to him, who proposed a meeting. It was always they who rose first to leave.'

'Betjeman has the flu', Waugh wrote to Nancy Mitford in November 1951, 'and has retired to the house of the Dowager Duchess of Devonshire where he is waited on & washed by Lady Elizabeth while the high-church butler reads *The Unlucky Family* aloud to him.'

A soft answer turneth away wrath, but Betjeman did more than this with Waugh. By ignoring Waugh's angrier taunts, and returning all Waugh's abusiveness with jokes and kindness, he won a victory. Waugh wrote to Penelope that he loved Betjeman but did not feel his love was returned. There is some truth in that – in his own paranoid old age, Betjeman railed against Waugh's books, his memory, his Catholicism – but it was more complicated than that. Friendships between writers are often marred and marked by edginess and rivalry. Both men revered one another, however, and respected what the other was doing. And on a surface level, both got on very well, having a shared sense of humour. Waugh was always a little abashed, however, by Betjeman's preparedness to switch on charm, or, more simply, to be charming. When he asked Betjeman to come to St Mary's, Ascot, to read poems and speak to the girls, his own daughters among them, he was bound to say, on Whit Sunday 1955, 'It was remarkably kind of you to come to Ascot & amuse my little girls & their friends. It was plain to me, watching their bright faces, that they enjoyed your poems rapturously & will remember your visit all their lives.'

Perhaps what created the edginess in their relationship was not their rivalry (if it ever existed) over Penelope, and not jealousy of one another's artistic reputation, but a shared sense that there were demons in both men. *The Ordeal of Gilbert Pinfold* concludes not with the simple medical discovery that Waugh/Pinfold's delusions had been 'caused' by an unwise admixture of chloral, alcohol and some sleeping pills prescribed by the doctor. Rather, there is the private, personal sense of a victory having been won by Pinfold himself, without the help of priest or psychiatrist. Betjeman's poems, as he approached his fiftieth year, are, in their different ways, dark, guilt-ridden, angry. They reflect as much unease about himself and about the world as do Waugh's dyspeptic diaries and letters.

A Few Late Chrysanthemums, of 1954, is the volume of poems whose contents reflect the range of his divided existence. It is a volume which contains solitary train-journeys, and games of seaside golf; there are hunter trials in Berkshire; there are splendidly evoked moments of seedy lust. There are evocations of agonising guilt about the emotional chaos of his private life. And there is above all, as the title suggests, a foreboding that in all these changing scenes of life, the grinning skull of death catches his eye to torture and mock.

The most terrible of all these lyrics, 'Late-Flowering Lust' (he was still less than fifty when it was published), confesses that sex is no fun any more, that the drunken fumblings with which he paws his love upon their reunion only serve to remind him of how soon they will both be skeletons, their eye sockets empty, their mouths tongueless.

> Too long we let our bodies cling,
>   We cannot hide disgust
> At all the thoughts that in us spring
>   From this late-flowering lust.

This is a truly chilling poem to have addressed to a lover who is still in her twenties. When one bears in mind that the experiences to which these poems refer all happened before he was fifty years old, and that he had thirty years of life in him after the volume was published, it might be thought that it was mere affectation which chose to see these vigorous stanzas composed by a highly popular poet in middle age as a few sprigs of autumnal flowering. But the fear of death, both in the poems and in Betjeman himself, was very real.

We cannot hide disgust . . .

And also, artists know themselves. Betjeman went on being able to write until he was about seventy. He continued to be a broadcaster of brilliance almost to the end. His distinctive vision of England, and his passionate concern about architectural vandalism, gathered pace in the second half of his life. It could therefore be said that the second half of his life was fuller than the first. But the autumnal title was accurate. Very few poets have been able to imitate Tennyson and continue to write well after their fortieth birthday. Although in

Betjeman's case there would be some good lyrics in the 1960s and 1970s, his crowded life ultimately left no room for the poetry to grow. He sensed this and it fuelled his self-doubt and self-reproach, which, though cloaked in the language of melodrama, were very decidedly not affectation. Against the background of all this, Penelope's voice warned him against the waste of life involved in the journalism, the social life and the adultery. Her letters to an increasingly absentee husband ring like a terrible chorus throughout the 1950s. At a certain point in Paul's schooldays, he does not quite remember when, his mother told him to stop writing joint letters home to his parents and to communicate with them separately.

MINDFUL OF THE CHURCH'S TEACHING

The arrangement of staying two or three nights each week as the lodger of friends in London, and the rest of the week in Wantage, was a restless one. Betjeman needed a proper London base. George Barnes introduced Betjeman to Lord Mottistone; he and his friend Paul Paget were partners in a firm of City architects, Seely & Paget. (They were the architects to St Paul's Cathedral.) Mottistone owned Cloth Fair, a narrow alleyway which had survived the Blitz, next to the great medieval priory church of St Bartholomew. They lived at number 45, and they let number 43 to Betjeman. The accommodation consisted of a narrow stairway, which Betjeman had papered with the William Morris willow pattern which he had in every house he ever occupied, an airy upstairs sitting-room which overlooked St Bart's churchyard, a tiny kitchen, and upstairs, a small bedroom and bathroom. The rent was £200 per annum (the equivalent of £8,978.67 in 2002, so – very reasonable).

There was a real feeling of homecoming. This was the first London base of his own which Betjeman had ever had. A Londoner through and through, he had hitherto either lived with his parents, or as a lodger in other people's flats and houses. A pre-war poem, 'City', was set in the churchyard of St Botolph Bishopsgate (the church where Keats was baptised) and as the great bell booms over the Portland stone, he waits

> For the spirit of my grandfather
> Toddling along from the Barbican.

Around us are Rovers and Austins afar

It isn't the greatest poem ever written, but *hear* him say it on one of the recordings, and you sense his exuberant love of the City of London. He was to live at 43 Cloth Fair for nearly twenty years. If Osbert Lancaster was right to say that Betjeman was married, had a mistress and was able to lead the life of a bachelor, then 43 Cloth Fair was what made this possible, and it was here that Betjeman the bachelor flourished. Without it, the rival claims of the two women in his life, and the guilt and depression which they induced, would very likely have sent him mad. In the new regime, in which he was his own master, the rival claims of wife and mistress could be set in perspective, often seeming, when they became complicated, like 'noises off' when compared with the central concerns of his life in this place. Number 43 Cloth Fair was his centre of operations, as a writer, as a campaigner against architectural wrecking, as a poet, as a friend of literally hundreds of people, as a broadcaster and public celebrity, as a Christian man doing good deeds by stealth. This last is worth mentioning at once in the context of his move to Cloth Fair. A few minutes' walk from the house is the hospital, founded in 1123, of St Bartholomew. His daughter Candida tells us that on Thursdays, he would disappear and tell no one where he went. He never discussed it with anyone, and she only discovered what he was doing years later – though Penelope evidently came to hear of it.

Soon after he moved to Cloth Fair, and started attending the Church of St Bartholomew, he asked the chaplain, Mr Bush, who was rather evangelical (JB enjoyed calling him *Father* Bush, though not to his face) if he might do hospital visiting. He was then introduced to Sister Mary Bland, a legendary ward sister who worked at Bart's for more than thirty years. ('She was madly loved by everyone', remembers a colleague, 'and was also a Christian.') Mary Bland recalled,

> John used to come and have coffee in my room every Thursday
> morning and then go round and visit the patients in my ward. He was
> able to make all the patients laugh – he was a wonderful mimic. He
> much enjoyed the names we had for the sisters. Nobody ever knew
> the real names, I was in fact Sister Percival Pott which was the name
> of my ward and John was intrigued by this. He named the Sister who
> was in charge of all the cleaning ladies, 'Sister Floors' and the Sister in
> charge of the skin department in the outpatients, 'Sister Skins'. He
> would say, 'Please can I go and see Sister Skins'. I think because of his
> horror of death it helped him to see dying patients.

Some of these were children. David Johnson, for instance, a patient in the Percival Pott Ward, was twelve years old and suffering from bone cancer when Betjeman started to visit him. As well as visiting the child, both in hospital and at home in the Vale, Hampstead, Betjeman also wrote him letters, full of drawings and jokes.

This reads the same backwards and is the longest sentence of its kind to do so which I know of – LIVE DIRT UP A SIDETRACK CARTED IS A PUTRID EVIL. The secretary of the Royal Fine Art Commission who is travelling with me [the letter is written in the train from Doncaster] and to whom I showed this sentence said did I know what Napoleon said when he was defeated? I expect you do. It was ABLE WAS I ERE I SAW ELBA. The skill of that one is that the words themselves fit. He also asked what was the first remark made by a man to a woman. And when I said I don't know, he told me it was, MADAM, I'M ADAM.

David Johnson died two months after reading this letter. Betjeman continued to visit and write to his family for years afterwards.

If his hospital visiting was one of the things he kept most private, Cloth Fair was also his home during the years of burgeoning fame as a public broadcaster. From this place he must have scripted and planned hundreds of wireless talks and television films. In 1955, he made twenty-six short films for Jack Beddington at Shell in a series called 'Discovering Britain', each one a brilliant piece of topographical analysis, and each one strengthening his confidence in the medium. George Barnes at BBC Television, envious of Shell for having milked so much of Betjeman's knowledge and energy, signed him up for similar topographical and architectural programmes, while also using his larky talents as a clown taking part in entertaining quiz shows and now forgotten studio-discussions. Naturally, the studio-buffoonery, what Betjeman called 'money for jam', was better paid and less hard work than the filming, which insisted on long hours on a tight budget. As was always to be the case, Betjeman found his temper fraying after the very tiring business of fronting a television film. After a visit to Cardiff Castle for the BBC, Betjeman returned the contract unsigned as a protest at the mean fees and the appalling treatment he believed himself to have suffered at the hands of the producer. He asked them to send the money to his old friend

Canon Freddy Hood, now vicar of St Mary Aldermary in the City, for his fabric fund.

> I am doing this as a protest against the disproportion of your television fees. If I take part in that delightful programme *Where on Earth?* there is virtually no rehearsing and I am given a good meal free, and even if I am asked to appear on the Christian Forum in the Isle of Wight there is virtually no rehearsing and I am offered eighteen guineas. Yet I had to make two visits to Cardiff in connection with the televising of the Castle, spend three nights in the city and rehearse almost the whole of Sunday. Between the final rehearsal at 6.15 and the programme at ten o'clock, I was offered not even a cup of tea, and only through the kindness of one of the local officials not appearing in the programme, did I manage to get a glass of beer at a club. Therefore I feel that either the standard of fees for doing things like *Where on Earth?* should be lower, or else that the fee for the extra work and specialist knowledge required over Cardiff should be higher.

John Piper used to say that he had seen two of his best friends being corrupted by television, Betjeman and Kenneth Clark. There is no doubt at all that television exacts Faustian compacts of its adepts. The 'better' the TV personality, the more the medium will ask its price. Those of us who enjoyed Betjeman on television – and speaking for myself, I enjoyed watching him more than anything I have ever seen on the small screen – are grateful for the sacrifice. But telly fame does not come without strange personal costs, and what is sinister about TV work is that those who are successful at it do not entirely realise what it is doing to them until it is too late.

At this time, Betjeman was often on jolly programmes with Gilbert Harding, a man who in the 1950s was probably one of the most famous broadcasters in England. Harding, a bulbous-eyed, moustachioed figure who looked like the most terrifying of head-masters, was used by the BBC as their stage 'angry' man. He was alcoholic, and if his producers could control the intake of drink, so that he was tight but not incapable when he went on air, entertainment could be guaranteed. The entertainment was surely morally on a par with those Bedlams in the eighteenth century who displayed the demented inmates to Sunday visitors. Harding's pathetic autobiography tells of his modest origins, of the cleverness which took him to Queens' College, Cambridge, and the piety which led him to study for the Anglican priesthood at Mirfield. It also chronicles his conversion to Roman Catholicism and his obsessive devotion to his mother. This was made clear to a wide audience in a programme called *Face to Face*, an interview-series in which John Freeman, editor of the *New Statesman*, subjected figures of the day to inquisitorial cross-examination. By reducing the normally belligerent Harding to tears at the very mention of his mother, who had just died, Freeman and his masters the Bedlam proprietors must have felt they had scored a particular triumph.

Harding's outbursts on radio and television were electrifying. 'As a priest of the Church of England', began one member of the public on *Any Questions?* . . . 'Sit down sir, you are no priest!' yelled back Harding.

Harding was very much Betjeman's sort of person, a vulnerable monster haunted by demons, a kind of Evelyn Waugh without the talent. A true friendship sprang up between the two men, and it is a token of how famous Harding was at that period that Candida used to boast to her schoolfriends that 'My dad knows Gilbert Harding'. He is forgotten now, as are almost all the men and women who ever made their name on television. In his autobiography, he of course makes no mention of his alcoholism or of his self-hating homosexuality, which led him into all kinds of humiliating scrapes. But did Betjeman, with his highly developed emotional intelligence, sense the danger of television work?

In the year that he moved to Cloth Fair, 1954, he appeared on *Desert Island Discs*, the radio programme in which a distinguished person imagines himself/herself as a castaway, marooned with eight favourite records, and a luxury. It is an exercise which often reveals the inner person more startlingly than a probing interview. When Roy Plomley, the inventor of the show, approached Betjeman, he received a very characteristic refusal at first. Betjeman pointed out to Plomley that 'Miss Howson, the stained glass artist lives in your road' (Deodar Road, Putney) and then said that he could not appear on the show, first because he had already recently been on a records request programme on the wireless, and secondly because 'Don't forget I'M NOT MUSICAL . . . "Tea for 2" is the kind of thing I like.' In the event, he did come on the show. Bach's *Jesu Joy of Man's Desiring*, arranged by Myra Hess, and Weber's *Der Freischütz* were the only really musical items he chose. He had country and town railway sound effects, the bells of Thaxted Church in Essex (the parish where the communist Anglo-Catholic vicar Conrad Noel hoisted the red flag on the tower), and the Padstow Obby-Oss ceremonies. His luxury was the lower half of the west window of Fairford Church in Gloucestershire.

Those who met Betjeman during these early years at Cloth Fair were struck by his air of perpetual business, his 'constant rushing here and there'. This wasn't surprising, since television work is demanding of time, and he was still doing a great deal of written journalism, as well as continuing his ever-expanding and ceaseless socialising. He was hyperactive, throwing himself fully into every enthusiasm which took him, whether it was developing a new friendship, saving a building, or finding a new place which excited him.

The rootedness in England which all this suggests was completely real. The fact that he loved Cloth Fair and the heady excitement of living in the middle of London with its opportunities to meet hundreds of new people, did not diminish the delight he took in Wantage.

Some new Wantage friends were a married couple called the Martins. Peter was a failed actor who dealt in antiques and his wife Dorothy, who aspired to be literary, ran a small lending library (sixpence a book to borrow). In imitation of the Catholic bookshop in Oxford which doubled as a café, Betjeman suggested that the Martins open a sort of C of E rival in Wantage, and rented an upstairs of a chemists shop on a traffic island. Dorothy took over the ground floor; the chemist went upstairs. The Martins' bookshop-cum-café was named King Alfred's Kitchen.

The business was a failure. Neither of the Martins could really cook, and Penelope, occupied with a duck farming venture which she had started at the Mead, was asked to help them train up some-one to provide meals. The Martins were buying nut-and-date loaves at the baker's opposite, removing the labels and selling them in King Alfred's Kitchen as 'Home Made'. Melodramatically, Penelope told Betjeman that if the truth leaked out it would destroy his career as a professional Anglican. She held before him the terrible example of Professor Joad, a philosopher who had shot to fame during the war as a broadcaster on a programme called the *Brains Trust* and who had then been disgraced when it had been discovered he used to forge his railway season ticket.

By the time the Martins had drifted off – Mr Martin to do a job at Culham, the atomic research station – Penelope was left with responsibility for the café. She found that Betjeman had signed a 'repairing lease' for the property and was liable for the cost of refurbishment when the floor of the upstairs café collapsed.

In 1956, when the whole place had been rebuilt, King Alfred's Kitchen was reopened by Father Trevor Huddleston, CR. Huddleston must have begun his career as a monk at Mirfield in Yorkshire at about the same time that Gilbert Harding was studying for the priesthood at the theological college there. Haunted by demons, as so many of Betjeman's friends and heroes were, this Anglican monk had written an unforgettable exposure of the South African regime in his book *Naught for Your Comfort*. Back in England he was restless, never particularly happy as confessor and spiritual director to Anglican nunneries and devout upper-class ladies, though this was one of the roles thrust upon him – hence his presence in Wantage as a spiritual director at the convent. His obsessions – with Africa, boys, the insufficiency of his Church's sympathy with him, religious doubt – make Huddleston the subject of, to date, at least two fascinating biographies and at least one fictitious exploration of his complicated nature.

Undoubtedly with the unhappiness went a profound spirituality and a near-sanctity. Betjeman would have been especially attuned to all this. As the lantern-jawed, skinny monk, with his deep-set eyes and his hypnotic voice, blessed King Alfred's Kitchen, many who crowded in to witness the spectacle must have felt little lower than the angels in the teashop's ingle-nook.

Inevitably, Penelope had painted 'Burnt cakes a speciality' on to the signboard for King Alfred's Kitchen. The enterprise lasted until 1961, when Penelope sold the 'caff' as she and Betjeman always called it. She was a good cook, and prided herself on giving value for money, offering four-course lunches for 3*s* 6*d*, in 2002 terms, by the standards of the retail price index, £2.69 per head. By this means, she could soon have the caff running at a loss, which, together with the cost of the repaired floor, guaranteed that more money would be wasted.

Meanwhile, in London, passing the showrooms of the Utility Vehicle Centre in Great Portland Street, perhaps on his way to admire the underground station designed by C.W. Clark in 1920, he spotted a Peugeot shooting-brake. 'My dear, dear Beddy', wrote Penelope in despair to Jack Beddington, 'PLEASE PLEASE PLEASE stop Johnny getting a Peugeot shooting brake. It is a real luxury car and FAR ABOVE OUR STATION. It may as he says only cost £800 [£12,281.26 in 2002 by the retail price index] but there is £300 purchase tax on top of that: total £11,00.' She meant £1,100. They bought the car, even though she had wanted a Morris Traveller. She was always worried by what she perceived as her husband's extravagance. 'John, in his new role as nouveau riche ordered, to my horror, 100 rock plants from Sutton's with two men to plant them. Among them were some frightful dwarf trees which I struck at and have dug up again', she complained a couple of years after the Peugeot purchase. As someone whose favoured tipple was ginger beer, she was always dismayed by Betjeman's generosity with alcohol. 'Loovely weather fer yer films', she wrote when he was out and about during the late 1950s. 'Yew as poured 1 doz bottles of Manzilla down the throats of the clergy since you got it 2 months ago. There was not a drop anywhere for Major Dent. He & she came to dinner last night to see my slides.' One can be sure that the Dents were not offered any alcohol with their well-cooked meal in Betjeman's absence.

They were the parents of Anita Dent, who worked as Betjeman's part-time secretary until she was married in 1957. She asked Betjeman to propose her toast at her wedding, which he did, but not before warning her, 'Penelope says it is *very middle class* to have a toast at a wedding. If you must make this mistake I will be honoured to commit the solecism for you.' In 1958, he took on another young secretary, Victoria (Tory) Dennistoun, a beautiful mischievous-faced person aged a little less than twenty, who lived with her parents at Antwick Stud House, Letcome Regis, Berks. She came on the recommendation of Molly Baring, promising, 'I am pretty hot on ecclesiastical affairs but am afraid I have forgotten most of my horse knowledge and know absolutely nothing about geese!'

It was a winning job application, guaranteed to appeal to her employer. They soon became friends. 'Have you done it yet?' he asked several times, and when the answer was 'Yes', he took her out to lunch at Coltman's, near Cloth Fair, to celebrate. She confesses to being a 'hopeless' secretary. 'Sometimes he would sigh and gaze wistfully at a photograph on the mantelpiece of a pretty girl, saying, "Oh, for Freckly Jill."' Archie the teddy bear gazed down on their work, and, she recalls, probably saw her forget to turn off the

Stenorette tape-recording machine which Betjeman used to dictate letters. 'I always suspected it was the cause of the fire which nearly destroyed the house', she says, 'but John never blamed me.' The fire caused such damage that Betjeman had to move out of Cloth Fair until it was put right. He was offered temporary accommodation by the son of one of his oldest friends, Anne, Countess of Rosse.

She was the sister of the designer Oliver Messel, and she will always be associated with beautifying or preserving two outstandingly interesting houses – Nymans, the estate in Sussex acquired by her Darmstadt-immigré stockbroking grandfather, and 18 Stafford Terrace, which had been the home of her other grandfather, Linley Sambourne, a celebrated *Punch* cartoonist. Her bachelor uncle Roy Sambourne kept this place entirely untouched by twentieth-century tastes or conveniences, so that when he died in 1946, she decided to keep it exactly as it had been since the mid-Victorian period. She and Betjeman, on the strength of this experience, founded the Victorian Society, with the aim of preserving and celebrating the best of Victorian taste and architecture, at that period wholly out of fashion. Anne Messel, whose character perhaps suggested something of Rosie Manasch in Anthony Powell's *A Dance to the Music of Time* – 'the lively, gleaming little Jewess in a scarlet frock' – was very much part of the London social scene when Powell, Betjeman and friends were coming down from Oxford in the late 1920s, early 1930s. Her marriage to Ronald Armstrong-Jones, a barrister of Welsh gentry background, was dissolved in 1934, and thereafter she married the sixth Earl of Rosse, who belonged to that category most beloved of Betjeman, the Irish peerage. (When she was being shown a tumbledown cabin where one of her husband's peasant tenants eked out a lowly existence, the man apologised for its rude simplicity. She exclaimed, 'My dear, don't change a thing!')

Her son, Antony Armstrong-Jones, was beginning to make a name for himself as a photographer, and by the late 1950s he led a raffish, Bohemian life, much of it centring around pubs and bars in the East End – most notably, the Waterman's Arms on the Isle of Dogs – run by his fellow photographer, Daniel Farson, who liked mixing artists, aristocrats, rough trade and sailors. Antony Armstrong-Jones fixed up for Betjeman to stay in a room in Rotherhithe Street, overlooking the River Thames. The friend, a journalist called William Glenton, was delighted by the 'beaming, well fed, almost Pickwickian figure of John Betjeman who . . . looked in no way like the conventional idea of the threadbare starving poet'. When Betjeman saw the room, and the river-view from it, he was as excited as a schoolboy and exclaimed, 'Oh, how jolly! This is going to be fun! I shan't want to go back to my own place!'

About two weeks after he had gone back to Cloth Fair, Betjeman made a reappearance at Rotherhithe, but this time he was not alone. He was accompanied by Tony Armstrong-Jones and by Elizabeth Cavendish. From this moment on, 'Tony's Room' changed its function in Glenton's house. Hitherto, it was a room which the young photographer had used to entertain a whole gang of Chelsea friends. Now it was to become a secret place known only to a few. There was a fishnet hammock in the corner of the room, into which Armstrong-Jones jumped lithely. Then Betjeman had a go, heaving his way in and out of the swinging bed, and then to Glenton's surprise – partly because he was in awe of her title, partly because she was so tall, and partly because her bearing was so dignified and old for her years – Lady Elizabeth too leapt into the hammock, but went right over the top and crashed to the floor on the other side. The second time, she succeeded in getting in, 'and she lay sprawled its full length like a highly bred saluki dog'.

There was a reason for the trio making their visit. They had been casing the joint and making it ready for the use of Armstrong-Jones's latest love. Some weeks later when Glenton came into the house, he met Elizabeth coming downstairs, who said she had just come in to 'tidy Tony's room'. Glenton noticed that some lilac-coloured lavatory

Princess Margaret and Antony Armstrong-Jones at the Badminton Horse Trials,
two weeks before their wedding

paper had been put in the loo. The large car waiting outside belonged
to Princess Margaret.

Betjeman and Elizabeth his girlfriend had seen the princess
through the upset of her decision not to marry Group Captain
Townsend in 1955. It was even said at the time by those 'in the
know' that Elizabeth had helped the princess draft her famous
public statement, of 31 October 1955, that she was renouncing
the group captain, 'mindful of the Church's teaching that Christian
marriage is indissoluble' and conscious of her duty to the

Commonwealth. If it is true that Elizabeth, or even Betjeman, had anything to do with the wording of that statement then it was indeed what some call an irony, given their own situation. Now, a few years on from the Townsend affair, Betjeman and Cavendish were once again at the heart of Princess Margaret's emotional life. On 26 February the Queen Mother announced the engagement of her 'beloved daughter' to Antony Armstrong-Jones, who later became the Earl of Snowdon. (Evidently they either had forgotten or did not agree with King George V's diktat that royal personages do not become engaged, they are betrothed.) The wedding of the Joneses, as John and Penelope Betjeman called them, took place on 6 May 1960.

⎇ ⎇ ⎇

The first five or six years in 43 Cloth Fair represented a peak in Betjeman's popularity as a poet which few of his loyal friends, who had purchased the privately printed *Mount Zion* in 1931, would have been able to predict. John Betjeman's *Collected Poems* were published in 1958, with a preface by his old friend Freddie Birkenhead. Though he had known Betjeman since Oxford days, there was something a little surprising about this choice, rather than, say, Tom Driberg, Evelyn Waugh, John Piper, Osbert Lancaster, Maurice Bowra or John Sparrow, all far more distinguished than Birkenhead, and all closer friends of Betjeman. But Birkenhead was the brother of the man who had introduced Betjeman to his new love. And he was a friend of Elizabeth's. *Collected Poems* sold at a rate of 1,000 per day in the month before Christmas 1958, and altogether, world-wide, it was destined to sell two million copies. A prize set up in memory of Duff Cooper by his widow Lady Diana, which had previously been given to Winston Churchill, was given in that year to Betjeman. The judges were all friends of Betjeman – Harold Nicolson, Maurice Bowra and Lord David Cecil, Elizabeth's uncle, and the prize was presented by

Princess Margaret, so the whole occasion was what some would describe as a bit incestuous.

'Don't buy my collected verse', he urged R.S. Thomas. 'I'll send it you. It's nothing like as good as your poetry.' He meant that.

'How nice of you', Betjeman wrote to his old friend Bryan Guinness, 'to write to me about my temporary success at poetry. I set no store by it. The slump in me will start in a month or two. But I can say, in the depths of it, that I have at least had my day. And your boom will Arrive.' He wrote from the Mead adding that 'we are all well'. But this was only ever true, from now on, up to a point.

There is no doubt that Betjeman felt, in retrospect, that he had been a neglectful father, especially to his son. Both Penelope and Betjeman himself derived pleasure from embarrassing the boy when he was at Eton by turning up on grand occasions such as the Fourth of June, wearing ragged clothes, old macs and battered hats. Eventually, he actually asked them not to visit him at school and embarrass him in front of his friends. After National Service, Paul got into Trinity College, Oxford to read Geography and increasingly began to go his own way. Betjeman was continually hard on him, as if genetically compelled to replicate the destructive rows he himself had had with Ernie. 'You're half my age and a twentieth my intelligence', he once raged at the Powlie, words which the son unconvincingly claims 'weren't offensive, because it was truthful'.

Candida, who would be allowed to leave school (St Mary's, Wantage) at fifteen, was a worry to her mother. Her printed memories of both her parents are loyal, while not being untruthful. She remembers a father who always took them to the Crazy Gang at Christmas time, who made jokes, who accompanied her to church in Wantage every Sunday while her mother went to RC Mass, who stuck up for her schoolfriends when they might otherwise have been expelled by the nuns, and who was in every respect an ideal Dad. Obviously she had a much closer relationship with her father than Paul did, but even so his frequent absences placed a great burden on

THE MEAD WANTAGE BERKS

34

TRINITY SUNDAY 1956

DARLING WIBZ ⊕ . I AM WRITING THIS IN THE
SUNK GARDEN IN FULL VIEW OF YOUR BEDROOM
WINDOW AS YOU CAN SEE ⊕⊕ IT IS LOVELY
& HOT & I AM VERY SAD THAT YOU ARE NOT
HERE BREATHING BUBBLE GUM OVER MY
SHOULDER AS I WRITE ⊕⊕ I RATHER LIKE
THE PICTURE OF APPLE BLOSSOM BY MISS LITHIBY

Trinity Sunday, 1956

[229]

Penelope, who, like most mothers, bore the brunt of the difficulties during Candida's moody adolescence. 'I go to London for telly on Sunday', he wrote to 'Darling Wibz', 'on the Great Western Plymouth to Paddington.' 'No peace when the Devil drives. I sometimes think I am sold to the Devil . . . No peace is left and you feel you are wasting the joy of being alive' — a better definition of television work was never written. But while he was rattling on trains with such thoughts, Penelope was at home, having the usual mother-daughter difficulties, only not usual because she had them at Penelope levels of high volume and overstatement.

> *LENTEN THOUGHT* I hate my daughter
> I hate her friends

> Therefore I will give her MONEY to lead her own life and keep out of the way as much as possible.

> IS THIS RIGHT???? WE have to answer to GOD ON THE JUDGEMENT DAY FOR OUR CHILDREN AND AS YOUR PRESENT ATTITUDE STANDS YOU WILL BE GUILTY OF GROSS NEGLECT.

So she wrote to Betjeman.

> All your hospital visiting and holy talks and inspiring people with religious sentiments through your poetry and other good works are worthless compared with what you owe your children and don't give them. Candida so often says, 'Daddy never comes home now. I am frightened of him when he goes on about hating my friends.' MY GOD HALF OF THEM DRIVE ME POTTY TOO but it is one's plain DUTY to provide a home background where she can bring them and entertain them. I know I like being here and enjoy having them until they drive me silly as last Sunday. But you MUST be here sometimes and HELP and SUPPORT me . . .

There were some levels on which Tewpie and Plymmie would always be at one, always sharing their distinctive enjoyment of remaining distinct from the rest of the world. This was particularly true when, astoundingly, they agreed to a proposal, which came via Stephen Spender, that he should spend a month being Poet in Residence at the University of Cincinnati and she go with him. This was precisely the way Spender loved passing his time, but one almost feels that the Betjemans, with their screams of horror about everything in America, especially the central heating, had gone to 'Cinci' simply in order to have another 'hilarious' incident to relate to their friends. 'I long to see you and Wantage again – my goodness I do', Betjeman wrote to Wibz. 'Don't forget Mummy and me. We think of you a lot and envy you *even* at school' – and to his secretary Anita Dent: 'This place' – Cincinnati – 'is HELL, an unrelieved hell, worse than Penelope and I thought it was going to be.' While he was away he wrote to 'Feebleness' every day.

Now, everything the Betjemans did, whether together or apart, reminded them of the difficulties of the triangle. Sometimes it was Feeble's turn to say she had had enough, and to break things off with Betjeman. He would write mournful poems about it – such as 'The Cockney Amorist' – and then it would be

> *Ausgang* we were out of love
> *Und eingang* we are in.

That one, 'In the Public Gardens', was written after a tour of Germany with Elizabeth, and her sister and brother-in-law, Anne and Michael Tree.

But the divided life was not without its cost. When Penelope, for example, had undertaken to have some French children, the Lurots, to stay, and Betjeman let fall that if they were in the house, he would not want to come home to Wantage for Christmas, it provoked one of Penelope's most alarming tirades, typed at furious speed on 20 December 1956 at the Mead, Wantage, Berks. One of the most frightening things about it is that it is in English rather than in Plymmie-ese, and the spellings are more or less orthodox, a token of how deadly serious she was.

Darling Tewps, If you won't come down for Christmas with the Lurot kiddies then DON'T. I am FED UP WITH YOUR BULLYING FOR NEARLY THIRTY YEARS AND AM AT LAST GOING TO TAKE A STRONG LINE. I have NEVER been able to have my friends to stay at Uffington, Farnborough or Wantage without a row. Dr Betty about once at Uff and after that always when you were away. I take all your new friends to my bosom, eg, the Demants, the Penning-Rowsells etc. etc. and get to like them then YOU get bored with them and play hell if I go on asking them to meals. I have had all your friends like Philip [Harding] Hanbury [Sparrow], Maurice [Bowra] to stay and/or meals whenever you have wanted them and mine and the kiddies mostly when you are away.

YOU ARE ABSOLUTELY MAD. Some silly sec rang up to-day and said, 'This is just to confirm that Mr Betjeman is going to the opera at Covent Garden tomorrow with Lord Drogheda'. You HATE opera. You have simply got yourself into a rich smart set with which you have little in common bar literary sympathies with the Cavendishes. Your LIFE IS NOT YOUR OWN AND IF YOU DO NOT CALL A HALT VERY SOON YOU WILL GO OFF YOUR ROCKER. You DARE to suggest that you cannot afford to feed two Frog kiddies when you must have spent about £15 on Christmas cards which are a SIN when they are such a waste of money; and had you had Maurice or Patrick or Philip to stay would have spent £20 on drink. As it is I am just getting a case of Coke in for Antoine, and P[owlie] will not be here so it will be QUITE unnecessary to offer A anything to drink except on C. Day when you always open a bottle for the Miss Butlers. We are not getting any more or less invitations because of the frog kiddies. The Barings have decided to give up their evening party on Chr Day as Dezzie is trying to economize on drinks VERY sensibly. They are just having a few intimate chums into drinks before Ch Day luncheon and will be delighted if you and Wibz and Antoine (Anne likes him very much) and Marian go while I am cooking. Nic to my great surprise says she would like to have A and Marian to cold supper on Chr night as the P. and Maurice won't be with us so she will have room for us five. The Stockings have invited us up on Boxing Night with Mr and Mrs King to sing Aussie songs. I KNEW you would like that, otherwise no outings thank God. Our daily cannot come for THREE DAYS AT CHRISTMAS as her husband will be home and does not want her to go out and she is much richer than us so does not need the money. Therefore I shall be VERY grateful for the help of the frogs as little Marian is very domesticated and Antoine is going to take the ENTIRE CHARGE OF MY HORSE which will be a GODSEND.

As always in their marriage, it was Penelope who made all the arrangements, and kept the show on the road. But this outpouring, with all its capital letters and all its anguish, goes much further than one of her usual outbursts. It screams with the painfulness of Betjeman and Elizabeth now being regarded as a couple by Princess Margaret and her friends. For all its anger with an errant husband, and heartbreak for a lost love, it also grieves for a Betjeman who is spoiling himself, wasting his time and his talents, frittering life away.

Re money it is idiotic to go and worry yourself sick over it. I shall give you SIX MONTHS IN WHICH TO GET OUT OF YOUR CAVENDISH ENTANGLEMENTS and fulfil your various commitments in London after which you must chuck up the flat and Sec and live BETWEEN HERE AND CORNWALL. STOP all this TV and stuff which you repeatedly tell me does not pay: make it your WHOLE OBJECT IN LIFE TO *GET OUT OF THE PUBLIC EYE*. Not until you are FORGOTTEN for a bit will you write anything worth while again. You are not living: you are EXISTING. Cut down the money you give me and I will sell some shares until such time as I can make some money writing myself *which I feel confident I can*.

Yewrs very truly Plymstoine

I WILL TAKE NO HALF MEASURES. I AM *FED UP* WITH YOUR DIVIDED LIFE AND COMPLETELY FALSE SET OF VALUES. Have the GUTS to tell your smart friends that you are tired of the rush and worry of London and that you are clearing out *AND WISH TO BE LEFT ALONE*.

DON'T PANIC ABOUT MONEY IT IS NOT WORTH IT. We cannot sell the Caff until the credit squeeze is over which I am told will last six months. After that if we DO sell it we will invest some of the capital in cutting this house in half and letting the front half as planned. I feel it is a better investment than any stocks and shares which go up and down. If we leave this to the kiddies with THREE little places to let furnished: two parts of this house and eventually G's cottage, it could bring in an income of £1000 p/a at least.

If you INSIST in going on with the London racket and Elizabeth and the Jones' then I shall ask for a legal separation and once Wibz is married I shall go and live in Spain on £300 p/a. But I don't WANT to do that. I would far rather we lived here WITHOUT a Tel. But WITH a Spanish maid to give ME time to write: and WITH an efficient woman sec daily to deal with your correspondence. Then I could go and ride round Spain for Sept and Oct each year and write about it and you could go to lots of places you want to see for British Council and/or to Cornwall where you have plenty of friends all round you.

But I'M DAMNED if I am going on with you in this perpetual dichotomy with insomnia, hysterical nerves, fear of losing your reputation etc., etc. We have both got only another 20 years to live if all goes well with our health and we are not run over by a bus or killed in a motor accident, and it is simply not worth being as MISERABLE AS YOU ARE OWING TO PHOBIAS LISTED ABOVE. Take it or leave it.

ELIZABETH OR ME.

Yewrs very truly Plymstoine

But he could not take it or leave it, and that for a reason which could only put terrible strain on all three of them, when things went badly, though of course it redeemed the whole situation when things went well, that is, when Betjeman's mood was happy, and in the company of one or the other he could enjoy 'laughter and the love of friends'. And that reason, that complicating factor, was the unbudgeable love he felt for Penelope. This was not a marriage which came unstuck because he fell in love with another woman, and which therefore ended in separation and estrangement. It was a marriage in which he never fell out of love with his wife, but in which he also loved another woman. While loving Penelope, he had fewer and fewer interests in common with her, whereas in Elizabeth's company he could not only see people he liked, he could worship with the woman he loved in the church they both loved together, and indulge in such harmless pleasures as golf. 'Dear, feeble Elizabeth and I did eighteen holes on a Municipal Putting course in Fulham Palace Gardens before she went away with her Little Friend.' One of his closest confidants, a priest called Harry Jarvis who came to work as his secretary after Tory Dennistoun got married, was quite clear about it. 'Elizabeth tried to encourage him to leave her, but he wouldn't.' What existed between him and Penelope was 'a very deep deep love . . . I don't think at any stage he wanted to leave Elizabeth – he never wanted to leave either of them in fact. I think he enjoyed dealing with the guilt to some extent.' Betjeman told Jarvis that his wife was not interested in sex any more, and that Elizabeth wanted a baby – blamed Betjeman as the years went by for not giving her this. But the situation was going to be one with which all three had to live for the rest of his life, and he would never resolve it.

What is more, it was a situation which, the longer it went on, the more social embarrassment it caused, in some cases actually poisoning friendship. Those who had enjoyed the friendship of both Betjemans felt a pull of loyalty when introduced to Elizabeth. She, therefore, very understandably preferred Betjeman to mix with new friends rather than those, such as Billa Harrod, who took a dim view of his new love. Penelope herself felt humiliated by not knowing how many of her supposed friends were actually colluding in the new arrangement. Never one to mince her words, she wrote to Michael Astor, a country neighbour, in December 1961:

Dressed for Princess Margaret's wedding

I find it hard to understand that you can invite John and me to
meals . . . and John and Elizabeth to stay together with you in
Scotland. I mean I think it indefensible to encourage a
relationship which can only bring unhappiness to three people,
most of all to Elizabeth, whose chances of falling in love with
someone unattached and making a happy marriage are becoming
remoter and remoter.

In such circumstances, especially at this date, when gay people
were firmly told their relationships were incompatible with
Christianity, when divorced people were excluded from the sacra-
ments, and even common parlance spoke of unmarried domestic
partners as 'living in sin', it would have been much easier to give up
church than to slog on with all its guilt-making complications. (Rose
Macaulay, one of Betjeman's friends and fellow enthusiasts for
Anglicanism, left behind letters which revealed a gap of thirty years
in her churchgoing, and indeed in her life of faith, because of the
sheer incompatibility of a married lover and a sacramental life.)
Some will always be puzzled by Betjeman's behaviour over this.
Others, in the Church, would explain it to themselves by asserting,
as did his old friend Freddy Hood, that the relationship with
Elizabeth was 'purely Platonic' – a judgement expressed, admittedly,
when Betjeman was old. As a judgement of the relationship from
the beginning, one priest who knew all three – Hood, Cavendish
and Betjeman – pronounced the idea of a Platonic relationship as
'twaddle'.

The doggedness of Betjeman's faith in these circumstances, his
regular attendance at Sunday Mass, almost without fail, his frequent
confessions, his Bible-readings, his prayers, are very notable. What-
ever else he was, Betjeman was a man who kept the faith.

It showed in his friendship with George Barnes, a fellow believer,
who, after becoming Principal of the University College of North
Staffordshire at Keele, developed cancer. The move of the Barneses

to Keele, taking them out of easy distance of London, might have estranged or cooled a friend who was rooted to one marital home or one workplace. But Betjeman always loved gadding about England, and Keele, whose Chancellor was none other than Princess Margaret, was conveniently close to Feeble's mother in Derbyshire, and their happy retreat at Moor View, Edensor.

'I love Stoke-on-Trent', he rhapsodised to the Commander, and to Anne Barnes, 'people in the Trent Valley are the nicest in England and the toofer, the naicer . . . When at Stoke you will love my Repton friends – the Lynam Thomases – both heavy drinkers and he the headmaster, she an ex-nurse and very pretty.'

In fact, Barnes was not especially happy at Keele, and came to regard the visits of Feeble and Little Friend there as almost the only 'escape' from the place. Of Princess Margaret, a decidedly 'hands-on' Chancellor, he wrote, 'I could not face Keele without her.' When cancer struck, Betjeman was not one of those friends who, through grief or shy awkwardness, avoided confronting the horrible reality of the situation. The letters he sent to the Commander about pain, and about dying, must rank among the most impressive things he ever wrote.

To Barnes in a nursing home, Nathan House, in Manchester, he wrote – 5 August 1959 –

My dear Commander, I am deeply touched that from a sick bed and in the space between pains you should write to me.

Like you, I've spent my life avoiding pain, mental and, particularly, physical. I only know tooth pains and have faint memories of my only other operation. I know enough however to know how awful pain is, I sometimes think it is the only thing which will reconcile me to dying – to get out of pain. But Anne is quite right. It either is or is not. And when it is not how wonderfully happy one is, even with a cream wall and beige dado which I expect you have at Nathan House. I cannot see that pain serves any purpose except to give one joy and thankfulness for not having it. And as all things on this earth have to be partly in shadow or one couldn't see them, I suppose there has to be pain. I don't think doctors know enough about pain . . . They don't seem to realise what it is. They get case-hardened otherwise matrons wouldn't use that word 'not so comfortable' for screaming agony. But Matron *did* tell me when I telephoned that you were going to get all right. That is something, even if you have to go through a few more tunnels of torture on the way.

How very rare, and how very brave it is, when speaking or writing to a sick friend to admit that 'tunnels of torture' are waiting. In another letter, he wrote:

Like sorrow it goes in waves. First a high wave of it and then it subsides and the next wave is nearly as high but not quite and the next a little less. Only when one is tired, as you are, it subsides far more slowly and being tired, you are less able to stand up to it and it seems worse. Poor Commander.

The next year, when the cancer continued its grim advance, Barnes 'told me how immensely grateful he was for having made his confession and wished I had urged him to make it in the past'. The Commander was visited by his old Repton School contemporary Archbishop Michael Ramsey, and by Father Trevor Huddleston who anointed him. Anne Barnes, a non-believer, watched these goings-on with mixed feelings. 'Though she *never* would admit it, she is greatly reconciled to the idea of a benevolent creator and the effectiveness of the Sacraments – though she calls them "magic", she admits they work', Betjeman wrote, when the Commander rallied a little after anointing. Anne, a month or so before the Commander's death, gave a different perspective. 'This morning he suddenly seized my hand & said, "this continuance of my life is utterly pointless" with a groan – backslip of the Management there I fear.' [The Management was Betjeman's word for God.]

When the Commander died, in autumn 1960, Betjeman wrote:

'Lord I am not high-minded . . .' the final lesson you taught me,
  When you bade the world good-bye,
Was humbly and calmly to trust in the soul's survival
  When my own hour comes to die.

Anne was less sanguine. 'Alas I *can't* possibly believe I'll see him again. I can believe certain things that you do, but *not* that. However, I am always open to a pleasant surprise . . . *Read Leonard Woolf's Autobiog. for some powerfully phrased views of the Management!*'

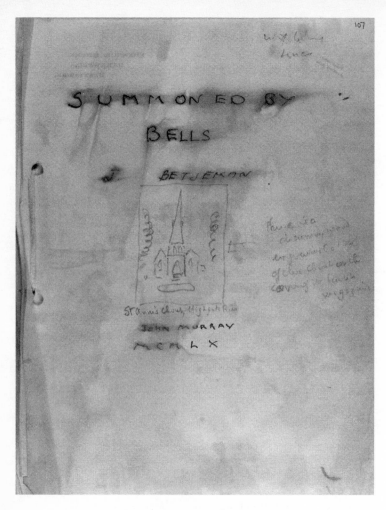

Opening page of 'The Epic'

SUMMONED BY BELLS

efore the Commander's slow, agonising death, there had been another death, which sealed off a whole area of Betjeman's past: Colonel Kolkhorst's in the autumn of 1958. As the remaining years unfolded, those who had first come to know Betjeman in the Colonel's smelly rooms in Beaumont Street, Oxford, acquired mythic status, like the few remaining members of Captain Flint's crew in *Treasure Island*, or like the Greek warriors who returned with Agamemnon from Troy. To Alan Pryce-Jones, for example, in 1976, a full eighteen years after Kolkhorst's demise, he wrote, 'Jim Knapp-Fisher has died, so have Christopher Wood, John Bryson and Colonel Kolkhorst. The Widow [John Lloyd], Crax [William Wicklow] and you and I remain with the Reverend Colin Gill on earth . . . On the other hand Osbert Lancaster is still with us.'

Colin Gill, now a clergyman and vicar of St Magnus the Martyr, London Bridge (the church which inspired Eliot's lines in *The Waste Land* with its 'inexplicable splendour of Ionian white and gold'), preached the panegyric at Kolkhorst's funeral, emphasising both the 'dark and the light' in the Colonel's character.

Crax (William Wicklow) wrote to Betjeman:

It is so hard to believe it is all over. The times we had at Yarnton – and you remember when you and, who was it, went over to Yarnton, and found the Colonel and sister with an enormous tea on the table between them. Then when you asked if the Colonel was in and were told, 'there's no Colonel here'. And I remember those wonderful

summer evenings, when the students came to dinner, with the
Colonel at the end of the table mopping his brow (you will remember
that gesture), driving shafts in to the pupils and opening his eyes
when anything doubtful was said. It is hard to believe he is gone . . .
And then there were the great days at Beaumont St; the sad thing is
that so many people are dead there can be very few people who
remember them, and so many people are scattered; do you remember
Kenneth Ewart's remarks in the Colonel's book (this mysteriously
disappeared). 'Artificial genuineness pays its tribute to genuine
artificiality'. And then the day when Rudolf Messel left and locked the
door, and the Colonel stood by the door making conversation and
pretending nothing had happened. Did you see Rudolf Messel has
died suddenly in Spain? I suppose it was heart.

And then one day (was it Andrew) Wordsworth arrived rather
gauchely at Beaumont St, where he hadn't been before, and asked if
John Betjeman was there – 'No', said the Colonel, 'but I have no
doubt he'll introduce you'. And then when we all used to sway from
side to side, calling out, 'The Colonel's tight, the Colonel's tight'.

Wicklow and Betjeman, only just past their fiftieth birthdays,
are reminiscing like Mr Justice Shallow and Falstaff recalling the
Chimes at Midnight. Ever since the early years of the war, Betjeman
had been at work on a long autobiographical poem which he some-
times referred to as the Epic. Kolkhorst's death was the final catalyst
which made him sit down and put it into publishable form, as always
with the help from John Sparrow and Tom Driberg, who cut and
altered and advised very extensively. The result was his verse autobi-
ography, taking him from infancy in Highgate West Hill to the
moment where he left Oxford and sought employment as a school-
master – *Summoned by Bells*. It is a perfect title, conveying the subject
matter exactly. As a child at school, and now as a young man trying
for a job in a prep school, his life was punctuated by the ringing of
school-bells. But equally, of course – and this is the real key and core

of the poem, and of Betjeman's life – he felt himself being led by
church bells: the bells of City churches in London, which called out
to the budding antiquarian youth 'by intersecting lanes / Among the
silent offices', and also the bells of High Church Oxford.

> Some know for all their lives that Christ is God,
> Some start upon that arduous love affair
> In clouds of doubt and argument; and some
> (My closest friends) seem not to want His love –
> And why this is I wish to God I knew.
> As at the Dragon School, so still for me
> The steps to truth were made by sculptured stone,
> Stained glass and vestments, holy-water stoups,
> Incense and crossings of myself – the things
> That hearty middle-stumpers most despise
> As 'all the inessentials of the Faith'.

'The secret of a man's nature lies in his religion, in what he really
believes about this world, and his own place in it', wrote J.A. Froude
in his *Life of Carlyle*, and it is certainly true that no one can begin to
understand Betjeman who does not see 'that arduous love affair' as
central to his existence, continued during earthly love affairs, and
after they faded or changed into affectionate companionship.

While he wrote the Epic, home life was stormy. Candida left
school, and went to Italy in the autumn of 1959. In Penelope's eyes,
Betjeman was not pulling his weight either as a husband or as a
father. On the Feast of St Michael Archangel 1959 (i.e. 29 September),
Candida's mother reported:

. . .Wibz has been misbehaving in Florence and insulting the Contessa
Marzotto . . . She now seems to have caused such disharmony in the
Marzotto household that one almost suspects there is an evil influence
at work within her and unless you as *HEAD OF THE FAMILY*, call her to
task very severely next holidays, anything may happen. You are so

weak you ALWAYS give in and start calling her Wibbly Wobbly and
laughing when she is infernally rude to me.

Meanwhile the (presumably menopausal?) Penelope had decided
that Paul, doing post-graduate research in geography at Trinity
College, Oxford, was also an enemy.

> I think it wants a sharp pulling up. I told you it arrived for lunch last
> Sunday at its own party to which it brought its very boring girl at
> *2.15pm*. I am writing to tell it that unless it does ten hours a week
> work for me sawing logs and gardening when fine next vacation and
> Easter it can stay down in its flat. I HOPE you will support me in this.
> It cannot and DOES NOT EVER work all day at its geography . . .

The prospect of Candida doing the 'season' in London horrified
Penelope.

> I think it would be far happier for all four of is [*sic*] if I retire
> gracefully to Italy within the next month . . . Wibz has been so
> terribly unkind to me since her return and you seem so dead against
> me going to London that I will retire gracefully and be very happy
> thank-you. It will do the P [that is, Paul – 'the Powlie'] the world of
> good to have to fend for itself next hols and live in cheap and
> uncomfortable digs while doing its thesis. I think it must be something
> to do with the decadence of the race the fact that most mothers
> nowadays get no support from their husbands in ticking off and
> reprimanding their kiddies. The Vicorian [*sic*] father had a lot to be said
> for him . . . I have no intention of letting C go and live in London
> with some other female while I live down here [i.e. at the Mead].
> Either she behaves properly, supported by you, and treats me with
> respect, and you must see that she does this. Or you can both make
> your own arrangements and I will leave you to it . . .

In old age, Lady Betjeman has marked this letter, now preserved
in the British Library, as 'Important'.

It is not surprising, given the fact that these were the 'noises off' while he was sitting at Moor View, Edensor, with Moucher Devonshire and Feeble, finishing *Summoned by Bells*, that the poem sees his pre-married youth in Oxford in such roseate tones. When he gave the poem to Penelope to read, she could not finish it, and even fell asleep at the first attempt, something which hurt him very much. She tried to reassure him by saying, 'Yew KNOW I have only to sit down by a warm fire after supper to go straight off EVEN WHEN I AM READING THEOLOGY.' But she could not resist adding, as if there was something odd about this, that Betjeman has a 'complex about yer poem'.

Betjeman's paranoia was stoked by the critical reactions to *Summoned by Bells* when it was published. It sold enormously. 'After a first printing of 80,000, we are furiously reprinting', crowed Jock Murray, its publisher. But the critics dipped their pens in poison.

'Tear-in-the-eye whimsicality is not poetry', wrote Julian Symons in *Punch*. John Wain in the *Observer* opined 'that so many people find Mr Betjeman the most (or only) attractive contemporary poet is merely one more sign that the mass middle-brow public distrusts and fears poetry'. It was left to Philip Larkin to salute the 'imaginative and precise evocation' of the past in the poem, and its 'splendid competence'. He rightly upbraided critics who were envious of a poet who had already sold 90,000 copies of his *Collected Poems*. He saw that 'the age has accepted him [Betjeman], in the most unambiguous way possible: it has made him a television personality', and he sees the point of the poem, namely that though the book ends in ostensible failure, 'it is really a triumph. Betjeman has made it. He has become Betjeman.'

Larkin's admiration for Betjeman was heartfelt, and it was reciprocated, Betjeman admiring the competence and control of Larkin's own verse, as well, of course, as its relentlessly pessimistic content. It should not be supposed that Larkin merely liked Betjeman as part

Larkin

of his innate Toryism. He really admired him as a craftsman, and saw how cleverly his poetry was made. At a time when confessional poetry such as Sylvia Plath's was fashionable, and the Beat poets beginning to make their mark, while sour old hangovers, imitating the great modernists but having none of their skill, tried to produce their own slim costive volumes, Betjeman and Larkin stand out not simply as two poets who were intelligible, but as two poets who valued, as all the great poets of the past had done, *form*. Larkin could also see that what made Betjeman's poetry live was an absolutely transparent sincerity.

The two men met for the first time in the spring of 1961. Larkin was surprised, finding Betjeman 'much gentler and quieter than I expected'.

Shy Larkin only appeared three times on television and twice it was with Betjeman. Patrick Garland made a memorable television film of the two poets after the publication of Larkin's *The Whitsun Weddings*. He filmed the Humber ferry looking towards Hull ('Larkin's country') and with Lincolnshire behind them ('Tennyson's country'). Afterwards, Larkin joked in a letter to his mother that the film should have been called 'To Hull with John Betjeman', but the scene of the two of them in a churchyard, seemingly vying with one another to see which could be gloomier, showed Betjeman just as keen to be a Larkin disciple as vice versa. The very fact that Betjeman misquoted a line of Larkin's, from his poem 'Ambulances' – 'So permanent and black and true' rather than 'So permanent and blank and true' – showed that Larkin's verse, albeit imperfectly, was lodged in Betjeman's head. The two were to be friends to the end of Betjeman's days. There was a side of Larkin which responded enthusiastically to clowning. He enjoyed it when Betjeman went into a bar and ordered drinks in what he thought was a North Country accent. 'We don't speak laike that here', said the ultra-genteel barmaid.

Larkin's poetic career as a laureate of provincial depression was matched in life by a need to be out of the metropolitan swim. He delighted in the fact, once he had become well known, that any 'bore' trying to visit him unannounced in Hull would have to change trains at Sheffield. Another uncompromising poet whom Betjeman greatly admired was R[onald] S[tuart] Thomas who has been described as the Solzhenitsyn of Wales 'because he was a troubler of the Welsh conscience' (Professor M. Wynn Thomas, no relation). Betjeman was drawn to Thomas's work from the time of his first publication, *The Stones of the Field* (1946). The poems confront with a directness which recalled Kierkegaard more than Solzhenitsyn the felt absence of God, but the impossibility of life without prayer. They are the confrontations of a soul waiting in silence, often in harsh Welsh landscape, and deserted Welsh churches. Some of the early poems are seen through the eyes of a Welsh farm labourer, who in his uncommunicative way has wrestled with the very moral and spiritual complexities which obsessed the mind of Immanuel Kant.

Thomas was an Anglican clergyman, another thing which endeared him to Betjeman. When anyone asked him what Thomas was like, Betjeman would reply, 'Like a dark-haired Stephen Spender if he was a priest.' His career took him into deeper and deeper rural obscurity, from curacies in the Welsh Marches (border with England) to being rector of Manafon, then of Eglwys Fach (Little Church) near Machynlleth, the seat of Owain Glyndwr's Parliament in the

Middle Ages but, by the time of the 1960s, a quiet market town in Montgomeryshire. Later still, he moved to the small parish of Aberdaron in the Lleyn peninsula.

One of Betjeman's Wantage friends, Hester Knight, recalled:

> The happiest evenings I ever spent were at the Mead when we sang or used to read poetry together after one of Penelope's excellent suppers. I remember the excitement of it, and how John would say, 'Do you know this?' And then the whole poem would come alive. And I particularly remember one morning years ago when there was a train strike on and I gave John a lift to London in my car. He had with him a copy of R.S. Thomas's latest little volume, and all the way he read extracts from it, finishing with one called 'Night and Morning' which begins, 'One night of tempest I arose and went / Along the Menai shore, on dreaming bent'. It is very short, and we learnt it by heart on the drive, and now whenever I see a seashore I remember it, and I remember that sunny morning driving into London on the old road, and John's voice, and the marvellous feeling of having been transported into a different world thanks to his guidance.

Thomas's poem 'Judgement Day' sees himself held up in a glass, indifferent to 'the claim of the world's sick / Or the world's poor', and longs for the mirror to be misted over. 'Oh thank you, thank you for your succinct, bleak, gloomy, soul-searching, memorable and terrifying "Judgement Day"', Betjeman wrote.

It was not an affectation. Judgement Day was quite real to Betjeman, and the situation in his private life now tore him between loyalty to a domestic life with his legal wife which was so often punctuated by pointless rows, or worries about the all-but-grown-up children, and the dream of peace, back in Cornwall, with Feeble.

The tremendous success of the *Collected Poems* and of *Summoned by Bells* meant that Betjeman now had money in the bank. He had always wanted a place of his own in Cornwall, and now he was able to buy Treen, Trebetherick, a house in his childhood seaside haunts.

Together but not together

His old friend Anne Channel, who lived at Rock, found it for him. 'Treen of all houses I should like best', he had told her.

It is a typical Trebetherick house. Neither Anthony Powell, who allegedly said that one of his ambitions was to live in a house with a drive, nor Evelyn Waugh, with his love of grandeur, would perhaps have seen the point of this modest, suburban seaside house with a small beautiful garden and a view across Daymer Bay. It was Betjeman's idea of the perfect house. He paid £8,000 for it; and he did so secretly without telling Penelope. At this period, it did not take much to make her angry, and his decision to keep her in the dark about so momentous a decision was bitterly hurtful – not least because she was finding the Mead a constant financial drain on her resources.

'I absolutely understand about E', she wrote to him, adding not altogether convincingly, and I am not at all jealous. But I do most *deeply* resent the fact that you bought the cottage in Cornwall without letting me know anything about it, just at a time when we need so much money spent on this property [the Mead, Wantage] and on the kiddies. It is all BUNK to say it is a good investment: you know as well as I do that one NEVER makes money on letting a house, especially a seaside one which one can let for at most two months in the year. However it is done and I wish to God I had sold this at the time when we were debating as to whether to stay on here or build a little 'contemporary' bijou residence. You said at the time that you liked this house so much you could not bear to leave it so I decided to go ahead and make it as nice as poss. But I was let in for FAR more structural work and repairs such as windowsills and repointing chimneys etc. than ever I bargained for and now I have no balance left at all. The money I got for land has just about paid for everything and the last lot I am raising from a mortgage on the house having been advised that I should stick to my ATV shares at all costs.

I keep reading and hearing how much you have made on your collected poems tho I KNOW you have to pay huge taxes on it. But it would have been nice if you had offered to give me a dress or two for this summer. As it is all you gave me at Xmas was one book of snaps, very nice horse snaps certainly but I cannot HELP feeling resentful. However if you really cannot pay for anything here I shall most CERTAINLY sell in the autumn. Your heart is in Cornwall and you had much better go there.

Yewrs very trewely and sadly Plymstoine.

To this letter, Lady Betjeman has added the note in old age, when she was widowed, 'JB bought TREEN, Trebetherick, 1960 for £8,000. He eventually made it over to E. It is now worth circa £80,000 so I was quite wrong saying it wasn't a good investment!' That was written shortly after his death. Although she threatened to sell the Mead in 1960, in fact they continued to live there, with Betjeman coming for weekends, for over a decade more.

What Osbert Lancaster had called Betjeman's capacity to live as if he were a bachelor continued in Cloth Fair throughout this period, in the intervals of more and more TV work, with its attendant travel, lecturing and speaking engagements.

In 1961, travelling commitments gave both Betjemans the excuse to spend time apart. Penelope, her children finally off her hands, could indulge the feet which, from her very first meeting with Betjeman, had been itching to travel. With a mule given her by the Duke of Wellington, she rode across Andalusia, partly in the hoof-steps or footsteps of that staunch anti-Catholic George Borrow whose *Bible in Spain* was a favourite book. The resultant volume from Penelope's pen was the highly distinctive *Two Middle-Aged Ladies in Andalusia*, a book which Betjeman genuinely and quite unpatronisingly admired. In November 1961, Betjeman visited Australia for the first time.

> One reason for going was the natural desire we all have to escape . . . besides that I was asked for November which was springtime down under. Another reason was that I would not have language difficulties which make the continent of Europe so difficult for one who has had the advantage of a public school education. The overriding reason was to see what it was like.

The visit, organised by the British Council, was a tremendous success. He visited New South Wales, Queensland, Victoria and Tasmania; he was taken on tours of Sydney, Canberra, Orange, Newcastle, Armadale, Brisbane, Mount Tambourine, Melbourne, Corio, Adelaide and Perth. The British Council afterwards reported that 'Mr Betjeman was the ideal visitor to Australia. He aroused in his audiences and acquaintances that pleasant sensation of nostalgia for "home" which is a feature of the old Australian character.' He did broadcasts on television and radio, public readings, lectures and talks. He marvelled at the beauty of the women. 'Yes', a girl in ABC make-up said to him as they were 'tarting him up' for a

Betjeman was an early fan of Barry Humphries

programme, 'we're the longest-legged English-speaking race.'

To Penelope, he wrote from New South Wales that it was like 'old Cornwall'. Orange, New South Wales was 'like Polzeath laid out on a grid system' – 'I'm *loving* Aussieland'. He loved the wild life – 'weird palm-like plants, no leaves and as big as sycamores'. He loved the exotic, 'most amazingly noisy' birds. He loved the fact that when you run the bath water out it whirls away in the opposite direction from that which it does in England. He loved the jokes, and developed a taste for a then unheard-of young comedian called Barry Humphries. He loved the religion, and found time to make a two-day retreat with the Kelham Fathers (Society of the Sacred Mission, founded Vassal Road, Kennington, 1894) in Adelaide. 'Aussieland is *much* nicer than America. The people are not boring.' Penelope wrote back to him about the infernal conditions in modern Spain. He replied, 'It's odd that I should travel thousands of miles to find Golders Green by the sea and you should go only a few hundred and find yourself back centuries.'

He told R.S. Thomas he felt

> ten years younger as the result of seeing such beautiful scenery, flowers, insects, birds, buildings and such kind and amusing people. Perhaps the best thing of all was the success of the dear old C of E there (except in

Sydney which is very low church) it is full & thriving & very friendly with R.C.s and Presbies. In fact I found my faith renewed.

Then he returned to England, and the divided life, trying to keep up the routine of weekends in Wantage, and with as many visits to the new house in Trebetherick, to Moor View, Edensor, Derbyshire, as were feasible.

For much of the time, in Cloth Fair, he was a bachelor, and could enjoy entertaining in his quite modest way. (Tins of Heinz tomato soup would be opened for guests at lunch.) He liked capricious acts of generosity and social surprises. For example, he was friends with all the Hornby brothers, who, as he knew, were fond of one another, but seldom met because they were so busy. He telephoned his stockbroker Sir Antony Hornby and asked him to lunch to meet 'someone who has wanted to meet you for some time'. And then he did the same to Michael Hornby, his Berkshire neighbour, and to the third brother, Edward Hornby, who stayed at White Horses, Trebetherick, each year. The lunch party consisted of just the four of them, Betjeman and the brothers Hornby, who were delighted, each in turn, coming into his room and finding their brothers waiting there.

'I realise', he wrote to Edward Hornby, 'how important all our companies are to each other.'

Dr Johnson said a man should keep his friendship in constant repair. For someone who was in constant demand as a public figure, presenting television programmes, travelling, giving public readings and making speeches, Betjeman's devotedness to his friends is impressive. It is only in the last decade of his life, when sickness and tiredness wore him down, that the friendships became frayed.

An example of the time-consuming activity in which he let himself be involved was the Festival of the City of London in 1962, in which he wrote and helped stage a masque, performed before the Queen at the Mansion House, starring John Gielgud, Tommy Steele and – typical of Betjeman to have included him – Randolph Sutton, a veteran of vaudeville. A newspaper reporter who attended rehearsals noted, 'Betjeman's nostalgia for his youth was immediately apparent in the advertisements from the 1920s which were flashed on a screen – Nestlé's chocolate, somebody's haircream, a poster for Noël Coward's *Vortex*.' 'And we'll throw in some Blitz noises as well', said Betjeman. 'Now what was the name of that music hall in Shoreditch High Street, Ran?' Randolph Sutton put on a topper with a flourish, answered Betjeman's question, and broke into 'On Mother Kelly's Doorstep'.

Randolph Sutton was a link with the fast-vanishing world of the music hall, one of those figures Betjeman especially cherished because they belonged to a very nearly vanished past.

The television interview Betjeman did with Randolph Sutton is one of the most memorable, giving the poet the chance to explore old Bristol (Sutton's home town) as well as indulge in his passion for the music hall. The film of Sutton in Bristol was one of a series which Betjeman made of West Country towns, including his old school of Marlborough, with 'a very nice Old Harrovian called Jonathan Stedall'. Stedall, together with Edward Mirzoeff and Patrick Garland, was one of the principal television directors with whom Betjeman did his best work.

The film about Sutton revealed that the old music-hall star had developed his singing talent as a choirboy (not surprisingly) at All Saints', Bristol, a famous Anglo-Catholic shrine – the church of which, incidentally, Betjeman's great friend Mervyn Stockwood was later the vicar. Sutton's father was a shopkeeper.

'And did you', asked Betj, 'when you were a small boy, slide down that gulley' – cut to Tuke-like boys sliding down a gully in the Downs, beneath Clifton suspension bridge – 'which has been worn smooth by a million Bristol bottoms?'

Ran was 'discovered' in a talent contest during a two-week summer holiday at Burnham-on-Sea. His most famous turn in the

Halls was 'On Mother Kelly's Doorstep'. It was a song composed by George Stephens, a man who made his living by hauling coal by day and who sat down in the Horn's Tavern, Kennington of an evening and wrote songs for which if he was lucky he got a fiver. ('There weren't royalties. A fiver was a godsend then.')

Although Betjeman is kind to the old singer, who says he has more offers of work than he can cope with, the haunting thing about the interview is that the old stager, and the tradition of entertainment he represents, is obviously as doomed as the old Bristol terraces from which he sprang. The two men, one mid-seventies, the other mid-fifties, stare down at a wrecked Bristol from the top of a fourteen-storey block. Randolph Sutton in his day was one of the most famous singers on the bill at the Theatre Royal, Bristol in the 1920s and 1930s. By the time the programme was made he was all but forgotten except by very, very old people. When he comes on the screen in top hat and tails to sing, with a flourish, the old song 'On Mother Kelly's Doorstep' the audience they have assembled to listen to him all look old enough to remember the Golden Jubilee of Queen Victoria; or even the first performances of Gilbert and Sullivan. Betjeman has once again pulled off the trick of cultivating an eccentric oddity (Kolkhorst, Bosie, Comper) and taking a snapshot of a lost England, that of the Halls.

Viewing the programme now, nearly half a century on, we can see that there is an artistic kinship between Betjeman and his hero. Telly like the Halls is an ephemeral medium. Betj was top of the bill on TV in the 1960s just as Ran was top of the bill at the Theatre Royal, Bristol in the 1920s. Such achievements get lost. You forget how very good Betj was until you see him again on DVD. Between him and music hall there is a deep bond. It is one of the sources, hymns being the other, for his poetry. He hardly drew from books, which is what make the verses so immediate. The lyric, the joke, comic monologue, all stand-bys of the music halls, these are all forms on which Betjeman drew in his poems and even if some of them are not easily imagined as 'turns' in the music hall, such poems as 'Felixstowe, *or* The Last of Her Order', about an Anglican nun living in a seaside boarding house because all the other Little Sisters of the Hanging Pyx have died out, are in fact 'monologues' in the music-hall formula.

And he continued to make new friends. (Before telling Sir Joshua Reynolds that a man should keep his friendships in good repair, Johnson had remarked, 'If a man does not make new acquaintance as he advances through life, he will soon find himself left alone.') John Osborne, the playwright who transformed the London stage with *Look Back in Anger*, became a friend. It is not hard to see why when one reads Osborne's memoirs and diaries. Osborne's celebrated play, much of it happening on a dingy Sunday afternoon in the 1950s, has much in common with the Betjeman who hymned 'dear old bloody old England'. Osborne, the shabby-genteel Fulham boy, bisexual, thrust by success into a much higher social milieu, while never losing his clear eye and his sardonic anger, had much in common with Betjeman. When the master of the double entendre, Max Miller, died in 1963 – a music-hall star whose acts consisted entirely of jokes and songs about sex, but in which he never said a 'dirty word' – Osborne noted, 'There'll never be another, as old John Betjeman says, an English genius as pure gold as Dickens or Shakespeare – or Betjeman come to that.' 'What did Trollope say – muddle-headed Johnny? It's deep honesty that distinguishes a gentleman. *He's* got it. He knows how to *revel* in life and have no expectations – and fear death at all times.'

Osborne had initially been Elizabeth's friend, but he and his wife Penelope Gilliatt soon formed a friendship *à quatre* with Betjeman and Elizabeth. They came to stay in Cornwall, and on the Sunday morning, they all four went to St Endellion's, the church where Betjeman always worshipped when down in Trebetherick. Perched on the hilltop above Port Quin, looking down into Port Isaac bay, it is a medieval collegiate church, pale grey granite, filled with light,

Betjeman attended Mass at St Endellion's regularly

and a potent, numinous atmosphere. The religion is Anglican Catholicism at its most unaffected. There is incense, the priest wears vestments, and the devotion of the church is focused on the Eucharist. 'I suppose you could say', one of the farmers who worships there once remarked to me, 'that I'm a perfectly straight down the line' – he paused, and one expected 'Church of England man'; but he said, 'Anglo-Catholic'. But it is an unobtrusive, unshowy Catholicism. It is not a place, to use Osborne's brilliant phrase, for Walsingham Matildas. When they entered their pew, Betjeman and Elizabeth were surprised to find they had not been joined by their friends. Osborne and his wife sat in the pew behind. Afterwards, Betj and Feeble realized it was because they were not sure when to stand up or sit down, and wanted to take their lead from their friends. Before that Mass, John Osborne was an unbeliever. Thereafter, he developed a religious seriousness, and the Church of England and its services were important to him.

John Osborne

When Osborne's play *Inadmissible Evidence* was staged at the Royal Court Theatre in September 1964, anyone who knew the private circumstances of Betjeman's life immediately recognised that this play was a version of it. Bill Maitland, a married man with two children, is tormented with guilt because he loves both his wife and a mistress called Liz. 'I have always been afraid of being found out' — a line which in real life Betjeman repeated like a mantra. Bill Maitland is a solicitor, obsessed by the ruina-tion of English architecture. Of a developer he says, 'I'm always seeing his name on building sites. Spends his time pulling down Regency squares — you know — and putting up slabs of concrete technological nougat. Like old, pumped-up air-raid shelters. Or municipal lavatories.'

'My dear old Top', Betjeman wrote to Osborne on 10 September 1964:

> Here, in the calm of the morning, I affirm what I said to you last night — that is a tremendous play. The best thing you — yes, even you — have ever written. Apart from the sentiments in the diatribe — which I heartily endorse — it is the most heart-rending and tender study of every man who is not atrophied. We want to avoid giving pain and we want to be left in peace. Love makes us restless and we resist it. I felt increasingly that the play was about me and that is what all the great playwrights and poets can do for their watchers and readers.

While it is true that everyone, while watching *Hamlet*, for example, is the Prince for the duration of the play, in the case of *Inadmissible Evidence*, it actually was about Betjeman, or Bill Maitland-Betjeman, as he signed himself.

Secretly proud, I showed off merrily

is one of the key lines in *Summoned by Bells*. He was a melancholic introvert with an exhibitionistic compulsion. It is a temperament which has often led to a career in the theatre. Ever since early childhood, he had both hugged to himself his inner life, his life of prayer, of wonder, of dread and depression. He had also been a natural clown, who loved attention, who wanted his poems to be performances, who, as a young man working for the *Architectural Review*, sang music-hall songs on the pavement outside cinemas, supposedly to collect enough money to see the film, but in truth to attract the attention of strangers. A television career could not have been more perfect for such a man. And yet, as always with those who wish to project themselves, did he want full exposure?

With a part of his nature, the answer to this question is obviously, yes. He kept a huge quantity of his correspondence – the archive of letters written to Betjeman, now at the University of Victoria, British Columbia, is enormous. His wife, likewise, kept all the records of their fights and quarrels, as well as of his marital infidelities. His hero Alfred, Lord Tennyson compared the art of biography to ripping someone open 'like a pig'. Tennyson was simply an introvert, without the exhibitionistic compulsion. Betjeman was a more complicated psychological case, and one reads in the letter to Osborne both panic and excitement that so much of his secret life had been paraded on the London stage. In life, such sailing near the wind filled the ever-timorous (as well as often exhibitionistic) Betjeman with terror. But, 'beyond the veil, beyond the veil . . .'? What does he want or think now?

Osborne's play dwelt upon the mystery of Betjeman's private

character. His continued exposure of himself on television in some ways built up a carapace by which the image could provide a mask. Since he was so good at television, it was not surprising that he was in constant demand. He said yes to most suggestions that he should appear on it, partly because it had become an addiction, a compulsion.

Penelope, free at last, had finished for the time being with her travels in Spain and had returned to India, her first and greatest love. He wrote to her regularly, as she rode 'on horseback among the jeep-infested Himalayas'. The more time they spent apart, the more their relationship changed and developed. They had been unable to stay together without quarrelling, and their paths were very different. From the beginning of their long love affair and marriage, she had made no secret of the fact that she wanted to ride about India on horseback studying antiquities, and being uncomfortable. This passion she could now guiltlessly indulge. He had wanted to stay in England, look at architecture, and see hundreds of friends. This he could now do, often with the companionship of the other woman he loved, Elizabeth. At its worst the situation was the guilt-ridden anguish of *Inadmissible Evidence*. At its best, it worked rather well for both the Betjemans, though for Elizabeth there was the grief of not being with her all-but-husband more than a fraction of the time, and not having the children she craved.

'After all the poverty you must be seeing in India', Betjeman wrote to Penelope:

> I expect there is a lot to be thankful for. Nehru was obviously a wonderful man (an Old Harrovian) and you will be able to see the papers on your return. [Nehru had just died.] Wibz had her snap in the *Daily Express* as an expectant mother. She is now mad on cooking and being a housewife and has forsworn literature it seems. I am away a lot at the moment and have hardly seen her. I go to Hull today for much of next week (the White Horse Hotel, Hull) for Telly and then to Truro for more Telly and I have to be in H[amp]s[hire] and Sussex

and Truro all on Telly. I have got a more efficient agent now who may well be able to help you. I love hearing from you and very much love you but want you to do what you feel suits you best about your book. You are truly gifted and don't know you are. Spansbury [John Sparrow] and Maurice [Bowra] have always realised this. I am so busy, I am quite happy and as I said, without you, the pull of Wantage is nought.

If the death of the Old Harrovian Nehru on 27 May 1964 was a cause for respectful remembrance, the death of T.S. Eliot on 4 January 1965 was a genuine shock. 'I feel very sad today', Betjeman wrote:

> He was an old friend and a delightfully funny man to be with, who kept one in fits of laughter with his slow, modulated stories generally against himself. The end of his life with his second wife was very happy, except for his chest trouble, and I am sure he didn't mind the idea of the next world and stepping across into it, though I much dread the process myself.

As his sixth decade drew towards its close, Betjeman was also facing not merely his own mortality, but the failures of his domestic and family life.

As their two children grew up and left home, the question of what remained of the Betjemans' marriage would pose itself with a new starkness. Candida married Rupert Lycett Green in May 1963. Their new life began. Rupert had done his National Service 'with that Guardsman's calm one expects of him', in his proud father-in-law's opinion. Candida and her husband were able to become friends with Penelope – more than Candida had ever been when she was single – and to befriend 'Darling Dadz and Liz', as she addressed the pair. Rupert had soon made a success of Blades, his fashionable tailoring business, and the pair produced five children. As young grown-ups in London, later in Wiltshire, they had a wide circle of friends, many of whom Betjeman shared. It was possible for their relationship to grow and move onwards.

Rupert and Candida Lycett Green's Wantage wedding

With Paul Betjeman, everything was rather different. After National Service in Germany, mainly with the US forces, he had gone to Trinity College, Oxford, to read Geography. It was not a subject which interested him, and he devoted more time to the saxophone than to his studies. It was gradually becoming clear to him that he wanted to devote his life to music. ('It was clear I'd earn my living as a player or a writer.') He went to New York, in the fall of 1962, without realising that he had begun a life of exile in America. Later he enrolled at Berklee School of Music (which became Berklee College of Music in 1973) in Boston, Mass. He had found his metier, and escaped the parents who had made a perpetual joke of him, calling him 'It' and 'the Powlie'. Moreover, he had begun to study music academically. His father 'didn't understand music. He wasn't a musical person', in Paul's vision, though it was with his father that Paul had begun to listen to Renaissance church music.

After Berklee, Paul had taught for a while at a prep school in Cambridge, Massachusetts. Betjeman made it clear to his son that he would not help him any more financially, and feared that Paul was 'becoming a perpetual student'.

Penelope, however, took a more sympathetic line. She saw that Paul was a late developer, who, after the 'important mistake' of reading Geography at Oxford, had only just begun to engage with things which interested him, namely philosophy and the academic study of music. He enrolled, at his

Paul

mother's expense, at the Harvard College of Education to train as a professional teacher and took a couple of courses on music history.

He joined various musical groups, and among the young musicians whom he got to know, he found some whose religious outlook awakened in him 'the beginning of the spiritual interest . . . A couple of them were very good musicians. It had a lot to do with the people around me, whom I liked. They were very vivid intellectually.' These people were Mormons. Paul's next step was to become a Mormon himself and to continue his study of music history at Brigham Young University, Utah.

It felt to the young man like a positive step in his own spiritual development; to the very publicly Anglican father it seemed like the ultimate rejection. Betjeman watched wistfully as other families of his acquaintance followed more conventional routes than Paul's. He took a great shine, for example, to R.S. Thomas's only son, who came to see him in London to ask about Magdalen College, Oxford, whither he was bound. 'He is a *wonderful fellow*', Betjeman wrote to Thomas, 'if he wants advice and thinks I can help, tell him to apply.' The next year, when the younger Thomas felt unhappy at Oxford, Betjeman wrote, '[W]hile your son is disillusioned by the Magdalen dons, mine has become a Mormon and is a student at Brigham Young University, Utah. Mors Janua vitae, and there are of course, lots of different januas to get to it.'

Betjeman had quarrelled violently with his own father. And he had himself always been obsessed by the byways of religious experience, sympathising with those who sought out strange ways to God. One of his earliest and most haunting poems was about the Sandemanian Meeting-House in Highbury Quadrant. He had himself been a Quaker. But in Paul's journey there was too strong an element of psychodrama for the father to be able to bear it easily. In old age, Betjeman liked to quote Larkin's lines, written in 1971:

> They fuck you up, your mum and dad.
> They may not mean to, but they do.
> They fill you with the faults they had
> And add some extra, just for you.

When I met Paul Betjeman in New York in November 2005, it was not long before he himself was quoting the lines, his eyes, very recognisably those of his father, filling with tears.

LAST YEARS
IN CLOTH FAIR

'In very early January 1966, Penelope had a motor accident in London, driving alone. Her head was cut, her teeth knocked out, and a rib was broken. She woke up in a dismal hospital near Kensal Green but is at last out and back to the Mead but still a bit tottery.' It was, Betjeman thought, typical of her that she implored the hospital not to telephone him in the middle of the night, but to wait until morning before telling him what had happened. Betjeman told this news to the vicar of St Augustine's, New Basford, near Nottingham, the Reverend Harry Jarvis.

There was a deep friendship between these two men. And this is one of the difficulties of describing the very full life of Betjeman as he entered his sixties. His capacity to form new friendships, and his determination to hold on to old friendships, was undimmed. It would be possible to write a whole Life of Betjeman, from 1966 to 1971, as seen through the eyes of Harry Jarvis, friends and neighbours in Berkshire, and his family, on the one hand, and with Elizabeth Cavendish on the other, with absolutely no reference to his public fame. He still continued to see old friends such as the Lancasters, the Pipers, Billa Harrod and the Barings. Church and local life at Wantage was part of his weekends. Driberg and Sparrow and Bowra still came to Sunday luncheons. And yet the fame took its toll, and, as well as constant television appearances, he also gravitated towards celebrities, public figures, televisionaries, members of the royal family. It was a tendency which Penelope had noted a good decade earlier and which she had done her best to stop, because she

BETJEMAN

felt it was wasting his gifts. It is the place of wives to wish their husbands other than what they are, but not their biographers. Betjeman was as he was. When Jonathan Stedall asked him if he did not regret spending so much time making television programmes when he could have been writing poems, he replied, 'I like to think they *are* poems.'

After the succession of female secretaries, Betjeman had turned to Freddy Hood, wondering if he could supply him with clergy who had, in Canon Hood's phrase, 'stepped aside'. This meant, stepped aside from the straight and narrow path; usually it meant getting themselves into scrapes over boys (very occasionally over women).

Betjeman had in fact first met Harry Jarvis in 1951 when he was a chaplain at Summer Fields, the prep school in North Oxford. Towards the end of that decade, Harry 'got myself into a little bit of trouble', and worked for Betjeman as a secretary for a few months. Then he was a curate at Worksop, a vicar choral at Southwell, and then the vicar of St Augustine's, New Basford, from 1965 onwards – when Jarvis was forty-five years old. In April of that year he married Jean Cunliffe, whom Betjeman called the Smasher, and they had a daughter, Rebekah, who became Betjeman's god-daughter. ('My love to the Smasher', he ended one letter. 'Kiss her downy cheeks for me, and then her full red lips.')

Betjeman would come over from Edensor, which was not far away from New Basford, and Harry Jarvis would quite often go over to Edensor. Harry Jarvis was at some stage Betjeman's confessor, but he was also the recipient of confidences outside the confessional, and it is from his very full interview with Candida Betjeman, preserved in the Betjeman papers, and largely quoted in her edition of her father's letters (Volume II) that we have such a clear picture of Betjeman's relationship with Elizabeth and Penelope. Jarvis in turn tried to counsel Betjeman –

I offered the Mass for you today and commended you to the Almighty
. . . I do offer a quick one for you every day but this was a bit more
special. I *do* sympathise with you and wish there were something that I
could say, or better still do, that would be of the slightest use or help.
Sometimes one gets caught in a lot of circs. which are completely out
of one's control and have no easy solution (even if they have a solution
at all) except death . . . At least one is normally spared the horror that
poor dear Cowper had to face that he would be carried off into hell
while still alive.

Harry Jarvis, perhaps more than any of the other counsellors,
confessors and friends, saw that Betjeman completely loved both
women in his life and was tormented by guilt at the agony this caused
them both, and himself. Any solution seemed wrong. Mindful of the
Church's teaching he could not contemplate divorce, even though
Penelope offered it. Even had his conscience allowed it, this was not
what he wanted. But nor was it thinkable that he should be separated
from Feeble, who had become his devoted companion, helpmate and
friend and whom he had allowed, for many years now, to sacrifice
the possibility of getting married and having children in order to
devote herself to him.

'Feeble is OK but v pressing about Penelope and me', he told
Harry Jarvis. 'She feels that I have deprived her of children and she
loves children and I can't bring myself to tell her that I love Penelope
as well as her.'

The Betjemans could not live together, but nor did they really
wish to face up to the implication of this fact, namely that they
should live apart. 'I had a horrid dream last night that you had
hidden yourself in a cupboard and refused to have me back',
Betjeman wrote to his wife. 'I was very offended.' She spent more
and more time travelling, especially to India. He threw himself with
manic fervour into television work and, in the recollection of his
daughter, 'could think of little else'.

It is not surprising that old friends such as the Pipers felt that he was being corrupted by television. They did not mean by this that he gave himself airs, any more than he had ever done, or that he thought of himself, as a famous person, too grand for old friends. Rather, they felt that he was dissipating his energies on stuff which was not of lasting value, and that he therefore had less time for the architectural and topographical studies, for old friends, and for poetry.

A constant leitmotiv, both of Betjeman's adult life and of his friendship with the Pipers, was the production of the *Shell Guides*. Betjeman himself rewrote his 1934 guide to Cornwall, and published it exactly thirty years later. The early self, who had been employed as a disciple of P. Morton Shand on the modernist *Architectural Review*, had been an austere guide to the duchy. Its aim had been to draw attention 'to the many buildings of the eighteenth and nineteenth centuries that have architectural merit'. The 1964 book found far more architectural merit in the great Victorians than had young Betjeman. Whereas in 1934 he had believed that Pearson's Truro Cathedral had been constructed in 'the E.E. style not suited to Cornwall . . .' and that it was no more than 'an interesting essay in the Victorian manner and the correct Gothic style', in 1964 he could see it for the masterpiece it is – 'the most interesting cathedral built since St Paul's in England'. Above all, the 1964 book breathes a love of Cornwall as a place, and not just as a setting for fine architecture. It evokes the wilds of Bodmin Moor, the beauty of slate-roofed cottages in remote villages, the smell of fish in ports, the dankness of holy wells, the sudden green of valleys such as St Kew, the deep fissures, white sands and rocky islands surrounding the granite coastline of St Levan. It is a celebration of his homecoming to Trebetherick, and of the church where he worshipped, St Endellion, 'a windswept parish high on the Atlantic coast with much to show inland and on its rugged slate coastline. The pinnacles of the granite church tower peep like a hare's ears over the hill crest and the churchyard has Georgian inscribed headstones, with particularly good rhymes on them.'

This is the essence of Betjeman. Brilliant as John Piper was, both as a painterly and a photographic eye (he photographed many of the best illustrations in the *Shell Guides*), he was primarily an artist. He was not a writer. He was a good-humoured and very lovable man, but he lacked the gifts which made Betjeman such an inspired general co-editor of the whole series, and which called forth some of the best titles in it, such as Billa Harrod's *Norfolk*, James Lees-Milne's *Worcestershire* and the Rev. Henry Thorold's *Lincolnshire*. The question of whether Betjeman went on with the *Guides* was one which he meditated with Hamlet-like agonisings, often in letters to Piper. In the years 1964-6, he wrote three very long letters to Piper all rehearsing the history of how the *Guides* came into being. 'I got a salary of £800 a year from Shell for editing and doing the make-up and writing the guides.' They were intended as 'prestige and advertising subsidised by Shell'. Of course, they became something much more than that, especially in the volumes which came out in the post-war years. Writers with a lifelong knowledge of, and love for, a particular county wrote highly distinctive and original topographical essays.

The financial situation had become problematic, it was true. By 1966, Betjeman was getting a fee of £200 a year.

> For this we are expected to find authors with money and time on their hands, as well as knowledge and ability. We are expected to brief them, and then go round the counties, seeing what they have left out and photographing places not obtainable in the agencies. Finally, we select the photographs at Fabers and decide which are to be big and which small, not forgetting that we read the proofs and alter them with the consent of the authors, when we think fit. This is all skilled work and we have hitherto done it for love of the thing because it cannot possibly pay us.

This particular dither occurred because James Lees-Milne's *Worcestershire* guide contained disparaging remarks about modern urban sprawl, roads, the proletariat, all of which might be thought offensive to 'the local authorities who may use Shell petrol'. The £200 which Betjeman received in 1966 was, by the index of average earnings, the equivalent in 2002 of £4,491.29. The 2002 equivalent of his 1934 payment of an annual £800 is £68,149.19. So Betjeman is talking about the difference between payment which is enough to support a writer's way of life, and something which is no more than a modest extra. By February 1966, he was warning John Piper that the enterprising publisher George Rainbird had, without consultation with Betjeman, appropriated the words *Shell Guide* for his guide-books to Scotland and Ireland. Meanwhile, the proper *Shell Guides*, those to the counties of England, edited by Betjeman and Piper, were altered without their permission by a combination of Faber, the publisher, and the faceless characters at Shell who wished to cut costs by reducing the illustrations, using inferior maps and even cutting the text.

Finally, on 11 March, Betjeman wrote to Piper to cut loose from the scheme altogether. 'The reason I can't go on with the Guides is purely financial. My work for the *Weekend Telegraph* and wireless and telly have to come first with me.'

In the nineteenth century, a figure such as Betjeman would probably have been given an adequate pension from the Civil List which would have been the equivalent of his old pre-war salary from Shell. As it was, in 1966, he had to make a living from journalism. There is something rather chilling, whatever the reasons, to read those words and realise they are written by the author of *Continual Dew* and *Summoned by Bells* and *First and Last Loves*: 'My work for the *Weekend Telegraph* and wireless and telly have to come first'.

He sat on so many committees that this, too, had become a burden and a chore. Many of his letters were written during meetings of the Oxford Diocesan Advisory Committee – 'Gabble, gabble, gabble – I can hear Harry Oxon [that is, Harry Carpenter, Bishop of Oxford] and the others at the end of the room taking a cup of tea with a layman'.

One of the many committees on which he agreed to sit was gathered at the offices of Lee, Bolton & Lee, Number One, the Sanctuary, in Westminster to discuss the future restorations of St Peter's, Vauxhall. One of those sitting on this committee was Canon Eric James, later well known as a religious broadcaster of a peculiarly sympathetic gentleness. The seat next to James was empty until two minutes to five, when Betjeman doddered in, took his seat, and began scribbling on a piece of paper. One of the sentences which he wrote, and shoved under James's nose, was 'Who are the Two Chairmen?' James wrote back, 'It's not two chairmen, one is the chairman, and the younger man is his secretary.' Betjeman scribbled back, 'Wrong. The Two Chairmen is a pub near here. If you have the courage to say that you are very sorry, but you have to leave, I'll come with you and we can go to the Two Chairmen.' Eric James is nothing if not courageous, and he made his excuses to the chairman of the meeting. He and Betjeman reached the pub at about 5.20 and stayed until 10 that night. It was a friendship entirely based on laughter. 'We drank quite a lot', James remembers, 'and we arranged to meet again.' 'Why not come to Cloth Fair on Christmas Eve?' Betjeman suggested to him. 'I'm always lonely on Christmas Eve.'

Opportunities to 'assemble my ideas about Victorian architecture together with slides' were provided by an invitation to give four lectures at the University of Belfast, but on top of all his other commitments what could have been an invigorating month, leading perhaps to a book, was merely 'an exhausting experience. Not very rewarding either.'

Of course, the television work which reversed Betjeman's priorities and gave him no time for church-crawling and friendships and leisurely reflection, was often itself of a high quality. In November 1966, he stayed in the American Colony Hotel in Jerusalem and made a film for the BBC about the Holy Land, visiting, as well as Jerusalem, Bethlehem and a Palestinian refugee camp.

I cannot recommend Jerusalem too highly. But this hotel is *the* place — old-fashioned, huge bedrooms, flowers and endless servants and quiet and run by Anglicized Americans.

Now this is the very odd thing about Jerusalem which makes me so glad I came. It really does make you aware that Christ (whether or not he was God is for the moment irrelevant) lived and walked here. There the devotion of centuries, despite raids by Persians, Romans, Moslems and modern conquerors, make one see that Christ was God, ie Man and God in one. And that is brought about by the churches here (Eastern Orthodox, Coptic, Syrian, Latin and the dear old C of E) all sucking honey from the rose of Jerusalem like bees. I am most surprised by how I love this city.

The love communicates itself, and nowhere more than in the sequence where the poet attends a service at St George's Cathedral and hears the words of the Book of Common Prayer. The programme was broadcast that Christmas.

In addition to the broadcasts, and the journalism, and the committee work, there was also the everlasting and ever-mounting work as the nation's most celebrated, but most exhausted, campaigner for the conservation of threatened buildings and town centres. The 1960s were a decade in which all the dreams of those early modernists, such as P. Morton Shand, were embodied in concrete, to the lasting regret of many who had supported the idea of architectural modernism in their youth.

Most of Betjeman's work, supported often by scores, hundreds or even thousands of those who loved the buildings or streets which he tried to save, was unsuccessful. He was closely associated with the campaign to save the Doric portico at Euston Station, though, as Bevis Hillier notes in his biography, apart from writing an article in the *Telegraph* about it, and speaking to the Royal Fine Art Commission and joining a deputation to the Prime Minister, Harold Macmillan, Betjeman was not the leader of that particular campaign.

Beside those spires so spick and span

Did he go easy about the Euston Arch for fear of embarrassing Uncle Harold? Macmillan, with whom Betjeman must have coincided on visits to Chatsworth, did nothing to save the arch. The portico came down in 1961, and for a whole generation it was not merely a loss in itself, but a symbol of what was being destroyed in the modernistic rebuild of Britain. Betjeman played a much bigger role in trying to rescue James Bunning's Coal Exchange (1849) in Lower Thames Street. This wonderful domed rotunda was demolished in 1962. If the campaigns for Euston and the Coal Exchange were notable setbacks, that to save Bedford Park, which began with the Bedford Park

Residents' Association in 1963, was successful. Today, the work of the Arts and Crafts architects who first built and inhabited the houses in the Bedford Park estates can be seen as beautiful.

Throughout the decade, Betjeman worked tirelessly with those who did not want to see nineteenth-century buildings replaced by modernist ones. A typical story, printed in the *Daily Herald* on 23 August 1961, occurred when thirteen-year-old William Norton tried to save the Victorian town hall at Lewisham, designed by George Elkington, from demolition. Accompanied by Peter Fleetwood-Hesketh, Secretary of the Victorian Society, Betjeman, with the inevitable shapeless hat and well-chewed cigarette, boarded the train from Holborn Viaduct Station ('arriving Catford at nine minutes past three'), clutching a large brown paper parcel tied with green string. 'A picture – a little memento for the boy', he explained.

It was a picture of one of the many memorials to Sir Walter Scott. 'This memorial to Sir Walter Scott was never put up. Let's hope that a memorial as great and impressive will one day be put up to William Norton in gratitude for his effort to save Elkington's work, the Lewisham town hall.' It was another unsuccessful campaign – Lewisham town hall was demolished in May 1962. William Norton, as well as being a thirteen-year-old boy with a passion for Victorian architecture, had another claim on Betjeman's affection. He was an Irvingite, a member of that diminishing band who belonged to the Catholic Apostolic Church. It had been founded by Carlyle's friend Edward Irving, and its most notable architectural shrines are in Albury Park, Surrey, and in Gordon Square, London where their cathedral has become the Anglican chaplaincy to the University of London. With his love of out-of-the-way Christian sects, Betjeman had a special fondness for the Irvingites, and, for example, went to visit his fellow North Londoner Helen Gardner when she was living outside Oxford at Eynsham for one last chance to see the small Irvingite church there before it was closed. He asked to visit not only the church, but also the Pym family who had been its chief pillars until some of them were converted to Roman Catholicism by the parish priest, Father Lopez (himself a convert from Anglicanism). 'Oh but *you are the one true church!*' Betjeman insisted when he met the Pyms, who ran the local shop-cum-post office. Young William Norton rose to become the Metropolitan of the Catholic Apostolics.

Probably, most of those who read these words would be on his side, nearly half a century after Betjeman's campaigns to save this and to preserve that. Most of the town planning in England during the 1960s was unimaginative, and many good Georgian and Victorian buildings were needlessly destroyed only to be replaced by non-descript lumps. In 1970, he accompanied Candida to Oving, to take part in a huge public protest against the building of a new airport at Wing, North Bucks, near the village of Olney where Cowper lamented the fallen poplars in his famous poem. Using the same rhythms, Betjeman declaimed –

> The birds are all killed and the flowers are all dead
> And the businessman's aeroplane booms overhead;
> With chemical sprays we have poisoned the soil,
> And the scent in our nostrils is diesel and oil.
>
> The roads are all widened, the lanes are all straight
> So that rising executive won't have to wait.
> For who'd use a footpath to Quainton or Brill
> When a jet can convey him as far as Brazil?

Was there a danger, as some said at the time, that by lending his voice to so many conservationist causes, Betjeman devalued the currency? 'Often', wrote Bernard Levin,

> the name of John Betjeman was attached to those appeals, and eventually Mr Eric Lyons, himself an architect, coined the phrase 'Betjemanic depressives' to stigmatise collectively those who would preserve at all costs everything from the past, be it a wrought-iron

lamp-post due for replacement in Chelsea, a Victorian church in Essex complete with its 'blue-jowled and bloody' stained glass, or the celebrated Doric portico at Euston Station.

Those words were written in 1970. From the perspective of this generation, Betjeman seems like a pioneer. So much has been wrecked, so much heedlessly destroyed that – yes, the old lamp-post in Chelsea probably is much better than anything which a modern designer could come up with, and yes, we do love the Victorian glass of a church in Essex. This shift in attitude towards conservation, as well as the incorporation of Victorian architecture into the canon of buildings which we all regard as worth saving, is part of a whole change in taste over the last generation; but if Betjeman did not achieve this shift single-handedly, he certainly was a major factor in it. To that extent, he was surely right to use the ephemeral medium of television to get the message across, even if sometimes telly is a crude weapon.

In those days, the 1960s, BBC television commissioned dozens of new plays to be performed on air each year. In 1965, Betjeman collaborated with Stewart Farrer on a satire called *Pity About the Abbey*, a play in which Westminster Abbey itself was sold stone by stone to Texas, so that the site could be redeveloped for traffic and offices. It was, Betjeman said, 'a very serious argument disguised as a comedy'. While architects and committee-bores protested to Betjeman about that play, millions of viewers saw the truth of what it conveyed. There was much about Betjeman, as he had emerged in his verse autobiography, and frequent television appearances, which must have jarred or seemed odd to 'the man in the street', especially in the 1960s. Few shared his wish that he could believe more fully in Christ's presence in the Eucharist; few – including apparently the bishops – believed in the divinity of Christ. Betjeman's love of peers, and grand houses, while striking a chord in some bosoms, would have been out of kilter with the egalitarian spirit of the times. But in

Betjeman's eye for modest station architecture

the matter of architecture, he spoke for England. While politicians such as Harold Macmillan stood silently by and allowed such desecrations as the demolition of the Euston Portico, and while the architectural 'establishment' contrived to ridicule Betjeman's views, representing them as a sort of camp joke, millions of television viewers felt that he spoke for them. They loved their Church, even if they did not pretend to believe its doctrines and did not wish to attend many of its services. They preferred Victorian railway stations designed by great architects to the brutalist 1960s alternatives designed by the fourth-rate. They liked their old corn exchanges and town halls more than multi-storey car parks and they could see that much of the demolition and rebuilding was done not because it was necessary but because it was going to make some unscrupulous planner, or borough engineer, or councillor a quick and dishonest buck. Many could see this. But it often seemed that Betjeman, in pointing it out, was a lone voice. For that, even if we do not love his poetry, the English will always be grateful.

A somewhat unwonted development in Betjeman's life during this period was that Elizabeth persuaded him to take holidays abroad with her mainly clergymanly friends. The exuberant Mervyn Stockwood, Bishop of Southwark, was usually of the party. So was Harry Williams, formerly the Dean of Trinity College, Cambridge, and later a monk of Mirfield. 'I am very surprised I like abroad so much', he wrote to Penelope from Simon Stuart's villa in Italy in August 1966. Stuart was a wealthy man, related to Guggenheims and Rothschilds, and it was a far cry from Trebetherick and Uffington. Betjeman called him 'bad Simon' to distinguish him from Simon Phipps, later a bishop, and because of his candour about homosexuality. Bad Simon always enjoyed Betjeman's euphemism for gay – 'I say, he was a bit unmarried, don't you think?' Stockwood was an amusing, bibulous and very unmarried companion, and there was no doubt that Betjeman had some fun with the Church of England Ramblers. The nickname had been first applied by Osbert Lancaster, who came upon them one year in Greece. Then, when they were in Calabria, and the manager of a restaurant where they had all been especially appreciative came forward with a visitors' book to sign, Betjeman signed it 'The Church of England Ramblers Association'. Thereafter the joke stuck.

These jaunts abroad, however, were not really Betjeman's idea of fun. Staying in expensive villas with the very rich, or, come to that, visiting Chatsworth, was on one level Betjeman's idea of heaven, since he loved to be comfortable. But he would also have seen the point of Penelope's manifesto, 'DOWN WITH GRACIOUS LIVING . . . I am all for Council estates and I want to live in one. Yew know yew said ow noice it was when yew stayed with G. Irvine.' In one of the sketch-books which he began in a desultory manner in Apulia in 1966, he did a sketch of Elizabeth looking anxious, pale and freckly.

Elizabeth Abroad

He also doodled what never quite turned into a poem, but which has a powerful eloquence of its own.

> I wish I were in England
> The country that I come from
> It's hells bells and Jolly Hotels
>> And aqua minerale
> But when will I be [illegible illegible] in a faithful [?]
>> Place where I can get a bun from?

He really had more fun visiting the Jarvises in Nottinghamshire – 'I didn't half enjoy myself in Claremont Road and neighbourhood. It is so quiet, so comfortable, so calm and the garden is so long and food and drink are so good and plentiful.' He went on to praise the church, 'the 1847 bit which needs a roof lift and the 1877 (or later) bit which is grand simple proportion whose effect is magnified by that glorious uplifting cross and candlesticks'. Typically, he also valued 'the niceness of the people up there' which 'restores my faith in mankind and God'.

Faith, always difficult to hold on to, had been shaken up by the Church of England at large during this decade. One of Mervyn Stockwood's suffragan bishops at Southwark, John Robinson, a Cambridge don turned Bishop of Woolwich, had caused great controversy with his book *Honest to God*, summed up in a famous newspaper headline, 'Our Image of God Must Go'. Harry Williams, another Cambridge don, had begun his ministry as a conservative Anglo-Catholic, but following a nervous breakdown and a course of psychoanalysis, he had 'come out' as a homosexual, and written a series of powerful sermons, which still enjoy a cult following to this day, with the titles *The True Wilderness* and *True Resurrection*. They do not specifically deny the objective truth of the old faith, though they do so implicitly, suggesting that the events of the Gospels make sense to us when they have become interiorised, and we have ourselves experienced the desolation of spirit of being in the Wilderness, when we have wrestled in our own Gethsemane. Both Betjeman and Elizabeth were much impressed.

Inevitably, being a famous person, a television personality, and a best-selling writer, as well as the lover of a lady-in-waiting to Princess Margaret, led Betjeman to have a very public profile, and the late 1960s were perhaps the height of his fame. It is remarkable that he had any time to be anything except the public 'persona' of John Betjeman, given the demands on his time. He became friends with the wife of the Prime Minister, Mary Wilson, who herself wrote verse.

John Wells and Richard Ingrams, who wrote a spoof *Mary Wilson's Diary* in *Private Eye* magazine naturally made merry with her attempts – 'If I could write before I die / One line of purest poetry', etc., etc. Betjeman defended her robustly against the mocking young men. He claimed to think highly of her poem: 'How like a man to choose a crowded train / To say that we could never meet again.' It was a genuine friendship between the two of them. Betjeman responded to the rather lonely, shy woman who had been swept up into the public realm because of the ambitions of her husband. Her love of poetry was quite genuine, and her fondness for the Scilly Isles, where she had a bungalow, matched his for Cornwall. It was not mere snooti-ness on the part of Betjeman's old friends, however, who felt that he was watering the mixture a little with his effusion to Mary Wilson on the occasion of making a train journey with her to Diss, in Norfolk —

> Dear Mary,
> Yes, it will be bliss
> To go with you by train to Diss.

As for his poem on the Investiture of the Prince of Wales, it reads more like a job application (for Poet Laureate) than something worthy of the poet who had written a great poem like the 'Death of King George V'. It begins after a dinner in the Rev. Harry Williams's rooms in Cambridge.

> The moon was in the Cambridge sky
>   And bathed Great Court in silver light
> When Hastings-Bass and Woods and I
>   And quiet Elizabeth, tall and white,
> With that sure clarity of mind
> Which comes to those who've truly dined,
>   Reluctant rose to say good-night;
> And all of us were bathed the while
> In the large moon of Harry's smile.
>
> Then, sir, you said what shook me through
>   So that my courage almost fails:
> 'I want a poem out of you
>   On my Investiture in Wales' . . .

And so on for three pages. R.S. Thomas, a fervent Welsh Nationalist who felt that the nationalist party, Plaid Cymru, did not go far enough in its opposition to England, had come to believe in the fire-bombing of holiday cottages to keep the English out of his beloved land. He might well have viewed with some scepticism Betjeman's enthusiasm for the prince, and his commendation of the young man to Thomas as Charles prepared for his Investiture as Prince of Wales in a ceremony at Caernarfon devised by David Lloyd George for the future Edward VIII. Of Prince Charles, Betjeman wrote,

> I have met him twice, dining with Harry Williams, Dean of Trinity, Camb. who is his moral tutor. Harry becomes a Mirfield monk next year. With C[harles] were two stalwart young undergraduate friends of his. I must tell you that whether he comes through his Wales affair safely or not [this was the Investiture which had excited some threats of demonstration by the Welsh nationalists] he is a winner of a person. Not handsome (like you & your glorious son) but humorous, sensitive to one's feelings, and obviously good. By 'good' I mean steadfast & unself-conscious & strong. I feel he has already mastered what it is like to be alone. Harry tells me he often serves at weekday celebrations in Trinity. Very curious it was to meet him twice at small private dinners. I think he looks forward to Wales. He clearly likes poetry. I copied out your 'One night of tempest' &c for Harry to give him, to whet his anticipation of Caernarfon. I often wonder why you did not include that shining lyric in your later volume.

The knighthood which Betjeman received in the same year as the Investiture, 1969, was more than deserved. 'It is of great help in restaurants and theatre ticket offices and airports. Better almost than a Lord.' If anyone in England deserved a knighthood, not only for his poetry, but also for his tireless campaigning, and for the enlighten-ment he brought to millions, it was Betjeman. But he did not need to write doggerel such as the poem on the Investiture. If one is to have a royal family at all, they need friends and courtiers. Betjeman, with his willingness to flatter, was a natural courtier, and that was something, especially with Princess Margaret, that he could do with Elizabeth. But the poetry had begun to dry.

To Harry Jarvis he explained, on 29 January 1970,

> I got a rather delightful thing called melancholia. I lost all confidence, couldn't bring myself to telephone or write a letter, dragged my feet as though I were eighty, and couldn't balance properly. It is being cured by pills which keep me asleep all day, and it will take a month to get all right. I am going to Iceland tomorrow, where I shall have to get pills to keep me awake, and then with Mervyn to Spain where I shall be able to sleep, but I don't think it wise to come up to you on the 4th or 5th. I am not really fit company for anyone. Apparently, I shall be quite all right in a month, the doctor is certain he can cure it. Feeble is very weak and it was at her instigation a doctor was called in. I was rapidly becoming even more intolerable than usual.

It was hardly a condition in which he should have taken on a major new undertaking: film making in Australia. But, without understanding the true nature of his condition, combined with his old melancholic self, and greatly exacerbated by alcohol, he set forth on what began as a whoopee and was to end as a sort of Calvary.

The previous visit to Australia, ten years before, had been a round of lectures, talks, television appearances, and poetry readings, and it had been exhausting for a man of fifty-five. At sixty-five, Betjeman was beginning to suffer from Parkinson's disease, though this was not yet known. He was also undertaking the much more tiring work of making television films. The producer in charge was Margaret McCall. She had not worked with Betjeman much before, and she did not appreciate that he was ill. There were several films to make. It had been written into the contract that Elizabeth should accompany Betjeman with all expenses paid. As well as Margaret McCall and the crew, there was an additional producer, Julian Jebb.

The grandson of the Catholic poet Hilaire Belloc, Jebb was both overshadowed by his past and in rebellion against it. He had a very carrying voice. The queue of penitents outside one of the confessionals in Westminster Cathedral were once astounded to hear him shouting, 'Are you telling me that it is a sin to BE a homosexual?' He stormed out of the church and never returned, being a paid-up agnostic ever afterwards. Slight, blonde, with large brown eyes and an excessively camp manner, Jebb was someone who had a deep knowledge of the literature and music of the nineteenth and twentieth centuries. He was an eerily good mimic, and sociable, adoring the company of aristocratic bohemia. He was a regular visitor to Lord David Cecil and his family, to Lady Diana Cooper, to Anthony and Violet Powell, to Vidia Naipaul, who depicted him with cruel accuracy in his novel *The Enigma of Arrival*. Julian used to say that he could not bear the idea of ageing, and that when he reached his fiftieth birthday, he would commit suicide. This he did, but not before a tortuous life-journey in which he confronted the fact that, clever as he was, he had never found any fulfilling outlet for his talents. The anti-depressant pills which he constantly popped did not seem to do anything for his depressions, and frequent visits to clinics, each more punitive than the last, did nothing to help him cure his ever more extreme alcoholism. He wanted not just friendship, but mother-love. When staying with one of his close friends, Jennifer Ross (briefly married to Robert Heber-Percy), he used to curl up to sleep at the end of her bed.

He loved Betjeman and Elizabeth and prided himself on being one of their intimates, calling – as he realised later – rather more often than they had wished to spend evenings with them at Elizabeth Cavendish's house in Radnor Walk.

At first all went well down under. The friendship with Barry Humphries, then living in Melbourne, was resumed. Betjeman's fondness for him and admiration for his comedic gifts increased. Julian Jebb, likewise, idolised Humphries.

From Sydney, on 29 September, Betjeman wrote to Candida,

We are all four very happy because Australian wine is so good. So is
Australian architecture right through to Moderne and real contemp.
I am ravished by it and you will be. The hotels are awful. The one at
Bendigo smelt of cats and my pillow smelt of pipe smoke . . . Julian is
our life and soul. Eliz organises us all and supports me when I lose my
balance (physically) and Margaret McCall is highly efficient and kind
and calm. We all get on very well and drink a lot.

Though, or because, the deep potations remained a constant
feature of the trip, the good humour did not last. Betjeman, like any
good public speaker or television performer, lived on his nerves and
found it a tremendous strain doing 'pieces to camera'. It looked
effortless when the viewers saw him in the finished films, but often
a speech lasting forty seconds on screen would have taken several
repetitive hours to shoot, with different 'takes'. If the speaker
remembers his lines, this does not guarantee that the light will be
right at just the moment he speaks the words. If words and light are
right, this will not stop a distant motor-bike or aeroplane cutting
through the sound. These are the habitual trials of the television
film-maker and they require much patience on all sides and, on the
part of the presenter, huge reserves of goodwill for (usually) very
uncongenial colleagues, and enormous stamina.

Jebb, a frustrated creative person himself, had an unmistakable
streak of sadism in his make-up, coupled with a deep envy of the
truly creative people he admired. To be a producer in such a
situation gives a man absolute power for the duration of the
filming. When they got to Tasmania, Margaret McCall allowed
Julian to be the producer of the film covering this part of the trip.
By now both Betjeman and Elizabeth had come to find their 'life
and soul' Jebb a bit too much of a good thing. Not to put too fine a
point on it, Betjeman had come to hate Jebb. There was a point when
Jebb knocked on Betjeman's bedroom door in Hobart, and it

opened. 'GO AWAY! GO AWAY! GET OUT OF IT!' shouted Sir John.

The mood was in any event darker in Hobart, since they were going to film the place where the convicts were imprisoned in the nineteenth century.

'The latent sadism in the human race', Betjeman wrote home to Mary Wilson.

> Port Arthur is the Belsen and Buchenwald of the 1830s – the English this time, but most unusually, the Irish doing the floggings and tortures. *For the Term of His Natural Life* by Marcus Clarke is a melodramatic classic about the prison life here and on Norfolk Island. Tourism has contributed its little offering – where men were flogged to death, and others turned cannibal, you can buy little model prisons as keyrings. It is horrible. We are filming it, and it's not for me to turn moralist but I *hate* the place and Tazzie generally.

Jebb wanted to film in a particularly cramped prison cell where the convicts awaited torture. Betjeman was made to squat down in this cell while the hot lights shone down on his face, and while the various technicians tried, in very difficult circumstances, to make sure that cameras, lights and microphones were in order. It was a terrible little scene, and in such circumstances, most people, even in perfect health, would have wilted after being made to do two or three 'takes'. Betjeman was tired and drunk. He kept fluffing his lines. Rather than give the thing up as a bad job, or decide to try again the next day, Jebb went on and on and on making the old poet try again to speak 'to camera'. They did *sixteen* takes.

When it was over, Betjeman staggered out of the cell and was helped back to the hotel. Later, assuming that they would be meeting as usual for dinner, Jebb made his way along a hotel corridor, where, elfin and tiny as he was, he encountered the tall and formidable figure of Lady Elizabeth Cavendish, JP. 'John and I would like you to know something', she said with terrifying calm. 'When we all go back to London, we do not want you to call on us. Please do not try to telephone, please do not visit. We do not want to see you EVER AGAIN.'

14

THE MISTRESS

The year 1972 brought two momentous changes. The Betjemans left Wantage, and in effect separated for the rest of their lives. And, in the autumn, Betjeman became Poet Laureate. For some time now, it had become impracticable to keep up the Mead, especially since Penelope herself was away more and more, travelling in India, making films and collecting material for her books. Betjeman had been coming home less and less. Nevertheless, for as long as the old place remained, at least notionally, 'home', and for as long as their shared furniture, his books, her riding tackle and Indian artefacts, were under the same roof, they could be said to have been a couple, living, as many do, a semidetached life, but still in some sense a married life. After Betjeman died, Penelope was officially regarded as the widow. It was in this role that she appeared at the grand memorial service in Westminster Abbey – though the Archbishop of Canterbury escorted Elizabeth from the abbey and gave her luncheon, a gesture which enraged Billa Harrod – 'most unbecoming in the Archbishop entertaining not the widow but the concubine'. Penelope in her no-nonsense way felt that it had been BOGUS – her capitalisation – to be given the seat of honour. When the Principal of Pusey House in Oxford invited her to a Requiem Mass for Betjeman, to hear the homily by their old friend Gerard Irvine, she accepted with alacrity, but said,

> As I am sure you know JB settled with Elizabeth Cavendish for the last
> ten or twelve years & although I saw him occasionally & we were on
> good terms, E did not like us meeting & she looked after him thro'out

the Parkinson period. Of course I told JB I would divorce him if he
wanted to marry E but he IMPLORED me not to. I have got to be in
a front pew in W A as I am John's official widow but I can't face it at
Pusey House as well.

This letter spells out as clearly and as mercilessly as it could
the state of things after 1972. Penelope turned down several good
offers for the Mead, preferring to accept the bid of a Tibetan family,
believing that they would care more for it. In fact, they sold it
quickly and realised a good profit. By then, Betjeman and his wife
had effectively gone their different ways. For about a year, Betjeman
stayed on at Cloth Fair, spending more and more time with the
Lycett Greens. The nocturnal noise of meat lorries trundling to
nearby Smithfield Market had always been one of the disadvantages
of living in Cloth Fair, and now he had begun to find it intolerable.
Parkinson's in its early stages incapacitated him. The shuffling walk,
which he had affected even in youth, was now for real. In 1954, the
first time he was the castaway on *Desert Island Discs*, he chose a
medieval stained glass window as his 'luxury'. In 1975 when he
returned to the show, he chose champagne. Alcohol helped deaden
some of the consciousness of what was happening to his body, but it
did not dissipate the gloom. When Penelope had bought a cottage
in the Welsh borders – New House, Cusop, near Hay-on-Wye – she
urged him to come and stay and have a health cure.

> We can ave er ealth food week tergether. Oone feels WOONDERFUL
> but MOOST stick tew it. No entertaining (other than invoitin other
> health food maniacs) and no going out and boothoney-sweetened
> lemonade ter drink. You *as* lapsed again drinking gin and whiskey.
> Oi am very sad: oi am NOT er pleasure killer oi simply think spirits
> are deleterious tew yr ealth and so does yer DOC.

The truth was that as Little Plymmie's ways became ever more
Spartan and primitive, Tewpie, fat and prematurely old and ill, was

ever more dependent on creature comforts – warm rooms, comfortable chairs and beds, hot tea and toast. While her idea of fun would be to rough it for three to six months in India, travelling by coracle or on horseback, and eating lentil dhal, Betjeman's would be to stay at Chatsworth and be brought champagne by the butler.

> My new position such is
> In halls of social fame
> That many a duke and duchess
> I know by Christian name.

In her cottage, which Betjeman and she nicknamed Kulu-on-Wye or Little Redoubt, Penelope had a downstairs bedroom and toilet installed but although he came a few times, he was too ill and it was too uncomfortable to regard it as a place to visit on a weekly or monthly basis, still less to call home.

Perhaps neither of them – not she, with her hopeful provision of an inadequate spare room, nor he, with his repeated assertions by letter and telephone, that he loved her – could quite bear the reality of what had happened. The clash of their egos had been going on for very nearly forty years by this stage, and neither, surely, had ever envisaged that in the end they would not in some sense be together. 'I miss Penelope', he wrote to a friend on 13 August 1972, 'who I feel has gone for ever.'

None of the three in the triangle could really tolerate the full reality of the situation, even though Penelope made the most articulate stab at doing so. Elizabeth still refused to meet Betjeman's wife, even though his illness really suggested that some broad strategy should be worked out for the future – how he would be looked after should his condition deteriorate, as it inevitably did. Moreover, whenever Betjeman tried to visit Little Plymmie, or to speak to her on the telephone, he was somehow made to feel 'guilty' by Elizabeth. Even for such occasions as family birthdays or Christmas, Elizabeth made him feel that she could not be left alone.

It is reediculous that she cannot be left halone as she as many friends living near & is very much a person in er own right being the Duke of D's sister with presumably a proivate hincome? It would be quoite different were she a Mary Berry (that was yer first girlfriend??) a poor parson's daughter, a nobody in the eyes of the world, without money or influential pals, whereas E as BOTH the latter in abundance. Boot, yew *MOOST BE FIRM* . . .

Of course, asking Betjeman to be firm in this area would have been like asking Penelope to see two sides of a religious question. The digs in this letter are deadly. (Presumably, Mary Berry is the 'Molly Higgins' with whom he had an affair at the very beginning of his marriage shortly after moving into Garrard's Farm, Uffington?)

For as long as he stayed in Cloth Fair, Betjeman could at least technically remain his own man. But, with Wantage sold, and nowhere *comfy* that he could call home, the outlook was alarming. Cloth Fair was all right as a book-lair and a bachelor pad during the week. But, like the flat 'high in Onslow Gardens' in one of his best poems, 'Eunice' – 'it's cream and green and cosy, but home is never there'.

In 1973, Elizabeth Cavendish acted decisively. A house ten doors along from her own terraced cottage, 19 Radnor Walk, came on the market, and she bought it and installed Betjeman in it – Number 29.

'My Darling Plymmie', he wrote to Penelope in April 1973.

I am now very nearly in 29 Radnor Walk, sw3 4bp [Tel] 352-5081 to give it its full titles. This is my first letter from it. The long delay is due to the horrors of moving. The new place is very tiny but very cheerful and much easier to reach than the City. Wibz has been very helpful and so has E. I am going to Cornwall while the workers are in on the toilets and other luxuries like shelves. There is no garden. That will have to be at Kulu-on-Wye.

But they both knew that was fantasy. No wonder there existed between Betjeman and Kingsley Amis such a rapport. Amis's novels,

especially the later ones which were written while he was friends
with Betjeman, cover the painful territory of men and women
failing to understand one another, and actually hating while needing
one another. They also confront failing powers of memory and sexual
potency, and they see, really, only one area of consolation: drink.
Although Kingsley Amis was a brusque person with strangers, this
manner hid a person who was full of terror (he could not sleep the
night alone in a flat or house) and who dreaded madness. There was
much in Betjeman, man and poet, to which he could respond. At the
time of his move from Cloth Fair, Betjeman often went and stayed
with Amis and his wife, Elizabeth Jane Howard, when they were
living at Lemmons, Hadley, Hertfordshire. Betjeman called it, not
inaptly, Gin-and-Lemons.

His friendship with Amis's friend Philip Larkin has already been
mentioned. When Cecil Day-Lewis, Poet Laureate, died in May
1972, Larkin and Betjeman were both spoken of as likely successors.
It was Betjeman who was chosen. He was pleased, but knew that
many of the poets laureate in the past had been nonentities. 'Alfred
Austin is my favourite laureate after Eusden', he wrote. Alfred Austin
(1835-1913) was the author of the lines about the appendicitis of the
future Edward VII – 'Across the wires the electric message came /
He is no better, he is much the same'. Laurence Eusden, who was
laureate 1718–30, was lampooned in Pope's *Dunciad* –

> Know Eusden thirsts no more for sack or praise;
> He sleeps among the dull of ancient days.

There were plenty of fools who would be prepared to take
Betjeman at his own estimation and place him among those
unintended jokes of literary history. As had happened before, it was
left to Larkin to see the point. Larkin wrote in the *Sunday Telegraph*,

> In a sense Betjeman was Poet Laureate already: he outsells the rest
> (without being required reading in the Universities) and his audience

overflows the poetry reading public to take in the Housman-Omar Khayyam belt, people who, so to speak, like a rattling good poem. In this he is like Kipling, and if Betjeman had not been appointed the two of them would have gone down the ages as the two unofficial Poets Laureate of the twentieth century. Lucky old England to have him.

It is true that he was already the laureate in the sense of being a poet who had been taken to the heart of the English people. Look at the poem 'To the Crazy Gang', of 1962. That is public poetry of a good jobbing kind. He was now sixty-six years old, and it is very unusual for any poet to write much which is any good past this age. 'I have become so public and overexposed that I am dry and self-piteous.' Tennyson and Goethe and Waller and Thomas Hardy are the exceptions. Most poetry is written by those who are young or middle-aged, and most poets are only any good for a very short period of their writing lives. Even Keats's *Annus mirabilis* of 1819 would probably never have been repeated even if he had lived – certainly nothing he wrote after it was much good.

How many poems of the two hundred or so which Betjeman published actually hit their mark, achieve what they are setting out to achieve?

I'd say about thirty out of a little over two hundred – 'Death in Leamington', 'Croydon', 'The Sandemanian Meeting-House in Highbury Quadrant', 'The Arrest of Oscar Wilde at the Cadogan Hotel', 'Death of King George V', 'Oxford: Sudden Illness at the Bus-Stop', 'Myfanwy' and 'Myfanwy at Oxford', 'Parliament Hill Fields', 'A Subaltern's Love-song', 'Ireland with Emily', 'Invasion Exercise on the Poultry Farm', 'Youth and Age on Beaulieu River, Hants', 'St Saviour's, Aberdeen Park, Highbury, London N.', 'Harrow-on-the-Hill', 'Christmas', 'The Licorice Fields at Pontefract', 'Middlesex', 'Late-Flowering Lust', 'Sun and Fun', 'Devonshire Street W.1', 'In Willesden Churchyard', 'Business Girls', 'Eunice', 'Felixstowe, or The Last of her Order', 'By the Ninth Green, St Enodoc', 'The

Cockney Amorist', 'Aldershot Crematorium', 'The Costa Blanca', 'Lenten Thoughts of a High Anglican', 'The Flight from Bootle', 'In a Bath Teashop'. This is not to say that the others are devoid of charm, or that they do not have good lines in them. But if most of Betjeman's poems were suits, you would say that they needed at least two more fittings at the tailor's. If you were trying to make a case for Betjeman, as I very much am, these thirty or so are the poems you would bring forward. By the standards of most poets, thirty good poems is quite a large number. Many famous poets of the twentieth century only produced two or three good poems, and some famous poets did not produce any good poems at all. In Betjeman's case the imperfect verse is simply doggerel, and often quite bad doggerel at that. The older he got, the lazier he became, and he concentrated all his creative energies on television.

When John Guest produced a John Murray book called *The Best of Betjeman* in 1978, Betjeman thanked him characteristically – 'Oh Gosh, thanks. Reading a book all by oneself – it feels as good as masturbating.' Some eighteen of the poems named above are chosen by Guest. What prompted him, for example, to choose 'Inland Waterway', a dull laureate poem about the opening of the Upper Avon at Stratford by the Queen Mother – 'Your Majesty, our friend of many years, / Confirms a triumph now the moment nears . . .'? At least Guest did not choose the absurd verses addressed to the wife of the Prime Minister, about going 'by train to Diss'.

The trouble with all these later duds is that they encouraged those who disparaged Betjeman to think of him as no more than a camp joke; and encouraged all those such as Mrs Wilson herself who wrote bad doggerel to think that they were poets. The second bit does not matter, the first does. Betjeman at his best was actually in tune with something, his ear was cocked, his eye was alertly open, his heart was beating; and the laziness which allowed the bad stuff into print did not do his reputation any good.

⚐ ⚐ ⚐

Your Majesty, our friend of many years . . .

After the move to Radnor Walk, Betjeman was regularly in London on a Sunday and took to attending Grosvenor Chapel in South Audley Street, the place where, in the 1950s, Rose Macaulay had recovered her faith. It is a robust eighteenth-century preaching-box (Wilkes is buried there) beautified by twentieth-century Anglo-Catholicism. The sanctuary was reordered by Betjeman's beloved Ninian Comper in 1912. Here the sensible, old eighteenth century of Dr Johnson and Bishop Butler, represented by dark-varnished box pews, and galleries supported by pillars, meets the mystery of T.S. Eliot's church or Charles Williams's represented by gilding and incense and Latin vestments. The priest in charge of Grosvenor Chapel at this date was John Gaskell, an exceptionally direct and intelligent preacher, as well as being a much sought-after confessor. With hair *en brosse* and an aquiline nose he resembles a slightly frightening Roman emperor until his face breaks into laughter. Betjeman and Elizabeth, sometimes accompanied by Princess

Margaret, would sit in the same box pew to the left. During the sermon, Betjeman sat with a slightly goofy frog-like expression on his face during the sermon, leaning forward and appearing to hang on every word the preacher spoke. 'Dear John, what a marvellous *opening & inspiring* sermon you gave us yesterday morning at the 11. The church is so full of beauty my heart misses a beat', he wrote in one letter, and in another, 'I love the Grosvenor Chapel and its plentiful incense'. On the way out, however, he would be all laughs. Betjeman used Father Gaskell as his confessor, sometimes coming to Gaskell's house for supper, and kneeling down before the meal in the kitchen to confess his sins. On one occasion, after the poet had been absolved from his sins, he rose from his knees, keeping one hand on the kitchen table, which had been covered with a cloth for dining. He made some observation, adding 'Touch wood!' Then he lifted the cloth to see that in fact the table was covered with formica. 'Bloody plastic!' he exclaimed. Religion fitted him like an old slipper. The priest, though no prig, was mildly startled that Betjeman should swear so soon after being absolved. But for him, the borderlines between the sacred and the profane were beginning to fade.

He moved easily from gawping attentively at the preacher to teasing him at the church door, just as he could not always stop himself, when at his devotions to the Blessed Sacrament, forming devotions of a more profane character. It was not long after he had begun worshipping at the Grosvenor Chapel before he formed one of his crushes, this time on the extremely beautiful Joan Prince, nicknamed, before Betjeman knew who she was, 'the Mistress'. Appropriately, she was the beauty editor of *Harper's Bazaar* and she was married to a man who was a sidesman at the Grosvenor Chapel, Michael Constantinidis.

Betjeman's poem about her appeared in his 1974 collection, *A Nip in the Air,* as 'Lenten Thoughts of a High Anglican'. It encapsulates something essentially Betjemanic. He is not the poet of the *grande passion*, he is the poet of the crush. It is the form of love which Englishmen learn at their boarding schools, and for many it remains a repeated emotional habit. It feels very often deeper, creates more of a glow, than consummated love affairs, certainly it is more exciting than the day-to-day life with mistress or wife. To the glorious company of Clemency the General's daughter, Emily in Ireland, Myfanwy leaning kind o'er the *kinderbank*, and of course Joan Hunter Dunn, was added another, though nameless, one —

Isn't she lovely, 'the Mistress'?
    With her wide-apart grey-green eyes,
The droop of her lips and, when she smiles,
    Her glance of amused surprise?

How nonchalantly she wears her clothes,
    How expensive they are as well!
And the sound of her voice is as soft and deep
    As the Christ Church tenor bell.

But why do I call her 'the Mistress'
    Who know not her way of life?
Because she has more of a cared-for air
    Than many a legal wife.

How elegantly she swings along
    In the vapoury incense veil;
The angel choir must pause in song
    When she kneels at the altar rail.

The parson said that we shouldn't stare
    Around when we come to church,
Or the Unknown God we are seeking
    May forever elude our search.

But I hope the preacher will not think
    It unorthodox or odd
If I add that I glimpse in 'the Mistress'
    A hint of the Unknown God.

Any Betjemaniac would see that he had here given us his Credo. It may not be his best poem but it is one of his most haunting and touching, and it is the last one where we really hear the voice of the master.

⚛ ⚛ ⚛

There was something fitting in the choice of title in the longest poem in his final volume, *A Nip in the Air* – 'Shattered Image'. This was now the telly age, and as one of the most successful TV 'personalities', Betjeman, like it or not, had become public property. He became naturally touchy about any attempt to dislodge the treasured picture of himself which existed in the minds of millions of delighted television-viewers. The homosexual side to his nature, for example, was something which he loved to play up in private. This joke was something which became more and more pronounced with the years.

'Diana Mosley has asked me to stay in Paris', he said mournfully one day to John Guest:

'Are you going?'

'No'.

'Why not?'

'I hate Paris – nasty food. Nasty architecture'.

'What would you rather be doing?'

'I'd like to go tenting in North Wales with Prince Edward'

– then barely a teenager.

With John Guest, Harry Williams and others he loved to camp it up. They read aloud to one another from *The Priest and the Acolyte* by John Francis Bloxam, a paederastic Victorian clergyman whose life had been ruined when J.K. Jerome, of *Three Men in a Boat* fame, threatened to 'expose' him. When Betjeman learned that Humphrey Carpenter was researching the biography of W.H. Auden which was published in 1981, he at first implored the fledgling biographer not to include the episode in which the two young poets had slept together at Oxford, and then threatened legal action if Carpenter did not come to heel.

When Betjeman and his friends had been young, there were strict rules governing gossip columns in the press. Details of other people's emotional or sexual lives could only be printed when they had been used in evidence in court – in divorce cases, for example, or cases of gross indecency.

Candida's friend Richard Ingrams, as one of the founders and (almost from the beginning) editor or pirate-chief of *Private Eye*, changed the limits of how far the boundaries of privacy could be stretched. *Private Eye* was published by a company called Pressdram Limited so Betjeman nicknamed Ingrams Pressdram or Dear ole Pressdram. The two men liked one another, and were in some ways natural soul-mates – both Anglicans, both melancholic solitaries who paradoxically throve on publicity and riotous company.

Evelyn Waugh's son Auberon wrote a scabrous 'Diary' for *Private Eye*, a cruelly Swiftian assault on all and sundry. Absolutely anyone was considered fair game – even the Queen, with whom Waugh claimed to be on intimate terms: she massaged his feet for him while bemoaning the commonness and stupidity of her children. Cardinals, close friends and neighbours could all find themselves held up for ridicule. Some of the ideas in the 'Diary' – that Churchill was a drunken, debauched old war criminal – were simple matters of opinion. Others, like Bron's idea that Mountbatten was a Soviet agent, had a sort of crazy plausibility in the minds of his fans even if they have never quite been substantiated in fact. Bron had a deep affection, and admiration, for Betjeman, but at this stage of his career, it was sometimes hard to know where the fictitious *Private Eye* Diary of Auberon Waugh ended and the kindly, amusing, affectionate young man Bron began.

The flavour of his friendship with Betjeman – both Betjeman's wariness and Bron's capacity to put the most wounding or damaging facts down on the printed page regardless of who got hurt – was conveyed in a letter Betjeman wrote on 6 December 1973, in response to an essay Bron had evidently written about him, in which he had let slip the idea that Betjeman had been the lover of his old schoolfriend from Dragon School days, Hugh Gaitskell.

> For your information, I never went to bed with the Leader of Her Majesty's Opposition. It's a good story but quite untrue and probably springs from the fact that Lionel Perry and I shared a flat with Hugh in Great Ormond Street for a few weeks when I was in transit from having been a private school master to starting journalism on the *Architectural Review* . . . Sex played no part in our lives and it was characteristic of Hugh's generosity to let me live rent free when I was penniless, having been despaired of by my parents. Hugh at the time was courting Dora, and I would hate to be involved in a libel action which my lawyer tells me this statement, which I have marked in brackets at the bottom of page 5, and the top of page 6, involves. I must therefore insist that 'From a rumbustiously homosexual youth – he is surely the only Poet Laureate who can claim to have been to bed with someone who was later to become leader of Her Majesty's Opposition' comes out.

It was Betjeman himself who was responsible for the 'libel'. He had once remarked to Osbert Lancaster that Hugh Gaitskell was 'the only Leader of Her Majesty's Opposition I ever went to bed with'. It was no doubt a joke. He loved playing up the whiff of bisexuality in his character. Lancaster was a great gossip, and loved amusing Ingrams, his young neighbour (at Aldworth, Berkshire), with titbits of this kind. It got repeated back to Bron and was in danger of being put into print. In his dealing with the young men at *Private Eye*, quite firmly suggesting that, if the story went into print, he would sue, Betjeman showed what Anthony Powell called Betjeman's Whim of Iron. Incidentally, though the jury will ever be out on the question of how homosexual Betjeman was in temperament, there is no evidence that he was ever, in grown-up life at least, a practising homosexual. And one priest who was very close to him avers, to me convincingly, that all his erotic interests were really in young women.

Bron's affection for Betjeman was deep and reciprocated, and, once the younger man had been called to order with the mention of a lawyer checking his writings, the friendship continued merrily as before. Indeed, Betjeman loved *Private Eye*, its indiscretions and all, and saw it as a useful weapon, which it was, against the spoliations and corruptions of modern architects, planners and shyster developers. On 13 February 1975, from 29 Radnor Walk:

Dear Bron,

I very much enjoyed yesterday's luncheon, so did my friend Harry Williams. We talked about it all the way back in that luxurious car to this place. It was very kind of you to ask me. I was silent and preoccupied. This was because, I now realise there was welling up in me a desire to let the cat out of the bag about an enormous land deal being made by British Railways over the sites of Liverpool Street and Broad Street Stations. It will not only mean goodbye to the Great Eastern Hotel with its dome of many coloured glass, to the Abercorn Rooms and the Masonic Temples; to that glorious elevated walk across from Bishopsgate; through the Miss Hook of Holland part of the station and on to those interlacing Gothic arches of the original Great Eastern. It will mean goodbye to Broad Street echoing and forgotten and to those Lombardic stairs that climb up its southern side to the North London Railway war memorial. Instead the whole area will be covered by offices. We know what they'll look like and under the offices there will be amid fumes and the tannoy system some platform for trains to East Anglia. It will be the new Euston only much worse, if that were possible, and much higher of course because the buggers will feel fully justified in being higher than the

Stock Exchange or the appalling new Barbican. Much ridicule will be poured on preservation-mad nostalgics such as yours truly, for admiring this essentially 'second-rate' collection of buildings, and for not seeing the glorious smooth-running-future the financiers see for their new slabs. I think there has been some pretty smart land dealing and I can't find out about it, but you can with your brilliant staff.

Ingrams got Betjeman to write the 'Piloti' column in *Private Eye*, exposing some of the more monstrous acts of architectural vandalism and the chicaneries of planners and civil servants. Betjeman soon handed this column on to his young friend and admirer Gavin Stamp, a fine architectural historian.

To this last decade of Betjeman's life, however, belong some of his best television work, and, even more remarkably, the setting of his poems to music by Jim Parker.

When asked at the beginning of 1975 to take part in a television programme with David Dimbleby called *Face Your Image*, Betjeman declined, saying, 'This is the sort of publicity I would rather avoid as I suffer from persecution mania. That is because my character is weak, pleasure-loving and grovelling and that would come out only too plainly in the course of an interview.' At about the same time, in that exceptionally cold, dank, misty early spring of 1975, Betjeman's old mentor, and first confessor, Freddy Hood began to sink towards death. Betjeman came to Hood's flat in Dolphin Square to make an emotional farewell. Hood, though at death's door, asked him to stay to luncheon. While Hood slumped in a chair and gazed weakly at the Thames through his window, Betjeman was accompanied down to the restaurant in Dolphin Square by one of Freddy Hood's closest friends, Canon John Lucas, vicar of St Thomas's, Becket Street, Oxford. As they entered the modernistic restaurant, the Poet Laureate said, 'Oh dear, is this what Purgatory is going to be like?' Saying goodbye to Freddy awoke in Betjeman the sense that he had not fulfilled the promise of what he might have been. His conversation returned to Pusey House in the 1920s and the very high standards, moral, aesthetic and professional, which Freddy had himself, and which he held up to his friends. 'And now, Canon,' said Betjeman sadly, looking into the middle distance with an expression of despondency, 'I'm just a Pop poet.'

Betjeman explained that he was in the middle of recording with Jim Parker. If he felt at that moment that he was 'just' a Pop, his self-reproach (partly affected?) could not have been more misplaced. For these records, made between 1974 and 1981, are among the very best things he ever did. If my harsh judgement is correct, and many of Betjeman's poems on the page need, to use tailor's jargon, a few more fittings, then Parker is the master tailor or Magger Tagger. Born in Hartlepool in 1934, Parker left school at sixteen, and after a spell in an accountant's office, joined the army and played in the band of the Dragoon Guards. Later he got a grant to study at the Guildhall School of Music, and joined the Birmingham Symphony Orchestra as an oboist. When he settled in London, he joined up with the Barrow poets, a group who read poems aloud, sometimes Betjeman's, and played background music to them. It is what the Germans call *Sprechgesang*, or spoken song. It was Parker's genius to get Betjeman himself to record his own poems, to richly varied background settings of Parker's composition.

The recordings were made in a studio in Willesden. In the Middle Ages, there was a shrine of Our Lady at Willesden to which pilgrimages were made. The modern Roman Catholic church at the end of Willesden High Road contains a shrine of sorts, but naturally Betjeman was not interested in that. Betjeman wanted to ask the vicar of Willesden to tell Parker about the appearance in the Middle Ages of the Black Madonna. Parker remembered Betjeman's indifference to the pouring rain as he 'ploughed on through the graveyard'. The rhythms of Betjeman's voice perfectly match the music of Parker, and vice versa. Many of the poems which are either too weird to be much appreciated in a silent reading – such as 'A Shropshire Lad', the one about the ghost of Captain Webb swimming along the old canal which carried the bricks to Lawley – or too slight – 'The Flight from Bootle' – come to life in a miraculous way when read aloud by Betjeman to Parker's accompaniment. The great poems, such as 'The Arrest of Oscar Wilde', the 'Death of King George V', 'Youth and Age on Beaulieu River, Hants' and the 'Subaltern's Love-song' are likewise enhanced to a positively sublime degree. No one confronted by medieval English lyrics, or the songs of Burns, can really appreciate them by simply sitting silently with the book open on the knee. They need to realise that these poems are songs. Parker has done much more than create a musical diversion around some spoken songs. He has brought out the inherent quality of lyrics which are, so many of them, the missing link between the songs of the music hall and *Hymns Ancient and Modern*. No one who has heard Parker's records can ever forget them. For ever afterwards, when you read Betjeman's lyrics on the page, the music starts.

The first few years at Radnor Walk were also the period when Betjeman made some of his finest television programmes. The most archetypical, and therefore the most celebrated, was *Metroland*, first screened on 23 February 1973 and directed by Edward Mirzoeff. Betjeman followed the line from Baker Street up to Amersham. If it is true that in death all the scenes of a past life flash before you, then this television-poem by Betjeman – it is too good to be described as simply a 'programme' – took him back through the suburban outskirts of London he had known and loved and love-hated since boyhood. He passes through St John's Wood, 'Sweet secret suburb on the City's rim', referring to its Victorian kept women, but no doubt also remembering the Woads. Out through Wembley, then to Harrow, where he had been at school in all but fact, and so on to Pinner, and Rickmansworth and beyond. 'The Croxley Green revels – a tradition that stretches back to 1952', a line which when first spoken, only twenty-one years after the tradition began, reduced Betjeman and the film crew to hysterics.

But though *Metroland* is perhaps his television masterpiece it is by no means the only great telly-poem he made during this last phase before his powers faded. *A Passion for Churches* was filmed largely in Norfolk. This enabled him to stay with his old friend Billa Harrod.

As a friend of both Betjemans, and as his ex-fiancée, Billa felt able, while he was staying, to speak out on the subject of Penelope. She felt Penelope was getting a raw deal, and that Betjeman was neglecting her in favour of Elizabeth. Billa was not a stranger herself to the complexities of the emotional life. For much of her marriage to Roy Harrod, she had been in love with another Oxford don, but as she said, 'You have affairs, and that is one thing. But you keep your marriage TOGETHER. You don't divorce or separate.'

Betjeman replied to her,

Your kindest action to me in our long and loving friendship was to speak to me so kindly and clearly of Penelope. I love her. *But I cannot live with her for long without quarrelling.* I sensed her anguish when we went to the cinema last night with Emily [Villiers-Stuart]. I cannot bear to hurt her. She kissed me on the cheek when she got out of the taxi last night and I went back to Radnor Walk.

You said being loved is a great burden. I have lived so long apart from Penelope, that Elizabeth now loves me more than anyone else in the world. I cannot hurt *her* either, any more than I can Penelope. I depend on Elizabeth for food for my body and mind. She is v much part of me too.

Both P and E feel threatened. Fear steps in and with it hatred and anger. It is difficult. I *think* Penelope would be wounded if we separated, though she says it is what she wants to do. I don't want to, but may have to if she precipitates it in rage at E and all the

Cavendishes. I can understand her rage and misery. She won't believe how much I love her. I think she needs to be given her rights and dignity. She is okay at Kulu-on-Wye and insecure in London within the enemy's camp. I must buy, if it ruins me, a camp for her in London where she can entertain her friends with me.

In this awful storm of misery, the one thing I cling to is my love for Penelope *and* for Elizabeth who has given up marriage and a family life with her own children, out of love for me.

I think, but am not sure, that P is more defenceless than E, and must therefore be propped up by a London base as well as Kulu-on-Wye. Radnor Walk would never do. It is too near the enemy, though P has tried to be friendly with E.

So still the problem raged on against the background of all his friendships, all his television appearances, all his communions and confessions, all his long periods of gloom. The fans who saw *A Passion for Churches* saw only their hero, approaching his seventieth birthday, and on the top of his form, not only as a performer, but as a man who was able to use television as a medium in which to tell the truth. There must be many for whom, as it was for me, *A Passion for Churches* was a formative experience.

The film, transmitted on 7 December 1974, is tremendously powerful. One of the best scenes is when Betjeman's voice-over says:

Every Anglican priest promises to say
Morning and Evening Prayer daily.
The Vicar of Flordon
Has rung the bell for Matins
Each day for the past eleven years.

The camera then comes back so that we can see the vicar reading the office to a completely empty church.

'Til all the world is C of E

> It doesn't matter that there's no one here
> It doesn't matter when they do not come
> The villagers know the parson is praying for them in their church.

The programme ends with a montage of people going to church on Easter Day and ends –

> And though for church we may not seem to care
> It's deeply part of us. Thank God it's there.

Betjeman understood, far more deeply than most of the bishops and synods and focus groups of the modern Church, what the C. of E. was, and why it was still central to the people of England. This programme was a reminder of the fact that Betjeman was much more than a poseur and a performer. 'Weak, pleasure-loving and grovelling' as he might in his worst 'persecution mania' have seen himself, he was also the best apologist for Anglicanism of his generation, far more persuasive, because far more modest, far less bossy, than his old tutor C.S. Lewis. If those two are the most finished and brilliant of all his TV programmes, I would not want to forget, either, the one, produced by Patrick Garland in 1976, about Parson Kilvert, in which Betjeman did very little except visit the Victorian curate's parish of Clyro, near Hay-on-Wye, and read from his diaries. In his love of children, in his fondness for rural life, in his delight in human eccentricities and in his susceptibility to form the most painful crushes on girls in the parish, Kilvert was an obviously sympathetic figure for Betjeman. He stayed with the film crew at the Three Cocks, the excellent local pub. The proximity of Penelope at Cusop meant that Tewpie could see Little Plymmie and avoid both the excruciating discomfort of his wife's domestic arrangements, and the jealousy of his mistress. That year, Plymmie said, 'For moi birthday oi would VERY mooch loike the COMPLETE EDITION OF KILVERT. BOOT oi believe it naow costs £20??? So if it does perhaps you could share the cost with Candida???' 'P.S. Oi read er poem of yewrs nearly hevery noight.'

LOVE IS EVERYTHING

The last years were ones of illness and pathos. The melancholia got worse, so did the persecution mania, as Parkinson's disease made its inexorable and debilitating progress. He had spent the Christmas of 1972, after becoming Poet Laureate, at the Wiltshire farmhouse of Tory and John Oaksey with Penelope, Rupert, Candida and the grandchildren. Through all the hilarity, it was obvious that he was much sicker than he had ever been, and Penelope wrote to Elizabeth Cavendish, suggesting that they should share the task of looking after him.

> I am writing to you to see if we cannot work something out for John whereby we take it in turns to look after him? He was in a really bad state at Christmas, worse than I have ever known him and really pathetic with his loss of balance, etc . . . I spoke to Jackie [his secretary] who for the first time opened her heart to me. I have naturally avoided discussing John's condition before and she said she had to give in her notice as she could not take it any longer . . . I expect you are having an equally trying time? I never thought it would really help his condition to become the Poet Laureate: twenty years ago, yes, had Masefield died sooner, but now he has reached the age of retirement it means that he can NEVER retire and relax completely, but must always have this yoke around his neck. And the correspondence it has involved him in has been enough to finish off anybody. I fear it is going to take at least a year to get the new wing built on to this tiny cottage. I am having a sound-proof bedroom built for him with a writing table in it so that he won't rave about the occasional

cars which go by! But until that is ready I do not suppose he will come down much, as with his loss of balance trouble he finds the stairs very difficult to negotiate. But I can always come up to London now he has got the ground floor of number 43 and look after him there . . .

In fact, he was about to move into Radnor Walk, to become Elizabeth's neighbour and dependant. Unable to see much of Penelope, he now loved her more and more, and he thought of his days of early married life with her in Uffington, the times, he said, when he had known most happiness. 'Oi often wish oi was back in those days when Gerald [Berners] was alive. Oi miss yew and those days. Achievement is nothing. Love is everything. Oi daownt give yew enough boot oi dew often think about yew with deep love.' Since he spent more and more time in Elizabeth's house, he offered the keys of Number 29 to three trusted friends, Harry Williams and Philip Larkin with his girlfriend Monica Jones, so that they had somewhere to stay in London whenever they wished.

As Penelope recognised, Elizabeth's life was not easy. 'John was very difficult to live with because of his guilt over Penelope about which he would never stop talking.'

Sex talk, too, formed a larger part of the repertoire as his powers failed. It was even more difficult than it had been in the days of Betjeman's vigour to know whether he meant, or 'meant', any of his professions of lust, whether hetero- or homosexual. Immobility made him a sitting target for any who wanted to call at Radnor Walk, and many of these were homosexuals. Had they been of a different persuasion, it is just as likely that the performance would have been adapted. When Richard Ingrams called on him to discuss John Piper about whom he was writing a book, the telephone rang. It was Betjeman's (female) agent. 'What are you wearing?' the Poet Laureate asked breathily into the telephone. 'Does it fit tightly?' 'Why did he say this?' Ingrams later asked. 'To show he was one of the lads? I felt rather embarrassed.'

With Rupert Lycett Green and grandchildren

Life was now punctuated by hospital visits. 'I have been in King's College Hospital, not at all nice. Go anywhere but there. The night staff is a mixture of IRA and emissaries of General Amin', he told John Sparrow. Some months later, in March 1978, he had a heart attack and was treated at the Brompton Hospital in Fulham Road. Candida, holding his soft hands, realised he had never done a day's manual work in his life.

In 1981 and 1982, Betjeman consented to make a series of no less than seven television programmes with the Old Harrovian producer Jonathan Stedall. By now, Betjeman was wheelchair bound, slightly impaired in speech and very much the worse for wear. Old friends and family gallantly came forward to be filmed with him. The Pipers wheeled him into the church at Harefield to see the magnificent tomb of the Countess of Derby, whose 'flaming ropes of hair' falling over her shoulders foreshadow the girl in the Licorice

Fields at Pontefract. Kingsley Amis and Barry Humphries tiptoed into the sitting-room of Radnor Walk, which was slightly too small to be filmed comfortably. And Stedall took him back to some of his favourite haunts, including Oxford and Cornwall, keeping up a seemingly unstoppable flow of questions.

Stedall: Do you have any regrets, John?
Betj: Yes I haven't had enough sex.

At the very end of it all, down at Trebetherick, Betjeman is asked to talk of his faith, and says, 'I hope "The Management" is benign and in charge of us. I do very much hope that.'

Stedall: Hope rather than believe?
Betj: Yes, certainly hope. Hope's my chief virtue.

Then he stares out across the garden, and murmurs, 'Lovely, here.'

Stedall: Finished?
Betjeman: Yes.

Jonathan Stedall has now said that he regrets not having made this film a couple of years earlier when Betjeman was less pathetically weak. Certainly, for some viewers, there was something very uncomfortable about watching a consummate performer paraded when he was not – as he so triumphantly is in the best films – in full control. But, of course, the reason that the television programme organisers wanted to devote so much airtime to this in many ways sad series was the simple one of Betjeman's huge popularity. The programmes will at least have prepared the fans for the knowledge that he had entered the valley of the shadow. His repeated theme, while he could still speak, and when he talked to priests, or old intimates, was guilt – guilt about Penelope and guilt about his son. Shortly after he moved into Radnor Walk, a letter arrived from Paul in America. At this stage of Betjeman's life, the correspondence had become overwhelming, and the letters were dealt with by Elizabeth

Cavendish and a secretary. When Elizabeth opened this letter from Paul, she felt it was too distressing for Betjeman to read, and she put it on one side.

Paul had for some years been feeling the burden of his childhood resentments and unhappinesses. They had grown, rather than diminished, during his exile. Whereas Candida had been able to put behind her the storms of adolescence and become a grown-up friend of both her parents, Paul, by being alone in the United States, had possessed no means to purge his demons. A letter, setting out the trouble, seemed the best way of doing so.

Thirty years after this painful episode, I asked Paul whether he had felt unappreciated; whether he was angry with John and Penelope for being bad parents. His face contorted as he recalled it all. 'Calling me It. That . . . I minded so much about that. I could not even articulate it to myself for years. It was not a question of them not appreciating me. It wasn't a question . . . he wanted to keep me *down*.' He forced his palm against the arm of his chair so forcefully that he might have broken it. '*Down*. That is where he wanted me. Either Elizabeth or a secretary would not let him see my letter. Eventually I got through to him on the telephone. It wasn't easy – eventually . . . I was angry with my father but I was chiefly angry with them for not letting him see what I wrote.'

As Elizabeth had feared, Betjeman was indeed deeply upset by what Paul wrote when she decided to show him his son's letter. Of course, it was she who had tried to protect Betjeman by initially concealing it. After a faltering conversation on the telephone between father and son, a deep silence descended. In 1974, Penelope went over to New York to give a lecture and reported, 'I spent most of the day with the P. yesterday and it was much nicer. I went to lunch in its flat – a GREAT improvement on the basement one it lived in in 1969 when I was last here. NO SNAKES . . .' By now Paul Betjeman was teaching at the prestigious Riverdale School, and would go on to become the head of the Music Department, and to teach philosophy there. Betjeman when he remembered it at all, referred to the school as Riverside. Penelope had at least made the effort to see 'the Powlie', and wrote that tomorrow she would be 'spending the day with it (Riverdale is in recess for spring vacation) & we are going to the Natural History Museum'. Later that year, she wrote from her Hay-on-Wye fastness, 'IT IS WONDERFUL NOT BEING ON THE TELEPHONE. NOT A WORD from the P. whom we must now call PAUL. Wibz said she was going to write and invite him over for Christmas.' He did not come. On 26 November that year, Penelope wrote to Betjeman from Vijayanagar, India, dating her letter 'Powlie's birthday'.

In 1977, however, Paul brought to England his American girl-friend Linda Shelton, a young woman with a passionate interest in Anglican church music. She got on well with Betjeman, and to Candida at least it appeared that a reconciliation had taken place. (Paul denies this, and says he has never really been reconciled to his father.) A few letters were at least exchanged, and a truce of a kind had been established. In May 1979, Penelope and Betjeman received a telegram: 'Linda and I are getting married on Saturday May 19th at the Advent Lutheran Church on 93rd Street and Broadway, New York. Please be there in spirit although we do not expect you there in body. Paul and Linda.' The word 'love' is surely very conspicuously absent from this telegram, and Candida does not tell us whether this telegram was really sent to both parents, or merely to Penelope. Paul and Linda are the parents of three children, Thomas, Timothy and Lily. Linda is the director of the choir, and the organist, at St Peter's Episcopal Church, Pearsekill, in a suburb outside New York. Whether Paul and his father have been reconciled is a matter for them, not us, to decide, but a long journey had been traversed since Paul left England and joined the Mormons. In the Anglican worship which has been so large a part of his family life, there has surely been an element of homecoming.

When I met Lily Betjeman in 2003, she described to me how she and her parents, both musicians, passed their time. She said that on Sundays, they all bundled into a Morris Traveller, and drove into New York. (They live some thirty miles out of town.) They then sang the service in one church after another, starting at the bottom of Manhattan and working their way northwards. I told her that in Oxford, in her grandfather's day, there had been a clergyman who was almost in the position of a medieval Mass-priest. Having a good voice, he was employed to sing the Prayer Book office of Morning Prayer in two of the colleges before bicycling off to do so in one of the parish churches in the town. His nickname was the Matins Machine. Lily, a golden-haired beauty of a sort which would inspire anyone to want to write a poem, replied, 'I guess you could say I'm a Matins Machine.' Paul smilingly said to me, a couple of years later, that Lily had been exaggerating.

In 1963, Betjeman had written to T.S. Eliot,

> I have been staying at St Michael's College, Tenbury Worc[estershire]. I can't recommend it too highly for a visit. There it is founded in 1853 by Sir Frederick Gore-Ouseley in Gothic buildings, also 1853 by H[enry] Woodyer, a Lancing under the Clee Hills and a daily matins and Evensong and anthem from a large choir of resident boys and men – an amazing and unknown beautiful C of E outpost.

Not now. St Michael's is still a school, but under different management, and the choir is no more. That tradition was carried on by Lily Betjeman and her parents in Manhattan.

> There in the nimbus and Comper tracery
> Gold Myfanwy blesses us all.

As Betjeman faded, his life was focused on places to which the chair could be wheeled. Grosvenor Chapel, as was stated in the first chapter, was given up in favour of Holy Trinity, Sloane Street, the Arts and Crafts (J.D. Sedding) church which had inspired one of his earliest poems. In times of liturgical innovation, this church still used the liturgy of the Book of Common Prayer which was liked by Betjeman, Elizabeth and by Princess Margaret who often accompanied them.

Penelope now felt excluded. Guilt made it impossible for Elizabeth to see her. She told James Lees-Milne that 'once, when Penelope had been to John's house, she, Feeble, from an upstairs window watched her walk away, looking so sad and weary that her heart bled'.

Penelope complained, 'Plymmie *would* like to be friends with her so that the feeling of your life being divided into two completely separate compartments *would* disappear. I would obviously never try to take you away from her which would be impossible anyway.'

So it was that the burden of nursing Betjeman in his latter years fell upon Elizabeth. She had experience with nursing, and engaging professional help, since while Betjeman declined, her long-lived mother Mowcher had also entered a phase of painful dementia which required round-the-clock attention. When they went to Moor View or to Chatsworth, Phyllis Foran, a nurse from Mexborough in Yorkshire, was engaged to be on hand. 'I had great affection for Sir John, he was always so kind and grateful whatever you did, however small his request. We had many a laugh as we talked to Archie.' In April 1981, he suffered a stroke while staying in Moor View, and was taken to the Royal Hallamshire Hospital in Sheffield. While he was here, Candida had the delicate task of organising the visits of Elizabeth and Penelope so that they did not coincide.

> I knew he worried about Elizabeth and I promised that I would always see she was all right and love her. I asked him why he hadn't married her. I never got an answer. I knew that my mother, in her great magnanimity had offered him a divorce soon after my marriage to Rupert. I knew also that he was desperate to avoid hurting my mother, because he loved her so much. He told me that he loved Elizabeth too. I remember thinking angrily at that point, that he was

an archetypal ostrich, and that he *should* be married to Elizabeth. But despite my anger I understood that for him, with his particular penchant for guilt, the situation was as insoluble as it had always been.

Deborah Devonshire — who felt 'the blinding *charm'*

'People kept expecting him to do the right thing, but maybe he did do the right thing — and maybe the right thing was not to make a decision', said Deborah Devonshire, Elizabeth's sister-in-law.

The year 1983 was spent largely sitting, often staring with his large, moist, despondent eyes into the middle distance. The letters, which were a curse to him even in his active days, continued to shower upon the mat of 29 Radnor Walk, and his secretary Elizabeth Moore attended most mornings to take his dictation of the ever-shorter replies to television-viewers, aspirant poets, conservation groups, clergymen. In September 1983 he had a heart attack and on 16 October another stroke from which he never really recovered.

All his life he had worried about money and believed himself to be poor, while being unable to contemplate doing anything so prosaic as a job. By the standards of today's best-selling authors, he was not rich. There is surely a sort of parable lurking in the fact that he left about the same sum of money in his will as Philip Larkin who was obsessed by what he called 'the toad work' and the need for poets to provide security for themselves by doing paid jobs — he as the very highly esteemed librarian of the Brynmor Jones Library in Hull. Larkin, who died a year after Betjeman in 1985, left £286,360. Betjeman was to leave £200,775, the equivalent in 2002, using the average earnings index, of £557,850.74.

In May 1984, he made the last journey to Trebetherick. Penelope wrote to him:

> I wish you wouldn't worry about me . . . I am very happy and have had a very full and happy life and am now indulging myself by going to India again and am very relieved to know that you will be well looked after by Elizabeth . . . Please relax in Cornwall and don't fuss about anything and don't drink any WHISKY.

Candida went down to Treen and read him the whole of *The Ordeal of Gilbert Pinfold*. It had been arranged that an ambulance would drive him back to London on 18 May. 'He must have heard it being arranged', Candida wrote. 'I know that at that point he decided he wanted to die at Treen.'

'His fear of death seemed to go', Elizabeth told their friend Father Gaskell. 'I had always dreaded that most for him for so many of his poems are so full of fear of it. But he was completely serene and at peace.' To Betjeman's old friend Billa Harrod, she wrote:

> I truly think that those last months he was more serene & at peace than I have ever known him. No one will ever know how wonderful the 2 nurses Carole and Vicky were to him & it was so lucky that they were both down in Cornwall & he died on the most beautiful sunny morning with the sun streaming into the room & the french windows open & the lovely smell of the garden everywhere & Carole was holding one of his hands & me the other & he had old Archy & Jumbo in each arm & Stanley the cat asleep on his tummy & he was conscious right up to the last moment. We none of us moved for nearly an hour afterwards & the sense of total peace was something I shall never forget. Then the nice Vicar came & said some beautiful prayers &

wouldn't even let me move Stanley the cat & for him, John, I have no doubt that his time had come to leave this world.

Carole read him all his Cornish poems on the previous afternoon which was too much for me but I read him all his favourite bits of Tennyson & Hardy & Matthew Arnold etc for at least an hour and a half in the evening – & he went to sleep quite content & then I went down in the night because his breathing was so bad & the doctor came & gave him an injection & he slept intermittently & finally died about 8 in the morning.

Betjeman wrestled all his life with melancholia, and self-doubt and fear. But he was also an incredibly lucky person, who with the manipulative skills of the only child, usually ended up getting precisely what he wanted in any given situation. There was a perfection in his dying where he had spent so many childhood hours of happiness.

The funeral took place at St Enodoc's, a short stroll across the golf course from Treen, on 22 May 1984, a day of driving wind and rain. Betjeman's two children, Candida and Paul, with their mother, followed the coffin and the drenched mourners into the dark little church which was not particularly full, the congregation being limited to family and close friends. It was so dark that the lady verger held up a torch, rather in the manner of an usherette at a cinema, to help them read from their hymn books. In 1975 he had written to Roy Plomley that he would like Isaac Watts's hymn, 'There is a Land of Pure Delight', not only on the Desert Island, but 'to be sung at my funeral'. In the event, they sang 'The Church's One Foundation' and 'Dear Lord and Father of Mankind / Forgive Our Foolish Ways'. The coffin was buried just to the east of the lych gate. Elizabeth and her sister, Anne Tree, entertained one lot of mourners at Treen, where a fire was burning in the grate and toasted sand-wiches and whisky were offered. The others went to a neighbouring house for luncheon with Penelope. James Lees-Milne remarked on 'the poignancy of sitting on John's little deathbed with Archie, teddy-bear, and Jumbo propped against the pillow. Anyway I have paid my respects to the best man who ever lived and the most lovable.'

Andrew Devonshire used to remark that Betjeman never talked about himself. There is a certain paradox here, since few men have had such success in projecting their personality into public consciousness. But it is a true observation of his behaviour in private, and it brings to life some of the mystery of a poet's life which will never be winkled out by biographers. Those who knew him remembered, as Deborah Devonshire did, 'the blinding charm. The *blinding* charm. The melancholy was there but he always hid it in company. You only saw it when he was walking away. The slouched shoulders. The crumpled old hat. The mac.'

Penelope Betjeman also had a death which seemed as if it had been scripted by a screenwriter who knew her character very well indeed. In 1985, after a return from one of her Indian trips, she decided to sell her house above Hay-on-Wye and give the money to Paul. She would go and live in a convent at Llandrindod Wells which had guest rooms. There was also a gabled Victorian hotel in the town for guests who did not want to enjoy the possibly austere hospitality of her new dwelling.

In fact, the house was difficult to sell and it was still unsold when she set off to the Himalayas in April 1986 in quest of temples. On her way to London, she met a friend in the train and remarked, 'I think I might never come back from this trip. The funny thing is, if I died on the mountains, I know that everyone will say what a wonderful death I have had. They'll say, what a wonderful way to go, it is just as she would have liked! But I don't want to die now at all, I've so much to do.'

'I feel as though I might be on my way to Heaven.'

She and a tour party, whom she was to lead round the temples of the Himalayas, assembled at Simla. There were fourteen of them in all, who set out the next day in a rackety old bus up the Hindustan/Tibet road to Narkanda. They camped in the mountains and Penelope gave them all a talk on the Hindu religion and the meaning of Hindu temples. For four days, they trekked on ponies higher and higher, eating simple, largely vegetarian food, sleeping in scorpion-infested rest-houses, washing in cold water. On 11 April, Penelope rose even earlier than usual when one of the tourists, Ronnie Watson, came upon her at 5.30 a.m.

'You're up terribly early', he said.

Somewhat distracted apparently, Penelope replied, 'I know, I feel as though I might be on my way to Heaven.'

The party began to climb after breakfast, their aim being to reach the remote village of Mutisher, 9,500 feet up. Penelope rode on ahead, and the others were to join her when they reached the village and be shown the temple. The temple *pujari* rushed out to meet her and bless her. He performed the service of puja in her honour and rang the temple bells. Penelope dismounted from her pony and climbed three high steps towards the temple. She sat down, closed her eyes with her head against the stone wall, and died.

There was wailing, and panic. The doctor in the party tried, without success to resuscitate her. Storm damage had destroyed all wires, and communication with the outside world at that juncture was impossible. They carried the body to the mountain village of Khang. There the group came to the decision to cremate her. Using Penelope's Bible, they improvised a Christian form of service within a Hindu cremation ceremony. They sang the psalm which begins 'I will lift up mine eyes unto the hills', and Paddy Singh, who had been educated by Jesuits, remembered the words of the Hail Mary: *Pray for us sinners, now and at the hour of our death.*

The trekkers made their way back down the hillside to their rest-house before the fire had burned itself out. It was for the villagers, Hindus and Buddhists, to sit in vigil around the flames and to gather her ashes which, some days later, were mingled with flower-petals and scattered into the raging Beas River at the bottom of the Kulu Valley.

Notes

CHAPTER ONE
BEGINNINGS
(Pages 1–20)

Radnor Walk, a small street . . . Princess Margaret to author, 1980

I hang on to faith . . . Betjeman Papers (hereafter BP), now in the Tom Brown Museum, Uffington, JB to a Mr Bramall, 26 October 1970

I did not like all the probing and prying . . . Candida Lycett Green (ed.), John Betjeman, *Letters, Volume One: 1926 to 1951* and *Letters, Volume Two: 1951– 1984* published by Methuen in 1994 and 1995 respectively (hereafter CLG I and CLG II), CLG II, p. 441

Excellent thing, excellent thing . . . Jonathan Cecil to author, 2005

He once threatened a younger journalist . . . Auberon Waugh

He's a lovely man, isn't he . . . Victor Stock, *Taking Stock: Confessions of a City Priest*, HarperCollins, 2001, p. 140

Unmitigated England . . . All quotations from the verse are taken, unless otherwise stated, from John Betjeman, *Collected Poems*, John Murray, reprinted 2001

A journalist called John Ezard . . . CLG II, p. 582

Elizabeth Cavendish . . . Conversation with author, 27 October 2005

You've always had guilt . . . BP, Wilhelmine Harrod to JB, 2 March 1982

I have just re-read Goldsmith's . . . CLG II, p. 541

Where wealth accumulates . . . Oliver Goldsmith, *The Deserted Village*

In every age, there are people . . . Arthur Machen, *The Secret Glory*, p.vi

The Betjemanns were cabinet-makers . . . Unless otherwise stated, all biographical details are taken from CLG I and CLG II.

To the actor James Fox . . . *Radio Times*, 28 August-3 September 1976

Before the First World War, we . . . Lady Diana Cooper to author, 1981

A rotten, low, deceitful . . . *Summoned by Bells* (hereafter SB)

One of Betjeman's closest upper-class . . . Diana Mosley to author

It is a most miserable thing . . . Charles Dickens, *Great Expectations*, ch. XIV

a little-known Victorian architect and his clerical patron . . . Bridget Cherry and
    Nikolaus Pevsner, *The Buildings of England, London 4: North*, p. 658
In Kentish Town, until the 1970s . . . Gillian Tindall, *The Fields Beneath: the
    history of one London village*, Phoenix Press, 2005, p. 169
To a member of the Camden History Society . . . quoted Tindall, p. 203

CHAPTER TWO

CORNWALL – AND THE DRAGON
(Pages 21–35)

The first of them would be a picture . . . John Lucas to author
I [sic] was a quiret [sic] eve when I went out . . . CLG I, p. 11
the healer of all wounds . . . CLG I, p. 6
I do want to buy a house in Trebetherick . . . CLG I, p. 537
Here at the end of the last century . . . John Betjeman, *Shell Guide to Cornwall*
    (revised), Faber and Faber, 1964
In 1863 the church was excavated . . . Nikolaus Pevsner, *The Buildings of
    England: Cornwall*, Penguin, 1951, p. 150
Beak's Bay . . . Michael Thomas to author, 2004
Little by little as business prospered . . . CLG I, p. 46
One of Betjeman's childhood playmates . . . Bevis Hillier, *Young Betjeman*, John
    Murray, 1988, p. 81. Bevis Hillier's life of Betjeman is in three volumes
    – *Young Betjeman, New Fame, New Love* and *The Bonus of Laughter*.
    Hereafter, HILLIER I, HILLIER II and HILLIER III
The cosy fuchsia-ed and tamarisked . . . CLG I, p. 46
Joan, a year older than John . . . HILLIER I, p. 81
now red-capped and jacketed like me . . . SB
I learned a lot from that tough . . . BBC Radio Talk, 24 August 1953
I couldn't see why Shakespeare . . . SB
I knew as soon as I could read and write . . . SB
The American master, Mr Eliot . . . SB
As a publisher, however . . . CLG I, p. 142
where the walls / Of Magnus Martyr . . . T.S. Eliot, *The Waste Land*
compulsive sociability . . . compare Roy Jenkins, John Julius Norwich, Melvyn
    Bragg, Archbishop Rowan Williams, Iris Murdoch, Anne McElvoy,
    Condoleezza Rice, Edmund Wilson, Elton John and other only children
Skipper's children, Joe and Audrey . . . CLG I

Wavell mi . . . Geoffrey Madan's Notebooks, ed. J.A. Gere and John Sparrow, Oxford University Press, 1981, p. 23

Hum was like a father to me . . . BP, undated

I liked the way you took . . . SB

a pleasing buxom wench . . . *The Draconian*, December 1918, p. 5117

The cleverest actor of all . . . quoted *The Draconian*, April 1920, p. 5260

Betjeman first achieved notice . . . J.P.W. Mallalieu, *On Larkhill*, 1983, p. 38

All that was crumbling, picturesque . . . SB

To my dear boy . . . BP

Thus were my London Sundays incomplete . . . SB

CHAPTER THREE

THE SECRET GLORY

(Pages 36–48)

When I announce . . . BP, JB to Auberon Waugh, 6 December 1973

I like things that are overshadowed . . . HILLIER III, p. 679

Doom, shivering doom . . . SB

At home, his parents . . . SB

Do you tickle your arse . . . SB

When he had children of his own, Betjeman taught them to sketch . . . CLG I, p. 7

Everybody thought he had absolutely fallen . . . Arthur Machen, *The Secret Glory*, Martin Secker, 1922, p. 160

There is no system known to human wit . . . Machen, *The Secret Glory*, p. 171

Dr Pevsner, his mind not attuned . . . Pevsner, *Cornwall*, p. 152

Boswell quotes Johnson as saying . . . James Boswell, *Boswell's Life of Johnson*, Oxford University Press, 1957, p. 51

I saw golden Mywanfy as she bathed . . . Machen, *The Secret Glory*, p. 188

The age demanded an image . . . Ezra Pound, *Personae*, Faber and Faber, 2001, p. 186

First tremulous desires in Autumn stillness . . . SB

Electric currents racing through my frame . . . British Library (hereafter BL) Add. MS 71645 f164

One day after lunch, his mother . . . HILLIER I, pp. 116–17

He signs his name 'Moth' because that is . . . Lord Alfred Douglas, Stopes Papers, BL Add. MS 58994 f75

Betjeman pasted into his copy of W.B. Yeats's . . . BP, JB to Rupert Hart-Davis,
20 June 1962

CHAPTER FOUR
OXFORD
(Pages 49–72)

Maurice Bowra, who had taken part in heavy fighting . . . Maurice Bowra,
Memories, Weidenfeld and Nicolson, p. 85
My diary, 'a red Oxford University one' . . . CLG II, p. 511
Looking back aged thirty-three . . . CLG I, p. 252
His friend and undergraduate contemporary Osbert Lancaster . . . Osbert
Lancaster, *With an Eye to the Future*, John Murray, 1967, p. 93
Dear Mr Betjemann, I am glad to have your poem . . . BP
Warren was a legendarily snobbish man . . . Oral tradition in Oxford
Lewis might not come across . . . For all the Lewis anecdotes, see my biography
C.S. Lewis, Collins, 1988
He made a particular cult of a Low Church . . . Gerard Irvine to author
Many who laughed, or smiled, at the sight . . . John Lucas to author
It was to Freddy Hood that he made . . . BP
Isaiah Berlin, in his tribute . . . Hugh Lloyd-Jones (ed.), *Maurice Bowra, A
Celebration*, Duckworth, 1974, p.76
Anthony Powell brilliantly captured . . . Lloyd-Jones, p. 111
Anthony Powell, pondering in old age . . . *Journals 1982–6*, Heinemann, p. 184
In grown-up life, some time in his fifties . . . James Lees-Milne, *Deep Romantic
Chasm: Diaries 1979–81*, John Murray, 2000, p. 101
The Anglo-Irish are the greatest race . . . BP, JB to Elizabeth Bowen, 12 June 1946
nowhere in your excellent book do you say anything appreciative . . . CLG I,
p. 251
I remember going to a dance . . . Elizabeth Longford, *The Pebbled Shore*,
Weidenfeld & Nicolson, 1982, p. 68
He picked up a waitress . . . Bowra, *Memories*, p. 169
Dear Betjemann, You must write to the Secretary . . . Duncan Andrews Collection,
quoted HILLIER I, p. 183
Betjeman did his best to make life awkward . . . Lancaster, *With an Eye to the
Future*, p. 93
A sustained and successful effort . . . Lancaster, *With an Eye to the Future*, p. 81

CHAPTER FIVE

MAKING A MARK – *ARCHIE REV*
(*Pages 73–92*)

Betjeman's biography. John demonstrates . . . Evelyn Waugh, *Diaries*, edited by
  Michael Davie, Penguin, 1986, p. 777

Waugh, three years older . . . Diana Mosley to author, 4 June 1990

My love to John . . . Evelyn Waugh, *Letters*, ed. Mark Amory, Penguin, 1980,
  p. 318

I had a suspicion . . . Anthony Powell, *A Question of Upbringing*, Heinemann,
  1951, p. 182

And being slightly off his head . . . CLG I, p. 52

I've the face of an angel . . . From an unpublished and undated letter to
  Betjeman from W. H. Auden, written during his time at the Downs
  School, Colwall, (1932–5) BL Add. MS 71646 f14

Do you know what Winters . . . CLG I, p. 44

The German lesbian film . . . HILLIER I, p. 246

Praise the Lord . . . CLG I, p. 77

Archibald looks like this . . . CLG I, p. 79

Archibald has accepted the Incumbency . . . CLG I, p. 87

He said he'd like to marry me . . . CLG I, p. 95

Four Quakers and he . . . HILLIER I, p. 214

Osbert Lancaster remembered . . . HILLIER I, p. 297

A year younger . . . For Edward James, I have used John Lowe, *Edward James,
  Poet, Patron, Eccentric*, Collins, 1991

Patrick Leigh Fermor . . . John Murray Archive, quoted HILLIER III, p. 590

If anyone asks me . . . BP, JB to Mr Boyne, 14 January 1974

P. Morton Shand will probably be best known . . . His son Major Bruce Middleton
  Hope Shand, born 22 January 1917, married Rosalind Maud Cubitt on
  2 January 1946. Camilla Rosemary, born 17 July 1947, was their first
  child

I have frightful nightmares . . . BP, P. Morton Shand to JB, 21 October 1958

To understand Leeds . . . Quoted Timothy Mowl, *Stylistic Cold Wars*, John
  Murray, 2000, p. 53

When Gothic architecture ceased to be fashionable . . . *Architectural Review* Vol. 70,
  October 1931, p. 92

I sometimes think that I should like . . . Peter Quennell in the *Sunday Telegraph*,
  28 October 1984, quoted HILLIER I, p. 258

Penelope Chetwode, I always think . . . Presentation copy of *Mount Zion* given to Penelope Betjeman

Grove, Collins, 1973, p. 55
The slowest part of the journey . . . CLG II, p. 513

CHAPTER SEVEN

MR PAHPER – THE DEFINING FRIENDSHIP
(*Pages 116–134*)

probate was complete . . . HM High Court of Justice Principal Probate Registry, 1934

Alan Pryce-Jones ('Bog') tells a remarkable story . . . Alan Pryce-Jones, *The Bonus of Laughter*, Hamish Hamilton, 1987, p. 231

Pierce Synnott, the Oxford friend who invited John Betjeman . . . Papers in the Huntington Library, San Marino, California, quoted HILLIER I, p. 199

My dear deaf father, how I loved him . . . SB

Shoot! Said my father . . . SB

I see / His kind grey eyes . . . SB

Born on 13 December 1903, and educated . . . All Piper information, unless otherwise stated, is taken from Richard Ingrams and John Piper, *Piper's Places*, Chatto & Windus/The Hogarth Press, 1983

Send me some S. Devon lighthouses . . . David Fraser Jenkins and Frances Spalding, *John Piper in the 1930s: Abstraction on the Beach*, Dulwich Picture Gallery, 2003 (hereafter Jenkins and Spalding), p. 54

Dear Artist . . . BP, 27 October 1936

In the October 1936 issue of Architectural Review . . . Jenkins and Spalding, p. 113

He drew absolutely certainly with a quill pen . . . Ingrams & Piper, p. 46

Where do we go from here? . . . Stephen Spender, 'A Talk with John Piper', *Encounter*, May 1963, p. 271

They had been at school together . . . Jenkins and Spalding, p. 57

Myfanwy was immensely impressed . . . HILLIER II, p. 101

'What's that?' asked the field marshal . . . HILLIER II, p. 101

Naow, Peter, what is orl this abaout not believing . . . Peter Quennell to author, 1980

Thank you for making our marriage so happy . . . HILLIER II, p. 85

We thought he was just . . . JB to Colin Gill, quoted to author by John Lucas

He was a much-loved parish priest . . . JB, *The Times*, 4 November 1958

My dear Penelope, I have been thinking over the question of playing the harmonium . . . Bowra, *Memories*, p. 172

Am very annoyed . . . BP, Penelope Betjeman to Pipers, 10 February 1940

The Pipers were intimidated . . . HILLIER II, p. 101

What a service you did us the day . . . BP, undated letter from Osbert Lancaster to JB, probably 1941

I can't do more than ten . . . Ingrams & Piper, p. 47

As their friend David Cecil once remarked . . . to A.L. Rowse, repeated to author

a partnership which did more to teach Englishmen . . . Ingrams & Piper, p. 50

What are the problems? For you, economic ones? . . . BL Harrod Papers Add. MS 71645

Till we all get a unified & intelligent . . . BP, C.R. Ashbee to JB, 7 March 1937

A letter from R.L.P. Jowitt . . . BP, the Georgian Group, 8 December 1939

Graham Greene . . . *The Spectator*, 16 September 1938

CHAPTER EIGHT

BETJEMAN AT WAR
(*Pages 135–155*)

At present fighting in a war seems to me . . . BP, 12 October 1939

Archie is very well and pro-Hitler . . . BP, JB to Gerard Irvine, 19 October 1940

There is no doubt that you have transformed . . . CLG I, p. 242

I saw as I sat in St Cyprian's . . . ibid.

the tabernacle as the centre . . . The tabernacle, abominated by Comper, was in fact added by a clergyman about twenty years after the church was built; but the doctrinal point stands, since the Eucharistic Altar was for Comper central.

What a joke about your being a Captain . . . CLG I, p. 251

Dear Betjeman, I do not know the origin . . . BP, K. Clark to JB, 9 September 1939

Jane and Sir K . . . BP, Maurice Bowra to JB, 17 July 1939

My dear John, I don't quite understand what part of the air force . . . BP, Philip Chetwode to JB, 3 October 1939

I cannot understand what you want . . . BP, Philip Chetwode to JB

Gosh, you know, I bet she is a doctor's daughter . . . Betjeman broadcast, BBC Home Service, 3 July 1961

We must all do our bit . . . BP, JB to Cyril Connolly, 6 October 1940

You will think it rude and not a little unkind . . . BP, Myfanwy Piper to JB, 19
    March 1940

a damn nice chap . . . CLG I, p. 167

Unpopular . . . except among politically minded tarts . . . BP, 20 April 1941

He told her afterwards that she was so beautiful . . . CLG I, p. 201

I think he should be very good . . . CLG I, p. 200

which they wrongly imagined . . . BP, 2 March 1941

I wish I cared more about the war . . . BP, 2 March 1941

As you probably know, the last big raid . . . BP, John Summerson to JB, 7 May
    1941. The 'we' who had photographed St-George's-in-the-East was the
    National Monuments Record.

It wasn't correct as Arabs hadn't been imported . . . HILLIER II, p. 224

They are all very fearful of British propaganda . . . BP, JB to John Lehmann, 12
    February 1941

I have to see pro-Germans, pro-Italians, pro-British . . . CLG I, p. 285

Oddly . . . you became a source of much anxiety . . . BP, Brennan to JB, 10
    December 1967

where everyone – Roman, Anglican . . . CLG I, p. 176

I spent a lot of time defending Dev . . . BP, JB to Geoffrey Taylor, CLG I, p. 354

We've had a happy time with them with no rancours . . . BP, Myfanwy Piper to
    JB, 6 November 1941

Oh how I miss you . . . It's really awfull . . . BP, Myfanwy Piper to JB, 8 March
    1941

I think a good deal about . . . BP, JB to Myfanwy Piper, undated [1941]

I cannot believe that such an expense . . . ibid.

my fondest love to luscious, bubble-breasted . . . BP, JB to John Piper, 29 March 1952

Did you go to Confession . . . BP, Penelope Betjeman to Myfanwy and John
    Piper, 16 April 1941

What a week! . . . BP, Osbert Lancaster to JB, undated [1942]

CHAPTER NINE
THE PATH TO ROME
(Pages 156–182)

Queen Mary said as she left Badminton House . . . James Pope-Hennessy, *Queen Mary*, George Allen & Unwin, 1959, p. 609

Known to his family as Ava . . . The full title is Marquess of Dufferin and Ava

he felt again the magic of that person . . . Lees-Milne, *Deep Romantic Chasm*, p. 101

You know the heavenly Campo Santo . . . BP, Maureen Dufferin to JB, 18 July 1945

A man of brilliance and of many friends . . . CLG I, p. 387

J. Coxeter & Co. . . . BP, 16 October 1946

like the clappers . . . CLG to author

1730ish . . . Pevsner says 1749; *The Buildings of England: Berkshire*, Penguin, 1966, p. 143

Betjeman wrote to Evelyn Waugh . . . BP

Having already settled £5,000 . . . Details of this and other inflationary equivalents of sums mentioned in the text are all culled from www.eh.net/hmit/ukcompare

When father went out on his basic . . . Chatsworth: typescript in Deborah Devonshire's copy of *Continual Dew* given her by Evelyn Waugh

The field marshal spent a week with them . . . BP, PB to Alan Pryce-Jones, 28 December 1945

grossly proletarian . . . *Diaries of Evelyn Waugh*, p. 660

My experience, Betjeman wrote to Gerard Irvine . . . CLG I, p. 508

If we were to desert it . . . CLG I, p. 411

The rift between the Betjemans after this crisis . . . Gerard Irvine to author

His Kingdom stretch from See to See . . . BP, date unintelligible but probably 1975. It is a picture postcard showing the enthronement of Donald Coggan as Archbishop of Canterbury.

I absolutely agree . . . JB to Harry Jarvis, 16 November 1963, CLG II, p. 264

This pensione, she once wrote from Florence . . . BL Add. MS 71648 f118, 22 September 1958

Pauline privilege he has only known that used once . . . BL Additional MS 71648

Bron's widow Teresa . . . Conversation with author, July 2005

pronounced by Powell 'Sar-deest' . . . Conversation with author

Isn't it nice that Penelope should be immortalised . . . BP, Bowra to JB, 19 October 1950

The Empress loses interest in such things . . . Waugh, *Letters*, p. 218

I am beginning to find that there is a lot to be said for sham half-timber . . . CLG I,
p. 412

He wrote urging Waugh to come to Farnborough . . . CLG I, p. 418

Just my subject and just my writer . . . CLG I, p. 430

What a wonderful book HELENA is . . . CLG I, p. 520

I must write to tell you what I find myself doing . . . CLG I, p. 438

What I cannot believe . . . Waugh, *Letters*, p. 245

Those were the days when that divine baroque . . . SB

If you accept an absurdity . . . Waugh, *Letters*, p. 244

Dearest Evelyn, I am very grateful . . . ibid. p. 250

Betjeman delivered a Christmas Message . . . Waugh, *Letters*, p. 264

Oi know oi was ysterical . . . BP, PB to JB, 29 October 1964

Dear Evelyn was never very high-brow . . . BP, Bowra to JB, 29 October 1950

Before 1948, everything was all right . . . Paul Betjeman to author, November
2005

Like Penelope Betjeman, Anne Barnes . . . Anthony Barnes to author, 22 February
2006

Betjeman became a frequent guest . . . Anthony Barnes to author, 22 February
2006

John seems very fond of that South African boy . . . BP, JB to John Piper

You really are an angel . . . BP, Diana Mosley to JB, 24 May 1946

The public seem very willing to buy it . . . BP, Sir Oswald Mosley to JB, 16
January 1947

A book printed by 'Mosley Publications Limited' . . . ibid.

old Comper has certainly not gone out of his way . . . BP, Charles Peers to JB,
3 May 1950

lost in admiration . . . BP, P. Morton Shand to JB, 3 January 1950

John Summerson went into the RIBA canteen . . . BP, John Summerson to JB,
5 January 1950

very sad it will be for Penelope . . . CLG I, p. 517

Woad was very please [sic] *oi went ter the garden party boot* . . . BP, PB to JB,
Friday [date?] 1950

CHAPTER TEN
DEFECTIONS
(*Pages 183–213*)

I have the most beautiful secretary . . . BP, JB to T.S. Eliot, 1 May 1951

Jill Menzies 'is very pure' . . . BP, JB to Anne Barnes, 11 August 1951

She is a very clever girl . . . BP, JB to John Guest, 2 October 1956

I think I was getting too fond of him . . . CLG II, p. 14, quoted HILLIER II, p. 501

sex 'only as a means of procreation' . . . Harry Jarvis interview with CLG

from 1953 for over a decade . . . Richard Ingrams, *Muggeridge: The Biography*, HarperCollins, 1995, p. 170

JB was very flattered . . . CLG II, p. 9

Is it not time you gave your heart a rest? . . . ibid.

just an upper class nanny . . . In conversation with Richard Ingrams. She used much the same language to me.

He made a brief plunge to Rome . . . Rose Macaulay, *Last Letters to a Friend*, Collins, 1962, p. 79

I love the Bog villa and also the people . . . BP, 25 May 1954

just an escape for JB . . . BP, Alan Pryce-Jones to CLG, scribbled during the 1980s on a letter of JB's dated 22 August 1953

Do I stand between you . . . BP, JB to Alan Pryce-Jones, 22 August 1953

Antonia Pakenham . . . Antonia Fraser to author, 2006

Osbert Lancaster, one of Betjeman's closest friends . . . Osbert Lancaster to Richard Ingrams

Darlin Tewpie oi AVE got confidence . . . BL Add. MS 71648

We must have this . . . CLG II, p. 3

The Roman Catholics were not taking part, 'and we . . . BP, JB to T.S. Eliot, 14 May 1951

The Archbishop – Ice creams – John Betjeman . . . BP, Earl Ferrers to JB, 28 September 1953

When I asked the Dowager Duchess . . . CLG II, p. 42

Nooni nooni nooni noewke . . . BP, JB to Penelope, 28 November 1953

When I'm depressed, Mr Rowse . . . A.L. Rowse to author

As they gathered round the wireless . . . Elizabeth Cavendish to author, 27 October 2005

Moucher took to Betjeman immediately . . . Deborah Devonshire to author, 24 October 2005

Dear, feeble, pale, soft-spoken Elizabeth . . . Letter at Chatsworth

Stevenage New Town in the rainy afternoon . . . CLG II, p. 42

HORRIFIED . . . This is not a personal matter with me . . . BP, JB to Alan Pryce-Jones, 22 August 1953

A very long letter written by Barnes . . . BP, from Director General of Television, 31 July 1951

Though Anne Barnes was Betjeman's confidante . . . Anthony Barnes to author, 22 February 2006

Oi habsolutely realise naow that the Anglican Church . . . BL Add. MS 71649

A great brain has made this place . . . BBC written archives, 12 May 1952

having decorated the house with rich wallpapers . . . CLG II, p. 3

Well, my dear fellow, all I can say . . . BP, Evelyn Waugh to JB, 16 November 1957

Oh no, old boy . . . CLG II, p. 47

Among the paranoid fantasies . . . Evelyn Waugh, *The Ordeal of Gilbert Pinfold*, Penguin, 1951, p. 83

He had made no new friends in late years . . . Waugh, *Pinfold*, p. 14

Betjeman has flu . . . *The Letters of Nancy Mitford and Evelyn Waugh*, ed. Charlotte Mosley, Houghton Mifflin, 1997, p. 244

It was remarkably kind of you to come to Ascot . . . BP, Evelyn Waugh to JB, Whit Sunday 1955

At a certain point . . . Paul Betjeman to author, November 2005

CHAPTER ELEVEN

MINDFUL OF THE CHURCH'S TEACHING
(*Pages 214–241*)

Soon after he moved to Cloth Fair . . . CLG II, p. 108

This reads the same backwards . . . CLG II, p. 124

As was always to be the case, Betjeman found his temper fraying . . . CLG II, p. 72

it is a token of how famous . . . CLG to author

Miss Howson, the stained glass artist . . . JB to Roy Plomley, St Swithin's Day, author's collection

Those who met Betjeman during those early years . . . William Glenton, *Tony's Room: The Love Story of Princess Margaret*, New York Pocket Books, 1965, p. 109

She found that Betjeman had signed a 'repairing lease' . . . HILLIER II, p. 471

at least two fascinating biographies and at least one fictitious exploration . . . The
  biographies are by Robin Denniston and by Piers McGrandle. The
  fictitious account, much altered, and with other priests contributing to
  the composite Huddleston-figure, is in my novel *My Name is Legion*,
  Hutchinson, 2004. See also the fascinating chapter on Huddleston in
  Eric James's *The House of My Friends*, Continuum, 2005

PLEASE PLEASE PLEASE . . . BP, Penelope to Jack Beddington, 3 August 1956

John, in his new role as nouveau riche . . . BP, Penelope to Jack Beddington,
  Bank Holiday 1958

Yew az poured 1 doz . . . BP, Penelope to JB undated

Penelope says it is very middle class . . . BP, JB to Anita Dent, 20 April 1957

I am pretty hot on ecclesiastical . . . BP, Victoria Dennistoun to JB, 11 May 1958

Have you done it yet? . . . Lady Oaksey to author, August 2005

I always suspected it was the cause of the fire . . . CLG II, p. 109

Oh, how jolly! This is going to be fun! . . . Glenton, *Tony's Room*, p. 33

The second time, she succeeded . . . Glenton, *Tony's Room*, p. 40

It was even said . . . that Elizabeth had helped . . . Alastair Forbes told me he had
  it from Betjeman himself that he (Betjeman) and Elizabeth had told the
  princess to add the phrase about 'mindful of the Church's teaching'.

'Don't buy my collected verse', he urged R.S. Thomas . . . Author's collection,
  22 December 1958

How nice of you to write to me . . . CLG II, p. 161

Betjeman was continually hard on him . . . Paul Betjeman to author, 18
  November 2005

I go to London for telly on Sunday . . . CLG II, p. 126

LENTEN THOUGHT . . . BL Add. MS 71649

I long to see you and Wantage again . . . CLG II, p. 123

Darling Tewps, If you won't come down for Christmas . . . BL Add. MS 71648 ff.
  93–4

Dear feeble Elizabeth and I . . . CLG II, p. 113

One of his closest confidants . . . Typed transcript of interview with CLG

she wrote to a country neighbour . . . BP, PB to Michael Astor, 11 December 1961

I love Stoke-on-Trent . . . CLG II, p. 89

I could not face Keele without her . . . CLG II, p. 187

My dear Commander . . . CLG II, p. 173

Like sorrow it goes in waves . . . CLG II, p. 186

Though she never would admit it . . . CLG II, p. 192

Alas I can't possibly believe . . . BP, Anne Barnes to JB, 17 September 1960

CHAPTER TWELVE
SUMMONED BY BELLS
(Pages 242–266)

Jim Knapp-Fisher has died . . . CLG II, p. 519

It is so hard to believe it is all over . . . BP, William Wicklow to JB, 3 October 1958

Artificial genuineness . . . Compare 'Approval of what is approved of / Is as false as a well-kept vow' in 'The Arrest of Oscar Wilde at the Cadogan Hotel'

Some know for all their lives . . . SB

The secret of a man's nature . . . J.A. Froude *Thomas Carlyle: A History of the first Forty Years of his Life, 1795–1835*, Longman, Green and Co., 1896, Vol. 1, p.89

Wibz has been misbehaving in Florence . . . BL Add. MS 71648

Important . . . ibid.

Yew KNOW I have only to sit down by a warm fire . . . BL Add. MS 71648

After a first printing of 80,000 . . . John Murray Archives, quoted HILLIER III, p. 102

Tear-in-the-eye whimsicality . . . Both reviews are quoted in HILLIER III, p. 104

It was left to Philip Larkin . . . *Required Writing*, Faber, 1983, p. 131

much gentler and quieter than I expected . . . CLG II, p. 201

So permanent and black and true . . . Andrew Motion, *Philip Larkin: A Writer's Life*, Faber, 1993, p. 347

He enjoyed it when . . . Philip Larkin to author

like a dark-haired Stephen Spender . . . JB to R.S. Thomas, author's collection

The Happiest evenings I ever Spent . . . CLG II, p. 103

Oh, thank you, thank you for your succinct . . . JB to R.S. Thomas, author's collection

Treen of all houses . . . CLG II, p. 171

I absolutely understand about E . . . BL Add. MS 71648

Mr Betjeman was the ideal . . . CLG II, p. 204

'Yes', a girl in ABC make-up . . . CLG II, p. 205

like Polzeath laid out on a grid system . . . CLG II, p. 220

Aussieland is much nicer . . . CLG II, p. 223

It's odd that I should travel . . . CLG II, p. 222

He told R.S. Thomas . . . Author's collection

For example, he was friends . . . Caroline Dawnay to author

I realise, he wrote to Edward Hornby . . . CLG II, p. 102

Dr Johnson said a man should keep . . . The remark was made to Joshua Reynolds in 1775 (*Boswell's Life of Johnson*, Oxford University Press, 1957, p. 214)

Now what was the name of that music-hall . . . *Sunday Times*, 8 July 1962, quoted in HILLIER III, p. 364

'And did you', asked Betj . . . 'The Lost Betjemans', 'Bristol My Home', HTV, 1994

There'll never be another . . . John Osborne, *Almost a Gentleman*, 1991, p. 243

My dear old Top, Betjeman wrote to Osborne . . . CLG II, p. 280

Secretly proud, I showed off merrily . . . SB

on horseback among the jeep-infested . . . CLG II, p. 276

for Elizabeth there was the grief . . . Harry Jarvis interview with CLG

After all the poverty you must be seeing in India . . . CLG II, p. 277

I feel very sad today . . . JB to R.S. Thomas, 4 January 1965, author's collection

Darling Dadz and Liz . . . BL Add. MS 71653, innumerable letters

After National Service . . . This and all subsequent information about Paul emerged in conversation, November 2005, in New York.

He is a wonderful fellow . . . JB to R.S. Thomas, 21 December 1967, author's collection

while your son is disillusioned . . . JB to R.S. Thomas, 4 January 1965, author's collection

CHAPTER THIRTEEN

LAST YEARS IN CLOTH FAIR
(*Pages 267–289*)

In very early January 1966 . . . CLG II, p. 300

When Jonathan Stedall asked him . . . *Time with Betjeman*, Episode One, quoted HILLIER III, p. 532

Betjeman had in fact first met Harry Jarvis . . . BP, Harry Jarvis to CLG

My love to the Smasher . . . BP, JB to Harry Jarvis, 28 August 1969

I offered the Mass for you today . . . BP, Harry Jarvis to JB, 28 September 1968

Feeble is OK but v pressing . . . BP, JB to Harry Jarvis, 13 January 1965

I had a horrid dream . . . CLG II, p. 315

could think of little else . . . CLG II, p. 311

The 1964 book found far more . . . *Cornwall: A Shell Guide*, 1964 p. 39 and passim

I got a salary of £800 . . . BP, JB to John Piper, 7 February 1965

the local authorities who may use Shell . . . ibid.

Meanwhile, the proper Shell guides . . . BP, JB to John Piper, 10 February 1966

The reason I can't go on with . . . BP, JB to John Piper, 11 March 1966

Gabble, gabble, gabble . . . BP, JB to Harry Jarvis, 2 March 1965

One of the many committees . . . Eric James to author, 2005

Opportunities to 'assemble my ideas' . . . BP, JB to Harry Jarvis, 22 February 1966

I cannot recommend Jerusalem . . . CLG II, p. 325

This memorial to Sir Walter Scott . . . HILLIER III, p. 262

Oh but you are the one true church . . . Helen Gardner to author

Young William . . . HILLIER III, p. 261

The birds are all killed and the flowers are all dead . . . CLG II, p. 375

'Often' wrote Bernard Levin . . . Bernard Levin, *The Pendulum Years*, Weidenfeld and Nicolson, 1970

Betjeman called him 'bad Simon' . . . HILLIER III, p. 315

DOWN WITH GRACIOUS LIVING . . . BP, Penelope Betjeman to JB, 'Soonday' some time in the mid-1960s. Gerard Irvine was sometime vicar of Cranford, a parish near Heathrow Airport.

I wish I were in England . . . BL Add. MS 71656 A f4

the 1847 bit which needs a roof lift . . . BP, letter from JB to Harry Jarvis, 1 April 1967

He claimed to think highly of her poem . . . Richard Ingrams to author

I have met him twice, dining with Harry Williams . . . JB to R.S. Thomas, 22 December 1968, author's collection

It is of great help in restaurants . . . JB to Roy Plomley, author's collection

I got a rather delightful thing . . . BP, JB to Harry Jarvis, 29 January 1970

We are all four very happy . . . CLG II, p. 421

When they got to Tasmania . . . Margaret McCall interview with HILLIER III, p. 301

GO AWAY! GO AWAY! . . . Ibid.

The latent sadism in the human race . . . CLG II, p. 425

Betjeman was tired and drunk . . . Julian Jebb to author shortly after returning from this trip to Australia

CHAPTER FOURTEEN
THE MISTRESS
(Pages 290–310)

most unbecoming in the Archbishop . . . James Lees-Milne, 29 June 1984

As I am sure you know . . . Pusey House Archives, quoted HILLIER III, p. 589

We can ave er ealth food week tergether . . . BP, Penelope Betjeman to JB, April
    or May 1975

I miss Penelope . . . BP, JB to Harry Jarvis, 13 August 1972

It is reediculous that she cannot . . . BP, Penelope Betjeman to JB, undated

I am now very nearly in 29 Radnor Walk . . . CLG II, p. 465

Alfred Austin is my favourite laureate after Eusden . . . Letter to Roy Plomley,
    author's collection

In a sense Betjeman was Poet Laureate already . . . Quoted CLG II, p. 438

I have become so public and overexposed that I am dry . . . JB to R.S. Thomas,
    author's collection

Oh Gosh, thanks. Reading a book . . . John Guest to author, 1978

Betjeman sat with a slightly goofy, froglike look . . . John Gaskell to author, 2005

Bloody plastic! . . . John Gaskell to author, 2005

I love the Grosvenor Chapel and its plentiful incense . . . JB to John Gaskell, 10
    September 1973 and 6 February 1974

With John Guest, Harry Williams . . . John Guest to author, 1978

For your information, I never went to bed . . . BP, JB to Auberon Waugh, 6
    December 1973

He had once remarked to Osbert Lancaster . . . Richard Ingrams to author, 2005

Dear Bron, I very much enjoyed yesterday's luncheon . . . BP, JB to Auberon
    Waugh, 13 February 1975

This is the sort of publicity . . . BP, JB to Anthony House, BBC, 28 February
    1975

As they entered the modernistic restaurant . . . 'I'm just a pop poet' . . . Quoted to
    the author by Canon John Lucas, 1975

Parker remembered Betjeman's indifference . . . HILLIER III, p. 481

Every Anglican priest . . . JB, reprinted in *Coming Home*, ed. Candida Lycett
    Green, Methuen, 1997, p. 516

And though for church . . . ibid., p. 521

For moi birthday oi would VERY . . . BP, Penelope Betjeman to JB, 3 February
    1975

CHAPTER FIFTEEN
LOVE IS EVERYTHING
(*Pages 311–324*)

I am writing to you to see if we cannot work out . . . CLG II, p. 439–40

Harry Williams and Philip Larkin . . . Philip Larkin to author, 1983

John was very difficult to live with . . . James Lees-Milne, *The Milk of Paradise*, John Murray, 2005, p. 174

With Harry Williams and John Guest . . . John Guest to author, 1979

When Richard Ingrams called on him . . . Richard Ingrams to author, 24 October 2005

I have been in King's College Hospital . . . BL, JB to John Sparrow, 21 February 1977

Jonathan Stedall has now said . . . CLG II, p. 554

Thirty years after this painful episode . . . Conversation between author and Paul Betjeman, New York, 6 November 2005

Penelope went over to New York . . . and reported . . . BP, Penelope Betjeman to JB, 20 March 1974

IT IS WONDERFUL NOT BEING . . . BP, Penelope Betjeman to JB, 24 August 2003

Powlie's birthday . . . BP, Penelope Betjeman to JB

In 1977, however . . . CLG II, p. 516

When I met Lily Betjeman . . . Lily Betjeman to author, Port Isaac, August 2003

Paul smilingly said to me . . . 6 November 2005

I have been staying at St Michael's College . . . CLG II, p. 263

once, when Penelope had been . . . Lees-Milne, *Milk of Paradise*, p. 174

Plymmie would like to be friends with her . . . BP, Penelope Betjeman to JB, undated

Candida had the delicate task . . . CLG to author, October 2005

I knew he was worried about Elizabeth . . . CLG II, p. 552

People kept expecting him . . . Deborah Devonshire to author, 24 October 2005

There is surely a sort of parable . . . Motion, *Philip Larkin*, p. 515

I wish you wouldn't worry about me . . . CLG II, p. 581

I know that at that point . . . ibid.

His fear of death seemed to go . . . Elizabeth Cavendish to John Gaskell, June 1984

I truly think that those last months . . . BP, Elizabeth Cavendish to Billa Harrod

In 1975 . . . JB to Roy Plomley, 5 March 1975, author's collection

the poignancy of sitting . . . James Lees-Milne, diary, 22 May 1984, *Holy Dread*, John Murray, 2001, p. 169

the blinding charm. The blinding *charm* . . . Deborah Devonshire to author, October 2005

I think I might never come back from this trip . . . Imogen Lycett Green, *Grandmother's Footsteps*, p. 354. All subsequent details of Penelope's death and funeral come from this source.

Acknowledgements

Alas! Many of those who have told me most, over the years, about Betjeman were dead before I began the formal research for this book. The more I have continued with my research, I have realised that it was a book which I have been writing, or preparing to write, ever since I became obsessed by Betjeman as a teenager. It has been my good fortune to have known several of his friends quite well, and to have met many others. One of the immediately noticeable things about Betjeman's friends was how frequently, and affectionately, they spoke about him. I list my debt to the following, some still with us, though many are on a brighter shore. All of them in different ways have helped me – Anthony Adolph, Anthony Barnes, Alan Bennett, Lily Betjeman, Paul Betjeman, Maurice Bowra, Glynn and Carrie Boyd-Harte, Elizabeth Cavendish, David Cecil, Hugh Cecil, Jonathan Cecil, Michael and Joan Constantinidis, Caroline Dawnay, Deborah Devonshire, Katherine Duncan-Jones, James and Maggie Fergusson, Donald Findlay, Alastair Forbes, Antonia Fraser, John Gaskell, Michael Gillingham, John Guest, Ruth Guilding, Desmond Guinness, Billa Harrod, Dominick Harrod, Henry Harrod, Selina Hastings (especial thanks for reading the typescript and improving it), Mark Heathcoat Amory, Susan Hussey, Richard Ingrams, Gerard Irvine, Eric James, Julian Jebb, Kathryn Johnson, Monica Jones, Lucy Lambton, to whom I owe a special debt because she took me to Radnor Walk to meet the great man, Philip Larkin, Deirdre Levi, John Lucas, Princess Margaret, Hugh Montefiore, Hugh Montgomery-Massingberd also suggested I wrote this book and persuaded Candida Lycett Green to commission it, Diana Mosley, Jock Murray, Tory Oaksey, Robin Penna, John and Myfanwy Piper, Anthony Powell, Alan Pryce-Jones, Peter Quennell, A. L. Rowse, Robert Runcie, Anne Scott James, Gavin Stamp, Michael Thomas, Rachel Trickett, Bron and Teresa Waugh, Rowan Williams, Sharon Wilson, Stephen Wilson.

All those helped in some way or another, either with an actual memory of Betjeman, or by giving me letters, or by some particular perception or insight. Candida Lycett Green gave help of a different order. In her house at Uffington, she assembled a Betjeman archive *sans pareil* which has now been moved to the Tom Brown Museum, Uffington. She has photocopied not only the Betjeman holding at the McPherson Library of the University of Victoria, British Columbia, but also relevant papers from many other sources, of which I found the Osbert Lancaster Archive at Lincoln College, and the Tom Driberg at Christ Church, Oxford, especially helpful. Her husband Rupert Lycett Green, as well as tolerating my constant presence in the attic, prepared delicious lunches, and children and grandchildren, both in Uffington and in Cornwall, helped with my Betjemanic preoccupations.

Amy Boyle, with her usual patience, efficiency and good humour, typed and retyped. Jenny Overton was a model and observant editor. James Nightingale, ever kind and unflappable, saw the book into production. The staff at the British Library, those who work in the Manuscript Room, and in the other reading rooms, and in the copying service, were all exemplary in their professionalism. Thanks too to the staff of the Bodleian Library, the Marylebone Public Library and the London Library.

Illustrations

Index

friendship with Anne Baring,
207; religious upbringing, 207;
on JB's hospital visiting at Bart's,
216; on JB's friendship with
Gilbert Harding, 219; relations
with parents, 228, 230, 263;
leaves school and goes to Italy,
245; as debutante, 246; preg-
nancies and children, 262-3;
marriage, 263; interviews Harry
Jarvis, 268; protests at proposed
Wing airport, 277; letters from
JB in Australia, 287; spends
Christmas 1972 with JB at
Oakseys', 311; visits JB in
hospital, 313; organises
Elizabeth's and Penelope's
hospital visits to JB, 318; visits
JB in Trebetherick, 320; attends
JB's funeral, 321
Lycett Green, Endellion (JB's
granddaughter), 114
Lycett Green, Rupert (Candida's
husband), 263, 311
Lynam, A.E. ('Hum'), 29-31
Lynam, Audrey, 29, 31
Lynam, Charles Cotterill
('Skipper'), 29-30
Lynam, Joe, 29, 31
Lynam, May, 29
Lyons, Eric, 277

M.

Macartney, Sir Mervyn: edits
Architectural Review, 85
Macaulay, (Dame) Rose, 189,
238, 297

McCall, Margaret, 285, 287
MacDonald, Ramsay, 82
Machen, Arthur, 11, 16; *The Secret
Glory*, 12, 41-3, 125
Macmillan, Harold (*later* 1st Earl
of Stockton), 274-5, 279
MacNeice, Louis: at Marlborough,
39; C.S. Lewis dislikes, 54;
poetic style, 72
Maffey, Sir John (*later* 1st Baron
Rugby), 145, 182
Magdalen College, Oxford, 48, 51
Mallalieu, J.P.W. (Per), 32
Margaret, Princess: visits JB, 1-2;
Elizabeth Cavendish as Lady-in-
Waiting to, 193; visits
Armstrong-Jones in Rotherhithe
Street, 226; engagement and
marriage to Armstrong-Jones,
227; presents Duff Cooper prize
to JB, 228; as Chancellor of
Keele University, 238; JB's
attitude to, 285; churchgoing,
298, 318
Marlborough College: alumni,
29-30; JB attends, 36-40; JB
makes TV film on, 256
Marshall, Sir John, 94, 105
Martin, Peter and Dorothy, 220-1
Martyn, Edward, 151
Mary, Queen of George V, 156
Masefield, John, 27
Mathew, David, Archbishop of
Apamea, 165
Mathew, Gervase, 165
Mauberley, Hugh Selwyn, 44
Mead, the *see* Wantage (the Mead)